Beginning Node.js

Basarat Ali Syed

Apress®

Beginning Node.js

ISBN-13 (pbk): 978-1-4842-0188-6

ISBN-13 (electronic): 978-1-4842-0187-9

Managing Director: Welmoed Spahr
Lead Editor: Louise Corrigan
Technical Reviewer: Martin Bean
Editorial Board: Steve Anglin, Mark Beckner, Ewan Buckingham, Gary Cornell, Louise Corrigan,
    Jim DeWolf, Jonathan Gennick, Robert Hutchinson, Michelle Lowman, James Markham, Matthew Moodie,
    Jeff Olson, Jeffrey Pepper, Douglas Pundick, Ben Renow-Clarke, Dominic Shakeshaft, Gwenan Spearing,
    Matt Wade, Steve Weiss
Coordinating Editor: Christine Ricketts
Copy Editor: Ann Dickson
Compositor: SPi Global
Indexer: SPi Global
Artist: SPi Global
Cover Designer: Anna Ishchenko

Distributed to the book trade worldwide by Springer Science+Business Media New York, 233 Spring Street, 6th Floor, New York, NY 10013. Phone 1-800-SPRINGER, fax (201) 348-4505, e-mail orders-ny@springer-sbm.com, or visit www.springeronline.com. Apress Media, LLC is a California LLC and the sole member (owner) is Springer Science + Business Media Finance Inc (SSBM Finance Inc). SSBM Finance Inc is a Delaware corporation.

For information on translations, please e-mail rights@apress.com, or visit www.apress.com.

Apress and friends of ED books may be purchased in bulk for academic, corporate, or promotional use. eBook versions and licenses are also available for most titles. For more information, reference our Special Bulk Sales–eBook Licensing web page at www.apress.com/bulk-sales.

Any source code or other supplementary material referenced by the author in this text is available to readers at www.apress.com. For detailed information about how to locate your book's source code, go to www.apress.com/source-code/.

Dedicated to my brother Babar Ali Syed who has always supported and loved me unconditionally, to my mother Hasnain Syedah who showed me the value of continued unquestioning effort, to my brother Baqar Ali Syed who has been a great friend to have at all times, to my sister Taskeen Syedah who has helped shape my opinion on how to lead a happy life, and to my loving wife Sana Basarat to whom I have dedicated my life.

Contents at a Glance

Contents

About the Author

Basarat Ali Syed is a senior developer and the go-to guy for front end at PicnicSoftware (http://picnicsoftware.com/) in Melbourne, Australia. He studied Master of Computing at Australian National University (the top Australian University) and graduated with high distinction in all courses. He is a familiar face at developer meet-ups and conferences in Australia and has been a speaker at events such as Alt.NET, DDDMelbourne, MelbJS, and Melbourne Node.js, among others. He is deeply passionate about web technologies and strongly believes that whenever given a choice, one should always bet on JavaScript. He is a respected member of the TypeScript community and works on the DefinitelyTyped team (https://github.com/DefinitelyTyped). He believes Node.js can do for the back end what Chrome did for the front end. In his spare time he enjoys bodybuilding and cycling, and he maintains a YouTube channel for helping fellow developers (http://youtube.com/basaratali). You can follow him on Twitter at https://twitter.com/basarat and https://github.com/basarat.

About the Technical Reviewer

Martin Bean is a web developer based in the North East of England. Having grown up and studied in Darlington, he moved to Newcastle upon Tyne at the age of 18, where he started his career with a well-respected digital agency. Although he entered with aspirations of being a designer, he switched to development, giving him skills in both disciplines.

After working at agencies for almost five years, Martin left to pursue a career as a freelance developer and consultant and hasn't looked back. Specializing in development, he has worked with global video game publishers and nationwide retailers on everything from simple web sites to bespoke e-commerce platforms.

Martin is active on various social networks. You can follow him on Twitter at `https://twitter.com/martinbean`.

About the Technical Reviewer

Acknowledgments

Man is limited by his fears.

—Babar Ali Syed

This work would not have been possible without the effort of some people very dear and close to me. I'd like to thank the kind folk at PicnicSoftware—Matt Walkenhorst, Nick Josevski, Andrew Browne, Scott Lowe, Tim Buddington, and Dave Churchill—who make my office feel like a second home. My brother Baqar Ali Syed who tolerated my long isolation periods where I would just research technology and then analyze the best way to present this material. Thanks to Steve Fenton, who inspired me to undertake the monumental task of authoring a book. All of the people from DefinitelyTyped—especially Boris Yankov, Masahiro Wakame, Bart van der Schoor, and John Reilly—who have been a constant source of inspiration. To all of the people at Apress—especially Christine Ricketts, Martin Bean, Ann Dickson, Louise Corrigan, and Dhaneesh Kumar—without whose effort this book would not be possible. Thanks to the Melbourne development community—especially Andrey Sidorov, Jim Pelletier, Leah Garrett and Michael Lyons—who make this awesome city even better.

Introduction

Undoubtedly, personal computing has revolutionized the way we live and work today. The Web has further revolutionized the way we use applications. When it was first introduced, the Internet was designed to present information in the form of documents. Later, JavaScript was added, which has been the key ingredient for the innovation we see on the Web today. Web applications are platform-independent, seamlessly updating, safe by default, and available anytime and everywhere. No wonder it is difficult to get started in a developer role today without some knowledge of how the Web works.

Because of the importance of the Web and the pivotal role that JavaScript plays in web development, you can find a solution for most technical problems in some open source JavaScript project. Node.js allows you to use all these innovative JavaScript projects on the server the same as on the client browser. Using JavaScript on the server also reduces the context switching that needs to happen in your brain as you change programming language and associated code conventions. This is the emotional side of why you should use Node.js.

This book is designed to be a gentle introduction to Node.js as well as JavaScript. No prior software development experience is assumed beyond a basic programming course. Since we clearly present the technical reasons behind the creation of Node.js, this book is also great if you are already comfortable programming in another environment, such as C# or Java, and are curious what all the fuss around Node.js is about. This book covers all the main areas of Node.js software development from setup to deployment so when you finish this book, you should be able to start using Node.js immediately and be ready to share your projects with the world.

CHAPTER 1

■ ■ ■

Setting Up for Node.js Development

In this chapter, we discuss how to set up a Node.js development environment as we guide you through the installation process of Node.js on various platforms. Then we give you a tour of the Node.js REPL (read-evaluate-print-loop) and show you how you can run Node.js applications. Finally, we provide examples of Integrated Development Environments (IDEs) that can help you deliver applications faster and make your journey more enjoyable.

Installing Node.js

You no longer need to build Node.js from source in order to develop Node.js applications. Node.js now provides installers for Windows as well as Mac OS X, and it can be installed in the same way as any other application on these platforms (Figure 1-1). You can download Node.js installers from `http://nodejs.org/download/`.

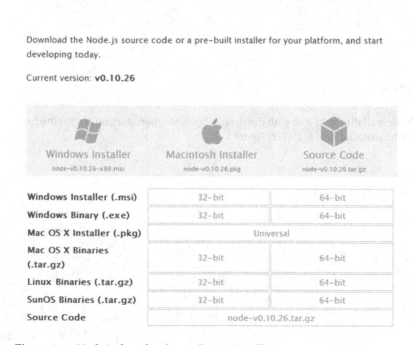

Figure 1-1. Node.js download page listing installers

1

In the next section, we will guide you through the important steps for your operating system (OS). You can safely skip the section not relevant to your current OS.

Installing on Windows

The website for Node.js lists "Windows Binary (.exe)" and "Windows Installer (.msi)." You do not want to use the windows binary (.exe) for development, as it does not contain important things such as Node Package Manager (NPM), which we cover in Chapter 4. Node.js provides separate installers (.msi) for 32-bit and 64-bit Windows. We recommend that you install based on your platform. You launch the installer as you would any other installer on Windows (Figure 1-2).

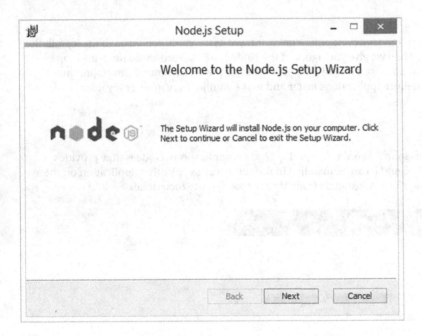

Figure 1-2. Node.js Setup Wizard on Windows

We recommend that you install to the default directory and with the default options when starting out for the first time. It is especially important that you let the installer *Add to PATH* (Figure 1-3).

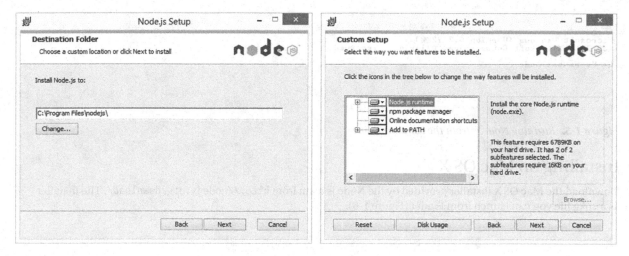

Figure 1-3. *Default options for Node.js installer on Windows*

After installation, uninstalling and reinstalling Node.js are extremely easy. If you run the installer again, you will be prompted with the *Remove* option, as shown in Figure 1-4.

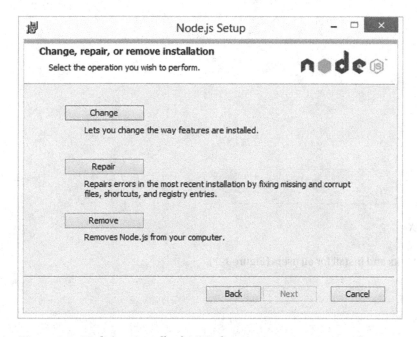

Figure 1-4. *Node.js uninstaller for Windows*

Since the installer set up the system PATH, you can run Node.js from the *command* prompt (search for "command prompt" in the Windows start menu). We can start up Node.js by simply typing node in cmd (Figure 1-5). This puts you in the REPL, which we explain in the next section.

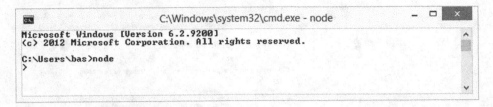

Figure 1-5. Running Node.js from the command line

Installing on Mac OS X

Download the Mac OS X installer provided by the Node.js team from `http://nodejs.org/download/`. The installer is a `.pkg` file you can launch from Finder (Figure 1-6).

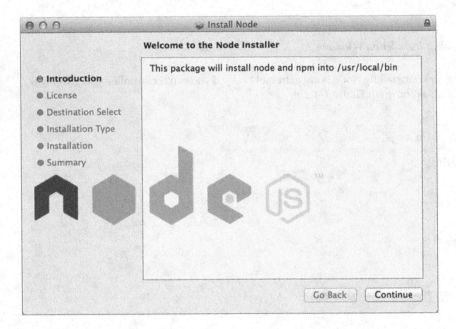

Figure 1-6. Node.js Installer for Mac OS X

When starting out, stick with the defaults and install for all users (Figure 1-7).

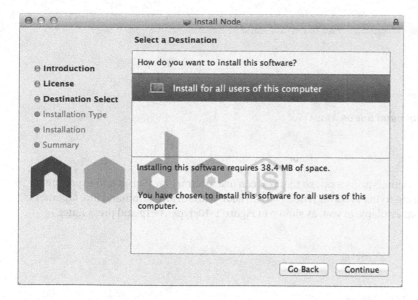

Figure 1-7. *Node.js setup for all users option*

Once complete, the installer will inform you of the two binaries it installed (node and npm), as shown in Figure 1-8.

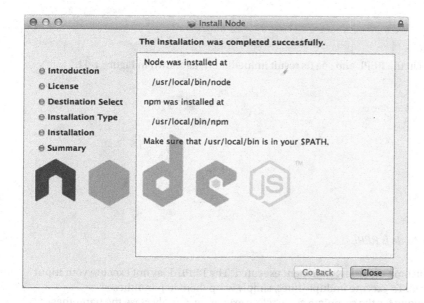

Figure 1-8. *Node.js binaries installed*

We will cover npm extensively in Chapter 4. Your main executable for running JavaScript in Node.js is node (Figure 1-9). For Mac OS X, you can start node from Terminal (use Mac OS X spotlight to search for Terminal). If you execute node in Terminal, it will start the Node.js REPL, which we discuss next.

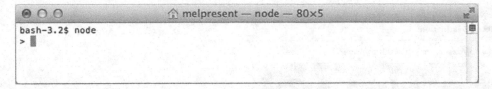

Figure 1-9. *Running Node.js from the command line on Mac OS X*

Using the REPL

Node.js provides you with a REPL (read-evaluate-print-loop) so that you can test arbitrary JavaScript and experiment and explore solutions to the problem you are trying to solve. When you run node without any command line arguments, it puts you in the REPL. To view the options available to you, as shown in Figure 1-10, type .help and press Enter.

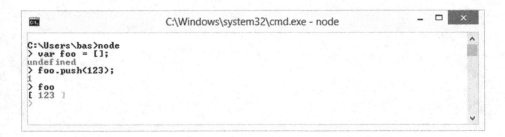

Figure 1-10. *Node.js REPL help*

You can execute arbitrary JavaScript in the REPL and see its result immediately, as shown in Figure 1-11.

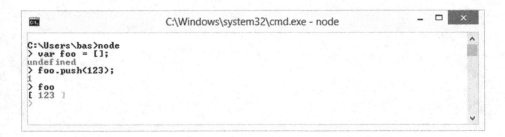

Figure 1-11. *Executing JavaScript in the Node.js REPL*

At each step, the REPL prints the outcome of the last statement executed. The REPL does not execute your input code until all brackets have been balanced. To execute multiple lines, simply wrap them in parentheses. The REPL uses (...) to denote that it is waiting for the complete code before executing. Simply close the parentheses and press Enter for the REPL to evaluate the entered JavaScript (see Figure 1-12). To exit from inside a block (...) without executing what you have already entered, simply type .break or press Ctrl+C.

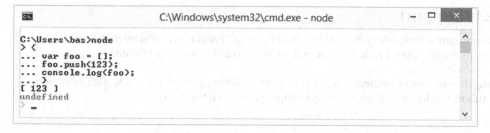

Figure 1-12. *Executing multiple lines in the Node.js REPL*

The REPL is great when you want to test some JavaScript and make sure that it functions the way you want it to. You can exit the REPL by typing `.exit` (or by pressing Ctrl+D).

Executing Node.js Scripts

We have seen how to execute JavaScript by typing it into the REPL. However, you will most commonly be writing Node.js programs (script files) and execute them with Node.js. You can execute a JavaScript source file in Node.js by simply passing the file to node on the command line (Figure 1-13). Create a new file called `helloworld.js` containing a simple `console.log` as shown in Listing 1-1.

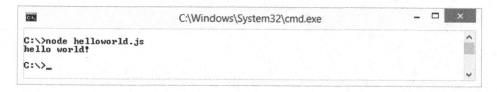

Figure 1-13. *Executing a script file in Node.js*

Listing 1-1. helloworld.js

```
console.log("hello world!");
```

Then run the file by running `node helloworld.js` on the command line from the same directory that you saved the file (`C:\`, in our case).

Notice that we use `console.log` in the same way as we would use if we were doing front-end web development. One of the philosophies of Node.js is that it should be intuitive to front-end developers. The Node.js team has tried to keep the API consistent with the browser whenever it made sense.

Node.js simply executes the input JavaScript from top to bottom as a browser would. It is, however, conventional to name the main file of your application `app.js` so people know which file to execute in order to run your application.

Setting Up an Integrated Development Environment

Node.js is great because it is really simple to get started with just a text editor and Terminal. (That does not mean that there aren't more full-featured development environments out there.) Node.js has seen fantastic support from JetBrains (creators of IntelliJ Idea, RubyMine, and PyCharm) in the form of WebStorm as well as from Microsoft in their Visual Studio. WebStorm is available on Windows, Mac OS X, and Linux, whereas Visual Studio is available for Windows only.

WebStorm Node.js Support

WebStorm claims to be "the smartest JavaScript IDE." It is based on IntelliJ IDEA platform and might be easy for you to migrate to if you are coming from a Java, Ruby, or Python background. You can get it from http://www.jetbrains.com/webstorm/.

WebStorm works using the concept of "projects." When you start WebStorm, you are presented with an option, *Create a New Project*. For this example, we will create a simple empty project (Figure 1-14).

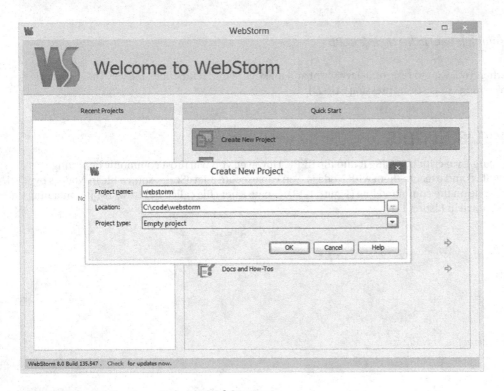

Figure 1-14. *Create a new project in WebStorm*

Now right-click the project name in the project window (shown in Figure 1-15) once it is open. Add a new JavaScript file and call this file "main" (also shown in Figure 1-15).

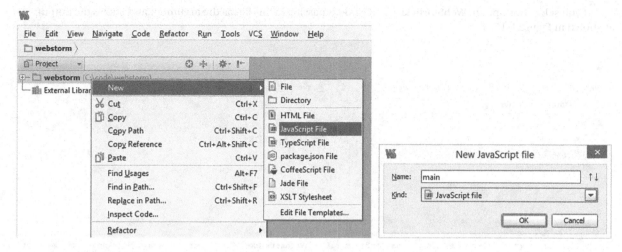

Figure 1-15. *Add a new file to a WebStorm project*

Clear the contents of the file and simply put in a `console.log`, as shown in Listing 1-2.

Listing 1-2.

```
console.log("Hello WebStorm!");
```

Since we already have Node.js installed, WebStorm is smart enough to figure it out. So, if you right-click anywhere inside the file, WebStorm shows the option *Run 'main.js'* (Figure 1-16).

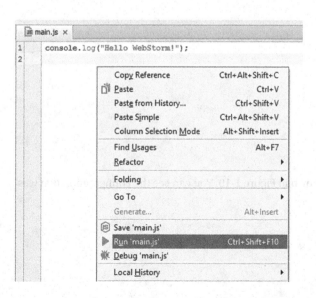

Figure 1-16. *Run a script file in Node.js from WebStorm*

If you select this option, WebStorm kicks off Node.js passing in this file as the argument and shows the output, as shown in Figure 1-17.

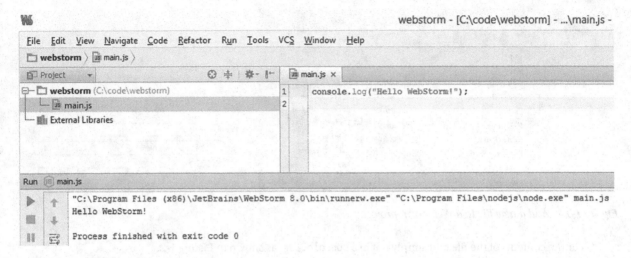

Figure 1-17. *Script execution result in WebStorm*

When you asked WebStorm to run the file, it actually created a run configuration. You can view this run configuration and customize it further by using Run ➤ Edit Configurations, as shown in Figure 1-18.

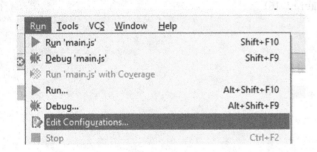

Figure 1-18. *Edit run configuration in WebStorm*

This will open up the Configuration Editor dialog, as shown in Figure 1-19. You can see the configuration that was created for you and edit it if you want.

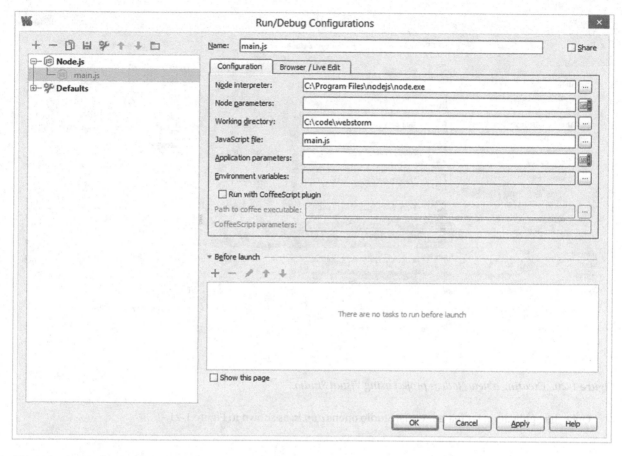

Figure 1-19. *Node.js configuration options in WebStorm*

WebStorm has more capacities than we have shown here, where the objective was to get you started quickly. WebStorm has excellent integration with the Node.js built-in debugger and will be explored in Chapter 11.

Visual Studio Node.js Support

If you are coming from a .NET background, you might be glad to hear that Visual Studio has first-class Node.js support. This support comes in the form of "Node.js Tools for Visual Studio," available for both Visual Studio 2012 and Visual Studio 2013 from Microsoft. You can download these tools from https://nodejstools.codeplex.com. Installing these tools couldn't be easier. Simply launch the downloaded .msi installer and click through to finish.

Now when you start Visual Studio and create a new project, you will see a new language option, *JavaScript*. Select it and create a Blank Node.js Console App, specifying its name and location as shown in Figure 1-20.

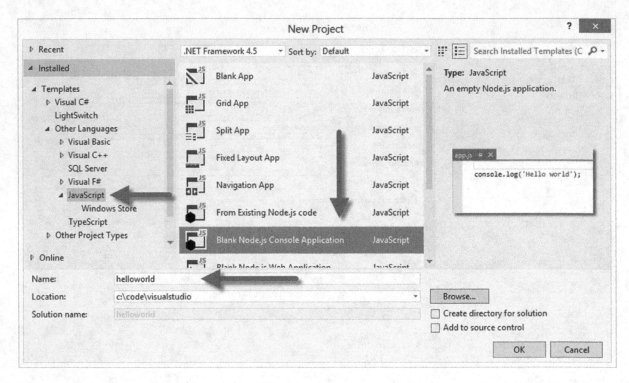

Figure 1-20. Creating a new Node.js project using Visual Studio

Once the application is created, Visual Studio opens *app.js*, as shown in Figure 1-21.

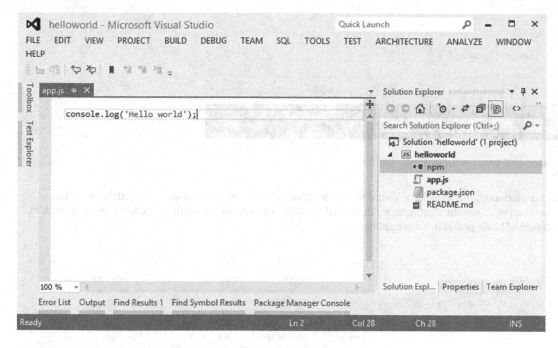

Figure 1-21. Node.js application created using Visual Studio

Do not worry about *package.json* and *npm* at this point. These options will be explained in Chapter 4. Now let's run this simple console application from Visual Studio. Click the sidebar in the editor to add a debug breakpoint, as shown in Figure 1-22.

Figure 1-22. Adding a debug breakpoint to a file in Visual Studio

To run this application in debug mode, press F5 and Visual Studio will pass app.js to Node.js and pause at the breakpoint as shown in Figure 1-23. Visual Studio uses the V8 debugger built into Node.js, which we will discuss in Chapter 11.

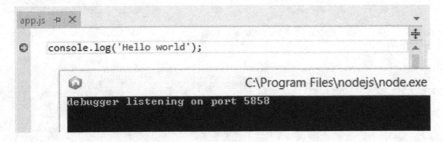

Figure 1-23. *Activated breakpoint in Visual Studio*

All the common debugging tools from Visual Studio, such as call stack, local variables, and watch, work fine with Node.js. You can even see the source code "inside" of Node.js. For example, module.js shown in the call stack in Figure 1-24 is a part of Node.js and not our application.

Figure 1-24. *Visual Studio showing local variables and the call stack*

Press F5 to continue. It will then print "Hello world" to the console and exit (Figure 1-25).

Figure 1-25. *Node.js application executed from Visual Studio*

One final thing to note when working with Visual Studio is the properties pane. You can right-click the project in the solution explorer and select *properties* to modify how Visual Studio interacts with node.exe, as shown in Figure 1-26.

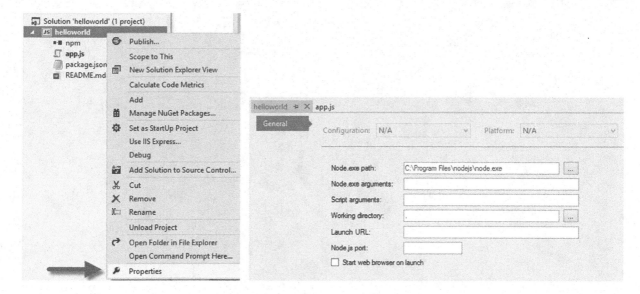

Figure 1-26. Node.js configuration options in Visual Studio

Summary

Node.js has seen fantastic community support since its beginning. Thanks to the installers, you no longer need to compile Node.js from source in order to create Node.js applications on your favorite platform. After setting up Node.js, we showed examples of IDEs that can make working with Node.js easier in order to get you up and running quickly.

In the next chapter, we will discuss important JavaScript concepts that you need to understand in order to be successful with Node.js.

CHAPTER 2

■ ■ ■

Understanding Node.js

To understand how Node.js works, first you need to understand a few key features of JavaScript that make it well suited for server-side development. JavaScript is a simple language, but it is also extremely flexible. This flexibility is the reason why it has stood the test of time. First-class functions and closures make it an ideal language for web applications.

JavaScript has a bad reputation for being unreliable. However, this notion couldn't be further from the truth. Actually, JavaScript's bad reputation comes from the DOM's unreliability. The DOM (docment object model) is the API (application programming interface) that browser vendors provide to interact with the browser using JavaScript. The DOM has idiosyncrasies between browser vendors. However, JavaScript the language is well-defined and can be used reliably across browsers and Node.js. In this chapter, we discuss a few fundamentals of JavaScript followed by how Node.js used JavaScript to provide a highly performant platform for web applications. Other people complain about how JavaScript handles programming errors (it tries to make invalid code work). However, in such cases, the developers are really to blame, as they need to be careful when working with a highly dynamic language.

Variables

Variables are defined in JavaScript using the var keyword. For example, the following code segment creates a variable foo and logs it to the console. (See Listing 2-1.) As you saw in the previous chapter, you would run this code from your console (terminal on Mac OS X and cmd on Windows) using node variable.js.

Listing 2-1. variable.js

```
var foo = 123;
console.log(foo); // 123
```

The JavaScript runtime (the browser or Node.js) has the opportunity to define a few global variables that we can use in our code. One of them is the console object, which we have been using up to this point. The console object contains a member function (log), which takes any number of arguments and prints them to the console. We will discuss more global objects as they are used. As you will see, JavaScript contains most things you expect a good programming language to have.

Numbers

All numbers in JavaScript have the same floating point number type. Arithmetic operations (+,-,*,/,%) work on numbers as you would expect, as shown in Listing 2-2.

Listing 2-2. numbers.js

```
var foo = 3;
var bar = 5;
console.log(foo + 1);    // 4
console.log(foo / bar); // 0.6
console.log(foo * bar); // 15
console.log(foo - bar); // -2;
console.log(foo % 2);    // remainder: 1
```

Boolean

Two literals are defined for boolean values: true and false. You can assign these to variables and apply boolean operations to them as you would expect. (See Listing 2-3.)

Listing 2-3. boolean.js

```
var foo = true;
console.log(foo); // true

// Boolean operations (&&, ||, !) work as expected:
console.log(true && true);    // true
console.log(true && false);  // false
console.log(true || false);  // true
console.log(false || false); // false
console.log(!true);           // false
console.log(!false);          // true
```

Arrays

You can create arrays quite easily in JavaScript using [ ]. Arrays have many useful functions, a few of which are shown in Listing 2-4.

Listing 2-4. arrays.js

```
var foo = [];

foo.push(1);          // add at the end
console.log(foo);     // prints [1]

foo.unshift(2);       // add to the top
console.log(foo);     // prints [2,1]

// Arrays are zero index based:
console.log(foo[0]); // prints 2
```

Object Literals

By explaining these few fundamental types, we have introduced you to object literals. The most common way of creating an object in JavaScript is using the object notation, {}. Objects can be extended arbitrarily at runtime. An example is shown in Listing 2-5.

Listing 2-5. objectLiterals1.js

```
var foo = {};
console.log(foo); // {}
foo.bar = 123;    // extend foo
console.log(foo); // { bar: 123 }
```

Instead of extending it at runtime, you can define which properties go on an object upfront by using the object literal notation shown in Listing 2-6.

Listing 2-6. objectLiterals2.js

```
var foo = {
    bar: 123
};
console.log(foo); // { bar: 123 }
```

You can additionally nest object literals inside object literals, as shown in Listing 2-7.

Listing 2-7. objectLiterals3.js

```
var foo = {
    bar: 123,
    bas: {
        bas1: 'some string',
        bas2: 345
    }
};
console.log(foo);
```

And, of course, you can have arrays inside object literals as well, as shown in Listing 2-8.

Listing 2-8. objectLiterals4.js

```
var foo = {
    bar: 123,
    bas: [1, 2, 3]
};
console.log(foo);
```

And, you can also have these arrays themselves contain object literals, as you can see in Listing 2-9.

Listing 2-9. objectLiterals5.js

```
var foo = {
    bar: 123,
    bas: [{
        qux: 1
    },
    {
        qux: 2
    },
```

```
    {
        qux: 3
    }]
};
console.log(foo.bar);        // 123
console.log(foo.bas[0].qux); // 1
console.log(foo.bas[2].qux); // 2
```

Object literals are extremely handy as function arguments and return values.

Functions

Functions are really powerful in JavaScript. Most of the power of JavaScript comes from the way it handles the function type. We will examine functions in JavaScript in progressively more involved examples that follow.

Functions 101

A normal function structure in JavaScript is defined in Listing 2-10.

Listing 2-10. functionBody.js

```
function functionName() {
    // function body
    // optional return;
}
```

All functions return a value in JavaScript. In the absence of an explicit return statement, a function returns undefined. When you execute the code in Listing 2-11, you get undefined on the console.

Listing 2-11. functionReturn.js

```
function foo() { return 123; }
console.log(foo()); // 123

function bar() { }
console.log(bar()); // undefined
```

We will discuss undefined functions more in this chapter when we look at default values.

Immediately Executing Function

You can execute a function immediately after you define it. Simply wrap the function in parentheses () and invoke it, as shown in Listing 2-12.

Listing 2-12. ief1.js

```
(function foo() {
    console.log('foo was executed!');
})();
```

The reason for having an immediately executing function is to create a new variable scope. An if, else, or while does not create a new variable scope in JavaScript. This fact is demonstrated in Listing 2-13.

Listing 2-13. ief2.js

```
var foo = 123;
if (true) {
    var foo = 456;
}
console.log(foo); // 456;
```

The only recommended way of creating a new variable scope in JavaScript is using a function. So, in order to create a new variable scope, we can use an immediately executing function, as shown in Listing 2-14.

Listing 2-14. ief3.js

```
var foo = 123;
if (true) {
    (function () { // create a new scope
        var foo = 456;
    })();
}
console.log(foo); // 123;
```

Notice that we choose to avoid needlessly naming the function. This is called an *anonymous function*, which we will explain next.

Anonymous Function

A function without a name is called an anonymous function. In JavaScript, you can assign a function to a variable. If you are going to use a function as a variable, you don't need to name the function. Listing 2-15 demonstrates two ways of defining a function inline. Both of these methods are equivalent.

Listing 2-15. anon.js

```
var foo1 = function namedFunction() { // no use of name, just wasted characters
    console.log('foo1');
}
foo1(); // foo1

var foo2 = function () {               // no function name given i.e. anonymous function
    console.log('foo2');
}
foo2(); // foo2
```

A programming language is said to have *first-class functions* if a function can be treated the same way as any other variable in the language. JavaScript has first-class functions.

Higher-Order Functions

Since JavaScript allows us to assign functions to variables, we can pass functions to other functions. Functions that take functions as arguments are called *higher-order functions*. A very common example of a higher-order function is setTimeout. This is shown in Listing 2-16.

Listing 2-16. higherOrder1.js

```
setTimeout(function () {
    console.log('2000 milliseconds have passed since this demo started');
}, 2000);
```

If you run this application in Node.js, you will see the console.log message after two seconds and then the application will exit. Note that we provided an anonymous function as the first argument to setTimeout. This makes setTimeout a higher-order function.

It is worth mentioning that there is nothing stopping us from creating a function and passing that in. An example is shown in Listing 2-17.

Listing 2-17. higherOrder2.js

```
function foo() {
    console.log('2000 milliseconds have passed since this demo started');
}
setTimeout(foo, 2000);
```

Now that we have a firm understanding of object literals and functions, we can examine the concept of closures.

Closures

Whenever we have a function defined inside another function, the inner function has access to the variables declared in the outer function. Closures are best explained with examples.

In Listing 2-18, you can see that the inner function has access to a variable (variableInOuterFunction) from the outer scope. The variables in the outer function have been closed by (or bound in) the inner function. Hence the term *closure*. The concept in itself is simple enough and fairly intuitive.

Listing 2-18. closure1.js

```
function outerFunction(arg) {
    var variableInOuterFunction = arg;

    function bar() {
        console.log(variableInOuterFunction); // Access a variable from the outer scope
    }

    // Call the local function to demonstrate that it has access to arg
    bar();
}

outerFunction('hello closure!');              // logs hello closure!
```

Now the awesome part: The inner function can access the variables from the outer scope *even after the outer function has returned*. This is because the variables are still bound in the inner function and not dependent on the outer function. Listing 2-19 shows an example.

Listing 2-19. closure2.js

```
function outerFunction(arg) {
    var variableInOuterFunction = arg;
    return function () {
        console.log(variableInOuterFunction);
    }
}

var innerFunction = outerFunction('hello closure!');

// Note the outerFunction has returned
innerFunction(); // logs hello closure!
```

Now that we have an understanding of first-class functions and closures, we can look at what makes JavaScript a great language for server-side programming.

Understanding Node.js Performance

Node.js is focused on creating highly performant applications. In the following section, we introduce the I/O scaling problem. Then we show how it has been solved traditionally, followed by how Node.js solves it.

The I/O Scaling Problem

Node.js is focused on being the best way to write highly performant web applications. To understand how it achieves this, we need to know about the I/O scaling problem. Let us look at a rough estimate of the speed at which we can access data from various sources in terms of CPU cycles (Figure 2-1).

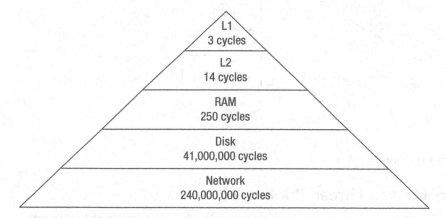

Figure 2-1. *Comparing common I/O sources*

You can clearly see that Disk and Network access is in a completely different category from accessing data that is available in RAM and CPU cache.

Most web applications depend on reading data from disk or from another network source (for example, a database query). When an HTTP request is received and we need to load data from a database, typically this request will be spent waiting for a disk read or a network access call to complete.

These open connections and pending requests consume server resources (memory and CPU). In order to handle a large number of requests from different clients using the same web server, we have the I/O scaling problem.

Traditional Web Servers Using a Process Per Request

Traditional servers used to spin up a new process to handle every single web request. Spinning a new process for each request is an expensive operation, both in terms of CPU and memory. This is the way technologies like PHP used to work when they were first created.

A demonstration of this concept is shown in Figure 2-2. In order to successfully reply to an HTTP request "A," we need some data from a database. This read can potentially take a long time. For this entire read duration, we will have a process taking up CPU and memory while idling and waiting for the database response. Also, processes are slow to start and have a significant overhead in terms of RAM space. This does not scale for very long and that is the reason why modern web applications use a thread pool.

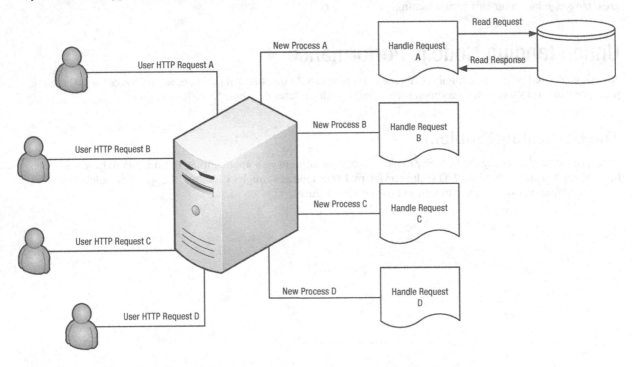

Figure 2-2. *Traditional web server using Processes*

Traditional Web Servers Using a Thread Pool

Modern servers use a thread from a thread pool to serve each request. Since we already have a few Operating System (OS) threads created (hence a thread pool), we do not pay the penalty of starting and stopping OS processes (which are expensive to create and take up much more memory than a thread). When a request comes in, we assign a thread to process this request. This thread is reserved for the request in the entire duration that the request is being handled, as demonstrated in Figure 2-3.

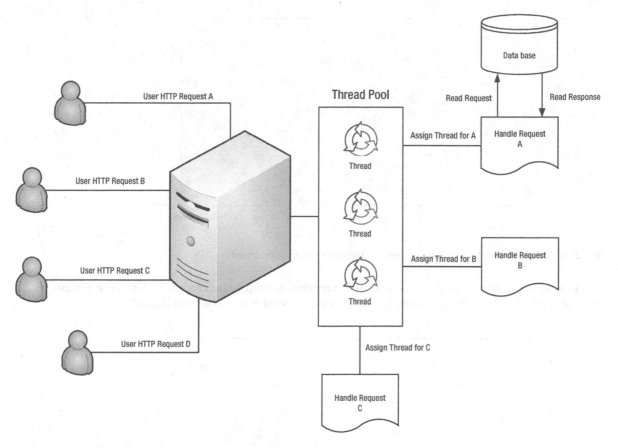

Figure 2-3. *Traditional web server using a thread pool*

Because we save the overhead of creating a new process every time and the threads are lighter than processes, this method is much better than the original server design. Most web servers used this method a few years back and many continue to use today. However, this method is not without drawbacks. Again there is wasting of RAM between threads. Also the OS needs to context switch between threads (even when they are idle), and this results in wasted CPU resources.

The Nginx Way

We have seen that creating separate processes and separate threads to handle requests results in wasted OS resources. The way Node.js works is that there is a single thread handling requests. The idea that a single threaded server can perform better than a thread pool server is not new to Node.js. Nginx is built on this principle.

Nginx is a single-threaded web server and can handle a tremendous amount of concurrent requests. A simple benchmark comparing Nginx to Apache, both serving a single static file from the file system, is shown in Figure 2-4.

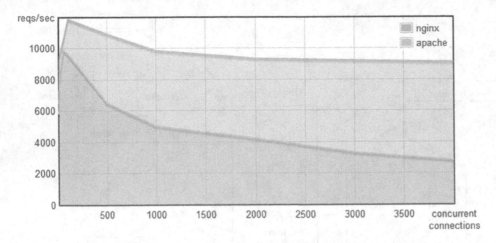

Figure 2-4. *Nginx vs. Apache requests/second vs. concurrent open connections*

As you can see, when the number of concurrent connections goes up, Nginx can handle a lot more requests per second than Apache. What is more interesting is the memory consumption, as shown in Figure 2-5.

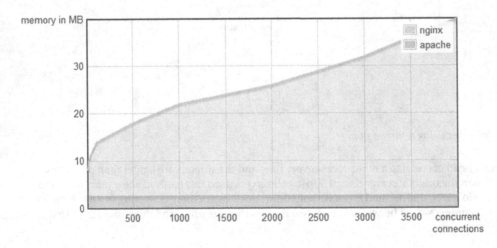

Figure 2-5. *Nginx vs. Apache memory usage vs. concurrent connections*

With more concurrent connections, Apache needs to manage more threads and therefore consumes much more memory, whereas Nginx stays at a steady level.

Node.js Performance Secret

There is a single execution thread in JavaScript. This is the way web browsers have traditionally worked. If you have a long-running operation (such as waiting for a timer to complete or a database query to return), you must continue operation using a callback. Listing 2-20 provides a simple demo that uses the JavaScript runtime setTimeout function to simulate a long-running operation. You can run this code using Node.js.

Listing 2-20. simulateUserClick.js

```javascript
function longRunningOperation(callback) {
    // simulate a 3 second operation
    setTimeout(callback, 3000);
}

function userClicked() {
    console.log('starting a long operation');
    longRunningOperation(function () {
        console.log('ending a long operation');
    });
}
// simulate a user action
userClicked();
```

This simulation is possible in JavaScript because we have first-class functions and passing functions—a callback is a well-supported pattern in the language. Things become interesting when you combine first-class functions with the concept of closures. Let us image that we are handling a web request and we have a long-running operation such as a database query that we need to do. A simulated version is shown in listing 2-21.

Listing 2-21. simulateWebRequest.js

```javascript
function longRunningOperation(callback) {
    // simulate a 3 second operation
    setTimeout(callback, 3000);
}

function webRequest(request) {
    console.log('starting a long operation for request:', request.id);
    longRunningOperation(function () {
        console.log('ending a long operation for request:', request.id);
    });
}
// simulate a web request
webRequest({ id: 1 });
// simulate a second web request
webRequest({ id: 2 });
```

In Listing 2-21, because of closures, we have access to the correct user request after the long-running operation completes. We just handled two requests on a single thread without breaking a sweat. Now you should understand the following statement: "Node.js is highly performant, and it uses JavaScript because JavaScript supports first-class functions and closures."

The immediate question that should come to mind when someone tells you that you only have a single thread to handle requests is, "But my computer has a quad core CPU. Using only a single thread will surely waste resources." And the answer is that yes it will. However, there is a well-supported way around it that we will examine in Chapter 13 when discussing deployment and scalability. Just a quick tip about what you will see there: It is actually really simple to use all the CPU cores with a separate JavaScript process for each CPU core using Node.js.

It is also important to note that there are threads managed by Node.js at the C level (such as for certain file system operations), but all the JavaScript executes in a single thread. This gives you the performance advantage of the JavaScript almost completely owning at least one thread.

More Node.js Internals

It is not terribly important to understand the internals of how Node.js works, but a bit more discussion make you more aware of the terminology when you discuss Node.js with your peers. At the heart of Node.js is an *event loop*.

Event loops enable any GUI application to work on any operating system. The OS calls a function within your application when something happens (for example, the user clicks a button), and then your application executes the logic contained inside this function to completion. Afterward, your application is ready to respond to new events that might have already arrived (and are there on the queue) or that might arrive later (based on user interaction).

Thread Starvation

Generally during the duration of a function called from an event in a GUI application, no other events can be processed. Consequently, if you do a long-running task within something like a click handler, the GUI will become unresponsive. This is something every computer user I have met has experienced at one point or another. This lack of availability of CPU resources is called *starvation*.

Node.js is built on the same event loop principle as you find in GUI programs. Therefore, it too can suffer from starvation. To understand it better, let's go through a few code examples. Listing 2-22 shows a small snippet of code that measures the time passed using console.time and console.timeEnd functions.

Listing 2-22. timeit.js

```
console.time('timer');
setTimeout(function(){
   console.timeEnd('timer');
},1000)
```

If you run this code, you should see a number quite close to what you would expect—in other words, 1000ms. This callback for the timeout is called from the Node.js event loop.

Now let's write some code that takes a long time to execute, for instance, a nonoptimized method of calculating the nth Fibonacci number as shown in Listing 2-23.

Listing 2-23. largeOperation.js

```
console.time('timeit');
function fibonacci(n) {
    if (n < 2)
        return 1;
    elses
        return fibonacci(n - 2) + fibonacci(n - 1);
}
fibonacci(44);            // modify this number based on your system performance
console.timeEnd('timeit'); // On my system it takes about 9000ms (i.e. 9 seconds)
```

Now we have an event that can be raised from the Node.js event loop (setTimeout) and a function that can keep the JavaScript thread busy (fibonacci). We can now demonstrate starvation in Node.js. Let's set up a time-out to execute. But before this time-out completes, we execute a function that takes a lot of CPU time and therefore holds up the CPU and the JavaScript thread. As this function is holding on to the JavaScript thread, the event loop cannot call anything else and therefore the time-out is delayed, as demonstrated in Listing 2-24.

Listing 2-24. starveit.js

```
// utility funcion
function fibonacci(n) {
    if (n < 2)
        return 1;
    else
        return fibonacci(n - 2) + fibonacci(n - 1);
}

// setup the timer
console.time('timer');
setTimeout(function () {
    console.timeEnd('timer'); // Prints much more than 1000ms
}, 1000)

// Start the long running operation
fibonacci(44);
```

One lesson here is that Node.js is not the best option if you have a high CPU task that you need to do *on a client request* in a multiclient server environment. However, if this is the case, you will be very hard-pressed to find a scalable software solution in any platform. Most high CPU tasks should take place offline and are generally offloaded to a database server using things such as materialized views, map reduce, and so on. Most web applications access the results of these computations over the network, and this is where Node.js shines—evented network I/O.

Now that you understand what an event loop means and the implications of the fact that JavaScript portion of Node.js is single-threaded, let's take another look at why Node.js is great for I/O applications.

Data-Intensive Applications

Node.js is great for data-intensive applications. As we have seen, using a single thread means that Node.js has an extremely low-memory footprint when used as a web server and can potentially serve a lot more requests. Consider the simple scenario of a data intensive application that serves a dataset from a database to clients via HTTP. We know that gathering the data needed to respond to the client query takes a long time compared to executing code and/or reading data from RAM. Figure 2-6 shows how a traditional web server with a thread pool would look while it is responding to just two requests.

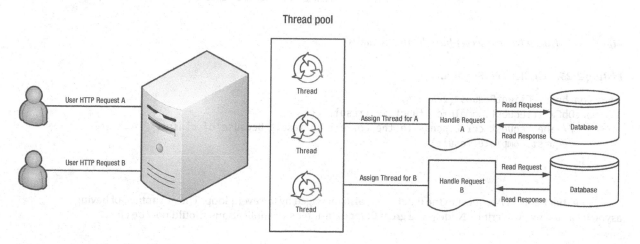

Figure 2-6. *How a traditional server handles two requests*

The same server in Node.js is shown in Figure 2-7. All the work is going to be inside a single thread, which results in lesser memory consumption and, due to the lack of thread context switching, lesser CPU load. Implementation-wise, the handleClientRequest is a simple function that calls out to the database (using a callback). When that callback returns, it completes the request using the request object it captured with a JavaScript closure. This is shown in the pseudocode in Listing 2-25.

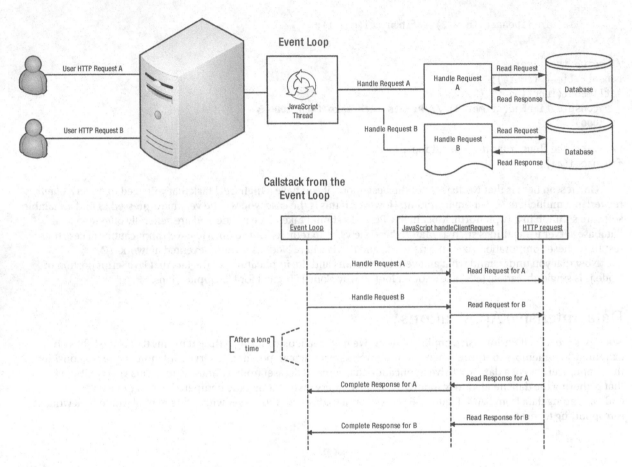

Figure 2-7. *How a Node.js server handles two requests*

Listing 2-25. handleClientRequest.js

```
function handleClientRequest(request) {
    makeDbCall(request.someInfo, function (result) {
        // The request corresponds to the correct db result because of closure
        request.complete(result);
    });
}
```

Note that the HTTP request to the database is also managed by the event loop. The advantage of having async IO and why JavaScript + Node.js is a great fit for data-intensive applications should now be clear.

The V8 JavaScript Engine

It is worth mentioning that all the JavaScript inside Node.js is executed by the V8 JavaScript engine. V8 came into being with the Google Chrome project. V8 is the part of Chrome that runs the JavaScript when you visit a web page.

Anybody who has done any web development knows how amazing Google Chrome has been for the web. The browser usage statistics reflect that quite clearly. According to w3schools.org (`www.w3schools.com/browsers/browsers_stats.asp`), nearly 56% of Internet users who visit their web site are now using Google Chrome. There are lots of reasons for this, but V8 and its speed is a very important factor. Besides speed, another reason for using V8 is that the Google engineers made it easy to integrate into other projects, and that it is platform independent.

More JavaScript

Now that we understand the motivation for using Node.js, let's delve further into JavaScript so that we can write maintainable applications. In addition to the fact that you need to be good at JavaScript if you want to become a Node.js developer, another reason to be good at JavaScript is to take advantage of the thriving ecosystem around Node.js and JavaScript in general. The language with the greatest number of projects on GitHub is JavaScript. Node.js is the most popular server-side technology on GitHub, as shown in Figure 2-8, and the third most popular repository overall.

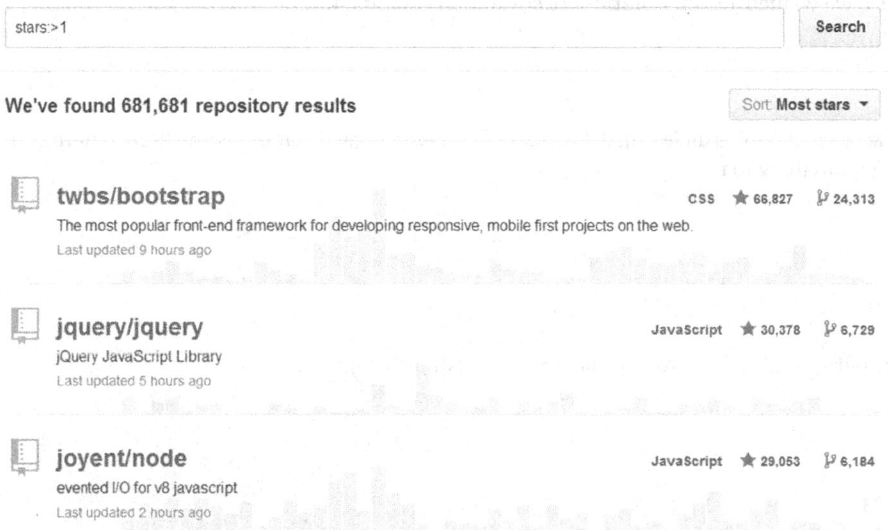

Figure 2-8. Most popular repositories on GitHub

Everything Is a Reference

JavaScript was designed to be simple and work with limited computer resources. Whenever we assign one variable to another, JavaScript copies a reference to the variable. To understand what this means, have a look at Listing 2-26.

Listing 2-26. reference1.js

```
var foo = { bas: 123 };
var bar = foo;
bar.bas = 456;
console.log(foo.bas); // 456
```

Passing objects around in function calls is extremely lightweight no matter what the size of the object, since we only copy the reference to the object and not every single property of the object. To make true copies of data (that break the reference link), you can just create a new object literal as shown in Listing 2-27.

Listing 2-27. reference2.js

```
var foo = { bas: 123 };
var bar = { bas: foo.bas }; // copy

bar.bas = 456;              // change copy
console.log(foo.bas);      // 123, original is unchanged
```

We can use quite a few third-party libraries to copy properties for arbitrary JavaScript objects. (It is a simple function we can write ourselves if we wanted.) Such libraries are covered in Chapter 4.

Default Values

The default value of any variable in JavaScript is undefined. You can see it being logged out in Listing 2-28, where you create a variable but do not assign anything to it.

Listing 2-28. default1.js

```
var foo;
console.log(foo); // undefined
```

Similarly, a nonexistent property on a variable returns undefined (Listing 2-29).

Listing 2-29. default2.js

```
var foo = { bar: 123 };
console.log(foo.bar); // 123
console.log(foo.bas); // undefined
```

Exact Equality

One thing to be careful about in JavaScript is the difference between == and ===. As JavaScript tries to be resilient against programming errors, == tries to do type coercion between two variables. For example, it converts a string to a number so that you can compare it with a number, as shown in Listing 2-30.

Listing 2-30. equal1.js

```
console.log(5 == '5');  // true
console.log(5 === '5'); // false
```

However, the choices it makes are not always ideal. For example, in Listing 2-31, the first statement is false because " and '0' are both strings and are clearly not equal. However, in the second case, both '0' and the empty string (") are falsy (in other words, they behave like false) and are therefore equal with respect to ==. Both statements are false when you use ===.

Listing 2-31. equal2.js

```
console.log('' == '0');  // false
console.log('' == 0);    // true

console.log('' === '0'); // false
console.log('' === 0);   // false
```

The tip here is to not compare different types to each another. Comparing different types of variables (such as a string with a number) is something you would not be able to do in a statically typed language anyway (a statically typed language is one where you *must* specify the type of a variable). If you keep this in mind, you can safely use ==. However, it is recommended that you always use === whenever possible.

Similar to == vs. ===, there are the inequality operators != and !==, which work in the same way. In other words, != does type coercion, whereas !== is strict.

null

null is a special JavaScript object used to denote an empty object. This is different from undefined, which is used by JavaScript for nonexistent and noninitialized values. You should not set anything to undefined because, by convention, undefined is the default value you should leave to the runtime. A good time to use null is when you want to explicitly say that something is not there, such as as a function argument. You will see its usage in the section on error handling in this chapter.

Truthy and Falsy

One important concept in JavaScript is truthy values and falsy values. Truthy values are those that behave like true in boolean operations and falsy values are those that behave like false in boolean operations. It is generally easier to use if / else / ! for null / undefined instead of doing an explicit check. An example of the falsy nature of these values is shown in Listing 2-32.

Listing 2-32. truthyandfalsy.js

```
console.log(null == undefined);  // true
console.log(null === undefined); // false

// Are these all falsy?
if (!false) {
    console.log('falsy');
}
if (!null) {
    console.log('falsy');
}
if (!undefined) {
    console.log('falsy');
}
```

Other important falsy values are 0 and the empty string (''). All object literals and arrays are truthy in JavaScript.

Revealing Module Pattern

Functions that return objects are a great way to create similar objects. An object here means data and functionality bundled into a nice package, which is the most basic form of Object Oriented Programming (OOP) that one can do. At the heart of the revealing module pattern is JavaScript's support for closures and ability to return arbitrary (function + data) object literals. Listing 2-33 is a simple example that shows how to create an object using this pattern.

Listing 2-33. revealingModules.js

```
function printableMessage() {
    var message = 'hello';
    function setMessage(newMessage) {
        if (!newMessage) throw new Error('cannot set empty message');
        message = newMessage;
    }
    function getMessage() {
        return message;
    }

    function printMessage() {
        console.log(message);
    }

    return {
        setMessage: setMessage,
        getMessage: getMessage,
        printMessage: printMessage
    };
}

// Pattern in use
var awesome1 = printableMessage();
awesome1.printMessage(); // hello

var awesome2 = printableMessage();
awesome2.setMessage('hi');
awesome2.printMessage(); // hi

// Since we get a new object everytime we call the module function
// awesome1 is unaffected by awesome2
awesome1.printMessage(); // hello
```

The great thing about this example is that it is a simple pattern to understand because it only utilizes closures, first-class functions, and object literals—concepts that are already familiar to you and that we covered extensively in the beginning of this chapter.

Understanding this

The JavaScript keyword **this** has a very special place in the language. It is something that is passed to the function depending upon how you call it (somewhat like a function argument). The simplest way to think of it is that it refers to the calling context. The calling context is the prefix used to call a function. Listing 2-34 demonstrates its basic usage.

Listing 2-34. this1.js

```
var foo = {
    bar: 123,
    bas: function () {
        console.log('inside this.bar is:', this.bar);
    }
}

console.log('foo.bar is: ', foo.bar); // foo.bar is: 123
foo.bas();                            // inside this.bar is: 123
```

Inside the function bas, this refers to foo since bas was called on foo and is therefore the calling context. So, what is the calling context if I call a function without any prefix? The default calling context is the Node.js global variable, as shown in Listing 2-35.

Listing 2-35. this2.js

```
function foo() {
    console.log('is this called from globals? : ', this === global); // true
}
foo();
```

Note that if we were running it in the browser, the global variable would be window instead of global.

Of course, since JavaScript has great support for first-class functions, we can attach a function to any object and change the calling context, as shown in Listing 2-36.

Listing 2-36. this3.js

```
var foo = {
    bar: 123
};

function bas() {
    if (this === global)
        console.log('called from global');
    if (this === foo)
        console.log('called from foo');
}

// global context
bas();     // called from global

// from foo
foo.bas = bas;
foo.bas(); // called from foo
```

There is one last thing you need to know about this in JavaScript. If you call a function with the new JavaScript operator, it creates a new JavaScript object and this within the function refers to this newly created object. Again, Listing 2-37 provides another simple example.

Listing 2-37. this4.js

```
function foo() {
    this.foo = 123;
    console.log('Is this global?: ', this == global);
}

// without the new operator
foo(); // Is this global?: true
console.log(global.foo); // 123

// with the new operator
var newFoo = new foo();  // Is this global?: false
console.log(newFoo.foo); // 123
```

You can see that we modified this.foo inside the function and newFoo.foo was set to that value.

Understanding Prototype

It is a common misunderstanding that JavaScript isn't object-oriented. It is indeed true that until recently JavaScript has not had the class keyword. But functions in JavaScript are more powerful than they are in many other languages and can be used to mimic traditional object oriented principles. The secret sauce is the new keyword (which you have already seen) and a property called the prototype. Every object in JavaScript has an internal link to another object called the *prototype*. Before we look at creating traditional classes in JavaScript, let's have a deeper look at prototype.

When you read a property on an object (for example, foo.bar reads the property bar from foo), JavaScript checks that this property exists on foo. If not, JavaScript checks if the property exists on foo.__proto__ and so on till __proto__ itself is not present. If a value is found at any level, it is returned. Otherwise, JavaScript returns undefined (see Listing 2-38).

Listing 2-38. prototype1.js

```
var foo = {};
foo.__proto__.bar= 123;
console.log(foo.bar); // 123
```

Although this works, the __ prefix in JavaScript is conventionally used for properties that should not be used by user code (in other words, private/internal implementation details). Therefore, you should not use __proto__ directly. The good news is that when you create an object using the new operator on a function, the __proto__ is set to the function's .prototype member, whichcan be verified with a simple bit of code, as shown in Listing 2-39.

Listing 2-39. prototype2.js

```
// Lets create a test function and set a member on its prototype
function foo() { };
foo.prototype.bar = 123;

// Lets create a object using `new`
// foo.prototype will be copied to bas.__proto__
var bas = new foo();

// Verify the prototype has been copied
console.log(bas.__proto__ === foo.prototype); // true
console.log(bas.bar);                          // 123
```

The reason why this is great is because prototypes are shared between all the objects (let's call these *instances*) created from the same function. This fact is shown in Listing 2-40.

Listing 2-40. prototype3.js

```
// Lets create a test function and set a member on its prototype
function foo() { };
foo.prototype.bar = 123;

// Lets create two instances
var bas = new foo();
var qux = new foo();

// Show original value
console.log(bas.bar); // 123
console.log(qux.bar); // 123

// Modify prototype
foo.prototype.bar = 456;

// All instances changed
console.log(bas.bar); // 456
console.log(qux.bar); // 456
```

Imagine you need 1,000 instances created. All the functionality you put on prototype is shared. And therefore lesson one:prototype saves memory.

Prototype is great for reading data off an object. However, if you set a property on the object, you break the link with the prototype because (as explained earlier) the prototype is only accessed if the property does not exist on the object. This disconnection from a prototype property caused by setting a property on an object is shown in Listing 2-41.

Listing 2-41. prototype4.js

```
// Lets create a test function and set a member on its prototype
function foo() { };
foo.prototype.bar = 123;

// Lets create two instances
var bas = new foo();
var qux = new foo();

// Overwrite the prototype value for bas
bas.bar = 456;
console.log(bas.bar); // 456 i.e. prototype not accessed

// Other objects remain unaffected
console.log(qux.bar); // 123
```

You can see that when we modified bas.bar, bas.__proto__.bar was no longer accessed. Hence, lesson two: .prototype is not good for properties you plan on writing to.

The question becomes what we should use for properties we need to write to. Recall from our discussion on this that this refers to the object that is created when the function is called with the new operator. So this is a perfect candidate for read/write properties and you should use it for all properties. But functions are generally not altered after creation. So functions are great candidates to go on .prototype. This way, functionality (functions/methods) is shared between all instances, and properties belong on individual objects. Now we can understand a pattern to write a class in JavaScript, which is shown in Listing 2-42.

Listing 2-42. class.js

```
// Class definition
function someClass() {
    // Properties go here
    this.someProperty = 'some initial value';
}
// Member functions go here:
someClass.prototype.someMemberFunction = function () {
    /* Do something using this */
    this.someProperty = 'modified value';
}

// Creation
var instance = new someClass();

// Usage
console.log(instance.someProperty); // some initial value
instance.someMemberFunction();
console.log(instance.someProperty); // modified value
```

Within the member function, we can get access to the current instance using this even though the same function body is shared between all instances. The reason should be obvious from our earlier discussion on this and the calling context. It is because we call a function on some instance, in other words, instance.someMemberFunction(). That is why inside the function this will refer to the instance used.

The main difference here vs. the revealing module pattern is that functions are shared between all the instances and don't take up memory for each new instance. This is because functions are only on .prototype and not on this. Most classes inside core Node.js are written using this pattern.

Error Handling

Error handling is an important part of any application. Errors can happen because of your code or even in code not in your controls, for example, database failure.

JavaScript has a great exception handling mechanism that you might already be familiar with from other programming languages. To throw an exception, you simply use the throw JavaScript keyword. To catch an exception, you can use the catch keyword. For code you want to run regardless of whether an exception was caught or not, you can use the finally keyword. Listing 2-43 is a simple example that demonstrates this.

Listing 2-43. error1.js

```
try {
    console.log('About to throw an error');
    throw new Error('Error thrown');
}
catch (e) {
    console.log('I will only execute if an error is thrown');
    console.log('Error caught: ', e.message);
}
finally {
    console.log('I will execute irrespective of an error thrown');
}
```

The catch section executes only if an error is thrown. The finally section executes despite any errors thrown within the try section. This method of exception handling is great for synchronous JavaScript. However, it will not work under an async workflow. Listing 2-44 demonstrates this shortcoming.

Listing 2-44. error2.js

```
try {
    setTimeout(function () {
        console.log('About to throw an error');
        throw new Error('Error thrown');
    }, 1000);
}
catch (e) {
    console.log('I will never execute!');
}

console.log('I am outside the try block');
```

The reason why it does not work is because at the point in time when the callback for setTimeout executes, we would already be outside the try/catch block. The setTimeout is going to call the function provided at a later point, and you can see that happen in this code sample since "I am outside the try block" is executed. The default behavior for uncaught exceptions in Node.js is to exit the process, and this is why our application crashes.

The correct way of doing this is to handle the error *inside* the callback, as shown shown in listing 2-45.

Listing 2-45. error3.js

```
setTimeout(function () {
    try {
        console.log('About to throw an error');
        throw new Error('Error thrown');
    }
    catch (e) {
        console.log('Error caught!');
    }
}, 1000);
```

This method works fine from inside an async function. But now we have an issue of finding a way to tell the code outside about the error. Let's look at a concrete example. Consider a simple getConnection function that takes a callback we need to call after a successful connection, as shown in Listing 2-46.

Listing 2-46. error4.js

```
function getConnection(callback) {
    var connection;
    try {
        // Lets assume that the connection failed
        throw new Error('connection failed');

        // Notify callback that connection succeeded?
    }
    catch (error) {
        // Notify callback about error?
    }
}
```

We need to notify the callback about success and failure. This is why Node.js has a convention of calling callbacks with the first argument of error *if* there is an error. If there is no error, we call back with the error set to null. As a result, a getConnection function designed for the Node.js ecosystem would be something like what is shown in Listing 2-47.

Listing 2-47. error5.js

```
function getConnection(callback) {
    var connection;
    try {
        // Lets assume that the connection failed
        throw new Error('connection failed');

        // Notify callback that connection succeeded?
        callback(null, connection);
    }
    catch (error) {
        // Notify callback about error?
        callback(error, null);
    }
}

// Usage
getConnection(function (error, connection) {
    if (error) {
        console.log('Error:', error.message);
    }
    else {
        console.log('Connection succeeded:', connection);
    }
});
```

Having the error as the first argument ensures consistency in error checking. This is the convention followed by all Node.js functions that have an error condition. A good example of this is the file system API, which we cover in Chapter 3. Also note that developers tend to use the falsy nature of null to check for errors.

Summary

In this chapter, we discussed important JavaScript concepts necessary to to be successful with Node.js. You should now have a deep understanding of what makes JavaScript and Node.js great for creating data-intensive applications and why it performs better than the technologies that preceded it. In the next chapter, we will discuss more Node.js specific patterns and practices for creating maintainable applications.

Works Cited

Ryan Dahl (2009) *Node.js* from JSConf.

"Nginx vs. Apache," http://blog.webfaction.com/2008/12/a-little-holiday-present-10000-reqssec-with-nginx-2/

"Browser Statistics," http://www.w3schools.com/browsers/browsers_stats.asp

"GitHub Repository Search by Stars," https://github.com/search?o=desc&q=stars%3A%3E1&s=stars&type=Repositories

CHAPTER 3

■ ■ ■

Core Node.js

Node.js ships with a number of built-in modules that provide a core set of features we can build upon. In this chapter, we will show the important parts of Node.js that every serious developer should be familiar with. The great thing about Node.js is that it is quite possible for the average developer to be completely aware of exactly how everything functions.

To successfully deliver large applications and work in sizable teams, we need a way of encapsulating complexity. JavaScript was originally designed to be read from top to bottom in a simplistic manner by a web browser, and files were loaded using `<script>` tags. As larger and larger applications have been written in JavaScript, two module systems (AMD and CommonJS) have been developed. They make code more manageable and reusable. Two patterns exist because the browser and server offer different challenges in terms of module-loading latency (network requests vs. file system). In this chapter, we will discuss these patterns and show how to reuse Node.js code in the browser.

One note about the code samples in this and every other chapter that uses multiple files is that the main entry point of the example is often called `app.js` following a Node.js community convention. So you should be able to run a sample as `node app.js`.

Node.js File-Based Module System

Kevin Dongaoor created CommonJS in 2009 with the goal to specify an ecosystem for JavaScript modules on the server. Node.js follows the CommonJS module specification. Following are a few salient points of the module system:

- Each file is its own module.

- Each file has access to the current module definition using the `module` variable.

- The export of the current module is determined by the `module.exports` variable.

- To import a module, use the globally available `require` function.

As always, it is best to jump right into the code. Let's consider a simple example where we want to share a function in file `foo.js` with various parts of our application. To export the function from the file, we simply assign it to `module.exports`, as shown in Listing 3-1.

Listing 3-1. intro/base/foo.js

```
module.exports = function () {
    console.log('a function in file foo');
};
```

In order to use this function from a file `bar.js`, we simply import `foo` using the globally available `require` function and store the returned value in a local variable, as shown in Listing 3-2.

Listing 3-2. intro/base/bar.js

```
var foo = require('./foo');
foo(); // logs out : "a function in file foo"
```

Node.js was designed to be simple, and this shows in its module system. Now that we have seen a simple example, let's dig deeper into various details, starting with the require function.

Node.js require Function

The Node.js require function is the main way of importing a module into the current file. There are three kinds of modules in Node.js: *core modules, file modules,* and external *node_modules,* all of which use the require function. We are discussing file modules at the moment.

When we make a require call with a relative path—for example, something like require('./filename') or require('../foldername/filename')—Node.js runs the destination JavaScript file in a new scope and returns whatever was the final value for module.exports in that file. This is the basis of file modules. Let's look at the ramifications of this design.

Node.js Is Safe

Modules in many programming environments are not safe and pollute the global scope. A simple example of this is PHP. Say you have a file foo.php that simply defines a function foo, as shown in Listing 3-3.

Listing 3-3. foo.php

```
function foo($something){
        return $something;
}
```

If you want to reuse this function in a file bar.php, you can simply include foo.php using the include function, and then everything from the file foo.php becomes a part of the (global) scope of bar.php. This allows you to use the function foo, as shown in Listing 3-4.

Listing 3-4. include Function in PHP

```
include('foo.php');
foo();
```

This design has quite a few negative implications. For example, what a variable foo means in a current file may change based on what you import. As a result, you cannot safely include two files, foo1 and foo2, if there is a chance that they have some variable with the same name. Additionally, *everything* gets imported, so you cannot have local only variables in a module. You can overcome this in PHP using namespaces, but Node.js avoids the potential of namespace pollution altogether.

Using the require function only gives you the module.exports variable, and you need to assign the result to a variable locally in order to use it in scope, as shown in Listing 3-5.

Listing 3-5. Code Snippet to Show That You Control the Name

```
var yourChoiceOfLocalName = require('./foo');
```

There is no accidental global scope—there are explicit names and files with similar internal local variable names that can coexist peacefully.

Conditionally Load a Module

require behaves just like any other function in JavaScript. It has no special properties. This means that you can choose to call it based on some condition and therefore load the module only if you need it, as shown in Listing 3-6.

Listing 3-6. Code Snippet to Lazy Load a Module

```
if(iReallyNeedThisModule){
    var foo = require('./foo');
}
```

This allows you to lazy load a module only on first use, based on your requirements.

Blocking

The require function blocks further code execution until the module has been loaded. This means that the code following the require call is not executed until the module has been loaded and executed. This allows you to avoid providing an unnecessary callback like you need to do for all async I/O in Node.js, which was discussed in Chapter 2. (See Listing 3-7.)

Listing 3-7. Code Snippet to Demonstrate That Modules Are Loaded Synchronously

```
// Blocks execution till module is loaded
var foo = require('./foo');

// Continue execution after it is loaded
console.log('loaded foo');
foo();
```

Cached

As you know from Chapter 2, reading something from the file system is an order of magnitude slower than reading it from RAM. Hence, after the first time a require call is made to a particular file, the module.exports is cached. The next time a call is made to require that resolves to the same file (in other words, it does not matter what the original relative file path passed to the require call is as long as the destination file is the same), the module.exports variable of the destination file is returned from memory, keeping things fast. Listing 3-8 shows this speed difference with a simple example.

Listing 3-8. intro/cached/bar.js

```
var t1 = new Date().getTime();
var foo1 = require('./foo');
console.log(new Date().getTime() - t1); // > 0

var t2 = new Date().getTime();
var foo2 = require('./foo');
console.log(new Date().getTime() - t2); // approx 0
```

Shared State

Having some mechanism to share state between modules is useful in various contexts. Since modules are cached, every module that require's foo.js will get the same (mutable) object if we return an object foo from a module foo.js. Listing 3-9 demonstrates this process with a simple example in which we export an object. This object is modified in app.js, as shown in Listing 3-10. This modification affects what is returned by require in bar.js, as shown in Listing 3-11. This allows you to share in-memory objects between modules that are useful for things like using modules for configuration. A sample execution is shown in Listing 3-12.

Listing 3-9. intro/shared/foo.js

```
module.exports = {
    something: 123
};
```

Listing 3-10. intro/shared/app.js

```
var foo = require('./foo');
console.log('initial something:', foo.something); // 123

// Now modify something:
foo.something = 456;

// Now load bar:
var bas = require('./bar');
```

Listing 3-11. intro/shared/bar.js

```
var foo = require('./foo');
console.log('in another module:', foo.something); // 456
```

Listing 3-12. Sample Run of intro/shared/app.js

```
$ node app.js
initial something: 123
in another module: 456
```

Object Factories

As we have shown, the same object is returned each time a require call resolves to the same file in a Node.js process. If you want some form of new object creation mechanism for each require function call, you can export a function from the source module that returns a new object. Then require the module at your destination and call this imported function to create a new object. An example is shown in Listing 3-13 where we export a function and then use this function to create a new object, as shown in Listing 3-14.

Listing 3-13. intro/factory/foo.js

```
module.exports = function () {
    return {
        something: 123
    };
};
```

Listing 3-14. intro/factory/app.js

```
var foo = require('./foo');

// create a new object
var obj = foo();

// use it
console.log(obj.something); // 123
```

Note that you can even do this in one step (in other words, require('./foo')();)

Node.js Exports

Now that we understand require a bit more, let's take a deeper look at module.exports.

module.exports

As stated earlier, each file in Node.js is a module. The items that we intend to export from a module should be attached to the module.exports variable. It is important to note that module.exports is already defined to be a new empty object in every file. That is, module.exports = {} is implicitly present. By default, every module exports an empty object, in other words, {}. (See Listing 3-15.)

Listing 3-15. intro/module.exports/app.js

```
console.log(module.exports); // {}
```

Exports Alias

So far, we have only been exporting a single object from a module. This can be done quite simply by assigning the object we need exported to module.exports. However, it is a common requirement to export more than one variable from a module. One way of achieving this is to create a new object literal and assign that to module.exports, as shown in Listing 3-16.

Listing 3-16. intro/exports/foo1.js

```
var a = function () {
    console.log('a called');
};

var b = function () {
    console.log('b called');
};

module.exports = {
    a: a,
    b: b
};
```

However, this is slightly cumbersome to manage because what the module *returns* can potentially be distant in terms of lines from what a module *contains*. In Listing 3-16, function a is defined a lot earlier than the point at which we actually export it to the outside world. So a common convention is to simply attach the objects we want to export to module.exports inline, as shown in Listing 3-17. This is possible because module.exports is implicitly set to {} by Node.js, as we saw earlier in Listing 3-15.

Listing 3-17. intro/exports/foo2.js

```
module.exports.a = function () {
    console.log('a called');
};

module.exports.b = function () {
    console.log('b called');
};
```

However, typing module.exports all the time becomes cumbersome as well. So Node.js helps us by creating an alias for module.exports called exports so instead of typing module.exports.something every time, you can simply use exports.something. This is shown in Listing 3-18.

Listing 3-18. intro/exports/foo3.js

```
exports.a = function () {
    console.log('a called');
};

exports.b = function () {
    console.log('b called');
};
```

It is important to note that exports is just like any other JavaScript variable; Node.js simply does exports = module.exports for us. If we add something for example, foo to exports, that is exports.foo = 123, we are effectively doing module.exports.foo = 123 since JavaScript variables are references, as discussed in Chapter 2.

However, if you do exports = 123, you break the reference to module.exports; that is, exports no longer points to module.exports. Also, it does not make module.exports = 123. Therefore, it is very important to know that you should only use the exports alias to *attach* stuff and not assign stuff to it directly. If you want to assign a single export, use module.exports = as we have been doing until this section.

Finally, you can run the code sample shown in Listing 3-19 to demonstrate that all of these methods are equivalent from consumption (import) point of view.

Listing 3-19. intro/exports/app.js

```
var foo1 = require('./foo1');
foo1.a();
foo1.b();

var foo2 = require('./foo2');
foo2.a();
foo2.b();

var foo3 = require('./foo3');
foo3.a();
foo3.b();
```

Modules Best Practices

Now that we understand the technology behind the Node.js file-based module system, let's look at a few best practices followed by the community. Node.js and JavaScript are quite resilient to programming errors and try to be flexible, which is why there are various ways that work. However, you should follow some conventions, and we highlight a few that are common in the community.

Do Not Use the .js Extension

It is better to do `require('./foo')` instead of `require('./foo.js')` even though both work fine for Node.js.

Reason: For browser-based module systems (such as RequireJS, which we look at later in this chapter), it is assumed that you do not provide the `.js` extension since we cannot look at the server filesystem to see what you meant. For the sake of consistency, avoid adding the .js extension in all your `require` calls.

Relative Paths

When using file-based modules, you need to use relative paths (in other words, do `require('./foo')` instead of `require('foo')`).

Reason: Non-relative paths are reserved for core modules and node_modules. We discuss core modules in this chapter and node_modules in the next chapter.

Utilize exports

Try and use the `exports` alias when you want to export more than one thing.

Reason: It keeps *what is exported* close to its *definition*. It is also conventional to have a local variable for each thing you export so that you can easily use it locally. Do this all in a single line, as shown in Listing 3-20.

Listing 3-20. Create a Local Variable and Also Export

```
var foo = exports.foo = /* whatever you want to export as `foo` from this module */ ;
```

Export an Entire Folder

If you have too many modules that go together that you keep importing into other files, try to avoid repeating the import, as shown in Listing 3-21.

Listing 3-21. Avoid Repeating Huge Import Blocks

```
var foo = require('../something/foo');
var bar = require('../something/bar');
var bas = require('../something/bas');
var qux = require('../something/qux');
```

Instead, create a single `index.js` in the `something` folder. In `index.js`, import all the modules once and then export them from this module, as shown in Listing 3-22.

Listing 3-22. Sample index.js

```
exports.foo = require('./foo');
exports.bar = require('./bar');
exports.bas = require('./bas');
exports.qux = require('./qux');
```

Now you can simply import this `index.js` whenever you need all these things:

```
var something = require('../something/index');
```

Reason: It is more maintainable. On the export side, individual modules (individual files) remain smaller—you do not need to put everything into a single file just so you can import it easily elsewhere. You just need to create an `index.js` file. On the import side, you have fewer `require` calls to write (and maintain).

Important Globals

Node.js provides a fair number of globally available utility variables. Some of these variables are true globals (shared between all modules) and some are local globals (variables specific to the current module). We have already seen an example of a few true globals, the `require` function. And we have seen a few module-level implicitly defined variables—module (used by `module.exports`) and exports. Let us examine a few more important globals.

console

`console` is one of the most useful globals available. Since it is so easy to start and restart a Node.js application from the command line, the console plays an important part in quickly showing what is happening in your application when you need to debug it. We have been using `console.log` throughout our examples for the same exact purpose. `console` has a lot more o functions, which we discuss in Chapter 11.

Timers

We've seen `setTimeout` before when we were discussing the Node.js event loop in Chapter 2. It sets up a function to be called after a specified delay in milliseconds. Note that this delay is the minimum interval after which the specified function is called. The actual duration after which it will be called depends upon the availability of the JavaScript thread as we saw in the section on thread starvation in Chapter 2. It also depends upon when the operating system schedules the Node.js process to execute (normally not an issue). A quick example of `setTimeout`, which calls a function after 1,000 milliseconds (in other words, one second) is shown in Listing 3-23.

Listing 3-23. globals/timers/setTimeout.js

```
setTimeout(function () {
    console.log('timeout completed');
}, 1000);
```

Similar to the `setTimeout` function is the `setInterval` function. `setTimeout` only executes the callback function *once* after the specified duration. But `setInterval` calls the callback repeatedly after *every* passing of the specified duration. This is shown in Listing 3-24 where we print out second passed after every second. Similar to `setTimeout`, the actual duration may exceed the specified value depending on the availability of the JavaScript thread.

Listing 3-24. globals/timers/setInterval.js

```
setInterval(function () {
    console.log('second passed');
}, 1000);
```

Both setTimeout and setInterval return an object that can be used to clear the timeout/interval using the clearTimeout/clearInterval functions. Listing 3-25 demonstrates how to use clearInterval to call a function after every second for five seconds, and then clear the interval after which the application will exit.

Listing 3-25. globals/timers/clearInterval.js

```
var count = 0;
var intervalObject = setInterval(function () {
    count++;
    console.log(count, 'seconds passed');
    if (count == 5) {
        console.log('exiting');
        clearInterval(intervalObject);
    }
}, 1000);
```

__filename and __dirname

These variables are available in each file and give you the full path to the file and directory for the current module. Being full paths means that they include everything right up to the root of the current drive this file resides on. Use the code in Listing 3-26 to see these values change as you move the file to different locations on your filesystem and run it.

Listing 3-26. globals/fileAndDir/app.js

```
console.log(__dirname);
console.log(__filename);
```

process

process is one of the most important globals provided by Node.js. In addition to a few useful member functions and properties that we will examine in the next section, it is a source of a few critical events that we examine in Chapter 5 when we take a deeper look at events.

Command Line Arguments

Since Node.js does not have a main function in the traditional C/C++/JAVA/C# sense, you use the process object to access the command line arguments. The arguments are available as the process.argv member property, which is an array. The first element is node (that is, the node executable), the second element is the name of the JavaScript file passed into Node.js to start the process, and the remaining elements are the command line arguments. As an example, consider a simple file argv.js, which simply logs these out to the console as shown in Listing 3-27. If you run it as node argv.js foo bar bas, you will get output similar to what is shown in Listing 3-28.

Listing 3-27. globals/process/argv.js

```
// argv.js
console.log(process.argv);
```

Listing 3-28. Sample Output from argv.js

```
[ 'node',
  '/path/to/file/on/your/filesystem/argv.js',
  'foo',
  'bar',
  'bas' ]
```

Some excellent libraries exist for processing the command line arguments in a meaningful way in Node.js. We will examine one such library when we learn more about NPM in the next chapter.

process.nextTick

`process.nextTick` is a simple function that takes a callback function. It is used to put the callback into the next cycle of the Node.js event loop. It is designed to be highly efficient, and it is used by a number of Node.js core libraries. Its usage is simple enough to demonstrate, and an example is shown in Listing 3-29. The output from this sample is shown in Listing 3-30.

Listing 3-29. globals/process/nexttick.js

```
// nexttick.js
process.nextTick(function () {
    console.log('next tick');
});
console.log('immediate');
```

Listing 3-30. Sample nexttick.js output

```
immediate
next tick
```

As you can see, the immediate call is executed first, whereas the `nextTick` callback is executed in the next run of the event loop. The reason why you should be aware of this function is because, due to the async nature of Node. js, this function will show up in the call stack quite commonly as this will be the starting point of a Node.js event loop. Everything before this function is in C. Everything after this function in the call stack is in JavaScript.

Buffer

Buffer World! Pure JavaScript is great for Unicode strings. However, to work with TCP streams and the file system, the developers added native and fast support to handle binary data. The developers did this in Node.js using the `Buffer` class, which is available globally.

As a Node.js developer working on applications, your main interaction with buffer will most likely be in the form of converting `Buffer` instances to `string` or strings to `Buffer` instances. In order to do either of these conversions, you need to need to tell the `Buffer` class about what each character means in terms of bytes. This information is called character encoding. Node.js supports all the popular encoding formats like ASCII, UTF-8, and UTF-16.

Converting strings to buffers is really simple. You just call the `Buffer` class constructor (see prototype discussion in Chapter 2 to review classes in JavaScript) passing in a string and an encoding. Converting a `Buffer` instance to a string is just as simple. You call the Buffer instance's `toString` method passing in an encoding scheme. Both of these are demonstrated in Listing 3-31.

Listing 3-31. globals/buffer/buffer.js

```
// a string
var str = "Hello Buffer World!";

// From string to buffer
var buffer = new Buffer(str, 'utf-8');

// From buffer to string
var roundTrip = buffer.toString('utf-8');
console.log(roundTrip); // Hello
```

global

The variable `global` is our handle to the global namespace in Node.js. If you are familiar with front-end JavaScript development, this is somewhat similar to the `window` object. All the true globals we have seen (`console`, `setTimeout`, and `process`) are members of the `global` variable. You can even add members to the global variable to make it available everywhere, as shown in Listing 3-32. The fact that this makes the variable `something` available everywhere is demonstrated in Listing 3-33.

Listing 3-32. globals/global/addToGlobal.js

```
global.something = 123;
```

Listing 3-33. globals/global/app.js

```
console.log(console === global.console);      // true
console.log(setTimeout === global.setTimeout); // true
console.log(process === global.process);       // true

// Add something to global
require('./addToGlobal');
console.log(something); // 123
```

Even though adding a member to global is something that you can do, it is *strongly* discouraged. The reason is that it makes it extremely difficult to know where a particular variable is coming from. The module system is designed to make it easy to analyze and maintain large codebases. Having globals all over the place is not maintainable, scalable, or reusable without risk. It is, however, useful to know the fact that it can be done and, more importantly, as a library developer you can extend Node.js any way you like.

Core Modules

The Node.js design philosophy is to ship with a few battle-tested core modules and let the community build on these to provide advanced functionality. In this section, we examine a few of the important core modules.

Consuming Core Modules

Consuming core modules is very similar to consuming file-based modules that you write yourself. You still use the `require` function. The only difference is that instead of a relative path to the file, you simply specify the name of the module to the `require` function. For example, to consume the core `path` module, you write a require statement like `var path = require('path')`. As with file-based modules, there is no implicit global namespace pollution and what you get is a local variable that you name yourself to access the contents of the module. For example, in `var path = require('path')` we are storing it in a local variable called path. Now let's examine a few core modules that you should be aware of to be successful with Node.js.

Path Module

Use `require('path')` to load this module. The path module exports functions that provide useful string transformations common when working with the file system. The key motivation for using the `path` module is to remove inconsistencies in handling file system paths. For example, `path.join` uses the forward slash `` `/` `` on UNIX-based systems like Mac OS X vs. backward slash `` `\` `` on Windows systems. Here is a quick discussion and sample of a few of the more useful functions.

path.normalize(str)

This function fixes up slashes to be OS specific, takes care of . and .. in the path, and also removes duplicate slashes. A quick example to demonstrate these features is shown in Listing 3-34.

Listing 3-34. core/path/normalize.js

```
var path = require('path');

// Fixes up .. and .
// logs on Unix: /foo
// logs on Windows: \foo
console.log(path.normalize('/foo/bar/..'));

// Also removes duplicate '//' slashes
// logs on Unix: /foo/bar
// logs on Windows: \foo\bar
console.log(path.normalize('/foo//bar/bas/..'));
```

path.join([str1], [str2], …)

This function joins any number of paths together, taking into account the operating system. A sample is shown in Listing 3-35.

Listing 3-35. core/path/join.js

```
var path = require('path');

// logs on Unix: foo/bar/bas
// logs on Windows: foo\bar\bas
console.log(path.join('foo', '/bar', 'bas'));
```

dirname, basename, and extname

These functions are three of the most useful functions in the path module. path.dirname gives you the directory portion of a specific path string (OS independent), and path.basename gives you the name of the file. path.extname gives you the file extension. An example of these functions is shown in Listing 3-36.

Listing 3-36. core/path/dir_base_ext.js

```
var path = require('path');

var completePath = '/foo/bar/bas.html';

// Logs : /foo/bar
console.log(path.dirname(completePath));

// Logs : bas.html
console.log(path.basename(completePath));

// Logs : .html
console.log(path.extname(completePath));
```

You should now have an understanding of how to use path and what its design goals are. Path has a few other useful functions that you can explore online using the official Node.js documentation (http://nodejs.org/api/path.html).

fs Module

The fs module provides access to the filesystem. Use require('fs') to load this module. The fs module has functions for renaming files, deleting files, reading files, and writing to files. A simple example to write to the file system and read from the file system is shown in Listing 3-37.

Listing 3-37. core/fs/create.js

```
var fs = require('fs');

// write
fs.writeFileSync('test.txt', 'Hello fs!');

// read
console.log(fs.readFileSync('test.txt').toString());
```

One of the great things about the fs module is that it has asynchronous as well as synchronous functions (using the -Sync postfix) for dealing with the file system. As an example, to delete a file you can use unlink or unlinkSync. A synchronous version is shown in Listing 3-38, and an asynchronous version of the same code is shown in Listing 3-39.

Listing 3-38. core/fs/deleteSync.js

```
var fs = require('fs');
try {
    fs.unlinkSync('./test.txt');
    console.log('test.txt successfully deleted');
}
catch (err) {
    console.log('Error:', err);
}
```

Listing 3-39. core/fs/delete.js

```
var fs = require('fs');
fs.unlink('./test.txt', function (err) {
    if (err) {
        console.log('Error:', err);
    }
    else {
        console.log('test.txt successfully deleted');
    }
});
```

The main difference is that the async version takes a callback and is passed the error object if there is one. We discussed this convention of error handling using a callback and an error argument in Chapter 2.

We also saw in Chapter 2 that accessing the file system is an order of magnitude slower than accessing RAM. Accessing the filesystem synchronously blocks the JavaScript thread until the request is complete. It is better to use the asynchronous functions whenever possible in busy processes such as in a web server scenario.

More information about the fs module can be found online in the official Node.js documentation (http://nodejs.org/api/fs.html).

os Module

The os module provides a few basic (but vital) operating-system related utility functions and properties. You can access it using a require('os') call. For example, if we want to know the current system memory usage, we can use os.totalmem() and os.freemem() functions. These are demonstrated in Listing 3-40.

Listing 3-40. core/os/memory.js

```
var os = require('os');
var gigaByte = 1 / (Math.pow(1024, 3));
console.log('Total Memory', os.totalmem() * gigaByte, 'GBs');
console.log('Available Memory', os.freemem() * gigaByte, 'GBs');
console.log('Percent consumed', 100 * (1 - os.freemem() / os.totalmem()));
```

A vital facility provided by the os module is information about the number of CPUs available, as shown in Listing 3-41.

Listing 3-41. core/os/cpus.js

```
var os = require('os');
console.log('This machine has', os.cpus().length, 'CPUs');
```

We will learn how to take advantage of this fact in Chapter 13 when we discuss scalability.

util Module

The util module contains a number of useful functions that are general purpose. You can access the util module using a require('util') call. To log out something to the console *with a timestamp,* you can use the util.log function, as shown in Listing 3-42.

Listing 3-42. core/util/log.js

```
var util = require('util');
util.log('sample message'); // 27 Apr 18:00:35 - sample message
```

Another extremely useful feature is string formatting using the util.format function. This function is similar to the C/C++ printf function. The first argument is a string that contains zero or more *placeholders*. Each placeholder is then replaced using the remaining arguments based on the meaning of the placeholder. Popular placeholders are %s (used for strings) and %d (used for numbers). These are demonstrated in Listing 3-43.

Listing 3-43. core/util/format.js

```
var util = require('util');
var name = 'nate';
var money = 33;

// prints: nate has 33 dollars
console.log(util.format('%s has %d dollars', name, money));
```

Additionally, util has a few functions to check if something is of a particular type (isArray, isDate, isError). These functions are demonstrated in Listing 3-44.

Listing 3-44. core/util/isType.js

```
var util = require('util');
console.log(util.isArray([])); // true
console.log(util.isArray({ length: 0 })); // false

console.log(util.isDate(new Date())); // true
console.log(util.isDate({})); // false

console.log(util.isError(new Error('This is an error'))); // true
console.log(util.isError({ message: 'I have a message' })); // false
```

Reusing Node.js Code in the Browser

Before we learn how to reuse Node.js code in the browser, we need to learn a bit more about the various module systems. We need to understand the need for AMD and what differentiates it from CommonJS.

Introducing AMD

As we discussed in the beginning of this chapter, Node.js follows the CommonJS module specification. This module system is great for the server environment when we have immediate access to the file system. We discussed that loading a module from the file system in Node.js is a blocking call for the first time. Consider the simple case of loading two modules, as shown in Listing 3-45.

Listing 3-45. Code Snippet to Show Loading Two Modules Using CommonJS

```
var foo = require('./foo');
var bar = require('./bar');
// continue code here
```

In this example bar.js is not parsed until all of foo.js has been loaded. In fact, Node.js doesn't even know that you will need bar.js until foo.js is loaded and the line require('./bar') is parsed. This behavior is acceptable in a server environment where it is considered a part of the bootstrap process for your application. You mostly require things when starting your server and afterward these are returned from memory.

However, if the same module system is used in the browser, each require statement would need to trigger an HTTP request to the server. This is an order of magnitude slower and less reliable than a file system access call. Loading a large number of modules can quickly degrade the user experience in the browser. The solution is async, in-parallel, and upfront loading of modules. To support this async loading, we need a way to declare that this file will depend upon ./foo and ./bar upfront and continue code execution using a callback. There is already a specification for exactly this called async module definition (AMD). The same example from Listing 3-45 in AMD format is shown in Listing 3-46.

Listing 3-46. code snippet to show loading two modules using AMD

```
define(['./foo', './bar'], function(foo, bar){
        // continue code here
});
```

The define function is not native to the browser. These must be provided by a third-party library. The most popular of these for the browser is RequireJS (http://requirejs.org/).

To reiterate, the browser has different latency requirements from a server startup. This necessitates a different syntax for loading modules in an async manner. The different nature of the require call is what makes reusing Node.js code in the browser slightly more involved. Before we dig deeper, let's set up a RequireJS bootstrap application.

Setting Up RequireJS

Since we need to serve HTML and JavaScript to a web browser, we need to create a basic web server. We will be using Chrome as our browser of choice as it is available on all platforms and has excellent developer tools support. The source code for this sample is available in the chapter3/amd/base folder.

Starting the Web Server

We will be using server.js, which is a very basic HTTP web server that we will write ourselves in Chapter 6. Start the server using Node.js (node server.js). The server will start listening for incoming requests from the browser on port 3000. If you visit http://localhost:3000, the server will try to serve index.html from the same folder as server.js if it is available.

Download RequireJS

You can download RequireJS from the official web site (http://requirejs.org/docs/download.html). It is a simple JavaScript file that you can include in your project. It is already present in chapter3/amd/base folder.

Bootstrapping RequireJS

Create a simple index.html in the same folder as server.js with the contents shown in Listing 3-47.

Listing 3-47. amd/base/index.html

```
<html>
<script
    src="./require.js"
    data-main="./client/app">
</script>
<body>
    <p>Press Ctrl + Shift + J (Windows) or Cmd + Opt + J (MacOSX) to open up the console</p>
</body>
</html>
```

We have a simple script tag to load require.js. When RequireJS loads, it looks at the data-main attribute on the script tag that loaded RequireJS and considers that as the application entry point. In our example, we set the data-main attribute to ./client/app and therefore RequireJS will try and load http://localhost:3000/client/app.js.

Client-Side Application Entry Point

As we set up RequireJS to load /client/app.js, let's create a client folder and an app.js inside that folder that simply logs out something to the console, as shown in Listing 3-48.

Listing 3-48. amd/base/client/app.js

```
console.log('Hello requirejs!');
```

Now if you open up the browser http://localhost:3000 and open the dev tools (press F12), you should see the message logged to the console, as shown in Figure 3-1.

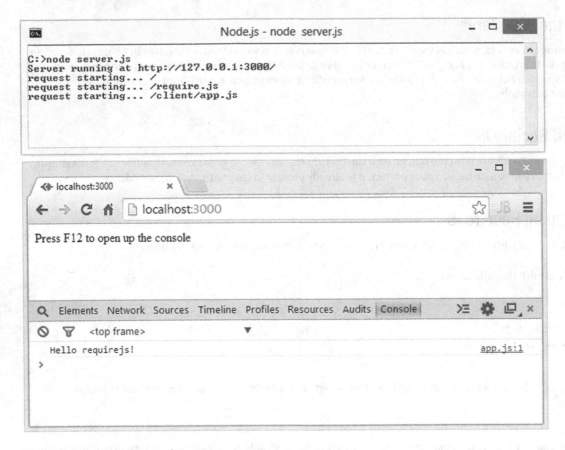

Figure 3-1. basic AMD sample

That is the basics of setting up RequireJS. This setup will be used in the remaining demos in this section. You only need to copy this `server.js` + `index.html` + `require.js` + `client/app.js` combination and start hacking to your heart's content.

There are a lot more configuration options for RequireJS and you are encouraged to explore the API documentation that is available online at `http://requirejs.org/docs/api.html`.

Playing with AMD

Now that we know how to start a RequireJS browser application, let's see how we can import/export variables in modules. We will create three modules: `app.js`, `foo.js`, and `bar.js`. We will use `foo.js` and `bar.js` from `app.js` using AMD. This demo is available in `chapter3/amd/play` folder.

To export something from a module, you can simply return it from the `define` callback. For example, let's create a file `foo.js` that exports a simple function, as shown in Listing 3-49.

Listing 3-49. amd/play/client/foo.js

```
define([], function () {
    var foo = function () {
        console.log('foo was called');
    };
    return foo; // function foo is exported
});
```

To be upfront about all the modules we need in a file, the root of the file contains a call to define. To load modules ./foo and ./bar in app.js in the same folder, the define call will be as shown in Listing 3-50.

Listing 3-50. amd/play/client/app.js

```
define(['./foo', './bar'], function (foo, bar) {
        // use foo and bar here
});
```

define can take a special argument called exports, which behaves similar to the exports variable in Node.js. Let's create the module bar.js using this syntax, as shown in Listing 3-51.

Listing 3-51. amd/play/client/bar.js

```
define(['exports'], function (exports) {
    var bar = exports.log = function () {
        console.log('bar.log was called');
    };
});
```

Note that you can only use exports to attach variables you want to export (for example, exports.log = /*something*/), but you cannot assign it to something else (exports = /*something*/) as that would break the reference the exports variable monitored by RequireJS. This is conceptually quite similar to the exports variable in Node.js. Now, let's complete app.js and consume both of these modules, as shown in Listing 3-52.

Listing 3-52. amd/play/client/app.js

```
define(['./foo', './bar'], function (foo, bar) {
    foo();
    bar.log();
});
```

If you run this application, you get the desired result shown in Figure 3-2.

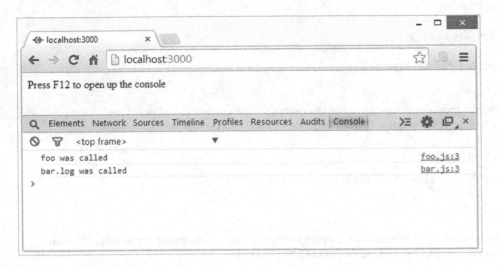

Figure 3-2. foo and bar used from app.js

The real benefit of using this alternate (AMD) syntax for modules becomes evident when we look at the network tab within the chrome debug tools, as shown in Figure 3-3.

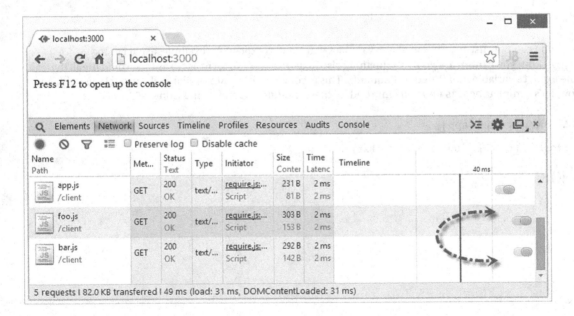

Figure 3-3. basic AMD sample

You can see that foo.js and bar.js were downloaded in parallel as soon as app.js was downloaded, and RequireJS found that app.js needs foo.js and bar.js to function because of the call to define.

More about AMD

Here are a few useful and interesting facts that you should know about AMD to complete your knowledge:

- Modules are cached. This is similar to how modules are cached in Node.js—that is, the same object is returned every time.

- Many of these arguments to define are optional and there are various ways to configure how modules are scanned in RequireJS.

- You can still do conditional loading of specific modules using a require call, which is another function provided by RequireJS as shown in Listing 3-53. This function is also async and is different from the Node.js version of require.

Listing 3-53. Snippet to show how you can conditionally load a module in AMD

```
define(['./foo', './bar'], function(foo, bar){
    if(iReallyNeedThisModule){
        require(['./bas'], function(bas){
            // continue code here.
        });
    }
});
```

The objective here was to give a quick overview of how you can use RequireJS and understand that the browser is different from Node.js.

Converting Node.js Code into Browser Code

As you can see, there are significant differences between the browser module systems (AMD) and the Node.js module system (CommonJS). However, the good news is that the Node.js community has developed a number of tools to take your CommonJS / Node.js code and transform it to be AMD / RequireJS compatible. The most commonly used one (and the one on which other tools rely) is Browserify (http://browserify.org/).

Browserify is a command line tool that is available as an NPM module. NPM modules are discussed in great detail in the next chapter. For now, it is sufficient to know that if you have Node.js installed as specified in Chapter 1, you already have npm available. To install Browserify as on the command line tool, simply execute the command shown in Listing 3-54. (Note: On Mac OS X you need to run this as root (sudo npm install -g browserify).

Listing 3-54. Installing Browserify

```
npm install -g browserify
```

This installs Browserify globally (a concept that will become clear in the next chapter) and makes it further available on the command line. Now if you run browserify, you should see output as shown in Figure 3-4 to indicate a successful installation.

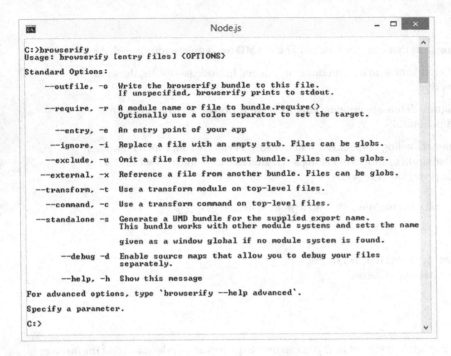

Figure 3-4. Using Browserify on the command prompt

The most common way to use browserify is to specify an entry point for your Node.js module and convert that file and all of its dependencies files into a single AMD compatible file using the -o (--outfile) parameter. As always, let's jump into a demo to get some hands-on experience.

Browserify Demo

In this section, we will create a few simple Node.js modules and then use Browserify to convert them to AMD syntax and run them in the browser. All of the code for this example is present in the chapter3/amd/browserify folder.

First off, we will create three files that follow the Node.js / CommonJS module specification (code is in the chapter3/amd/browserify/node folder). We are using foo.js (Listing 3-55) and bar.js (Listing 3-56) from app.js (Listing 3-57) using CommonJS. You can run this code in Node.js to see that it works as expected.

Listing 3-55. amd/browserify/node/foo.js

```
module.exports = function () {
    console.log('foo was called');
}
```

Listing 3-56. amd/browserify/node/bar.js

```
exports.log = function () {
    console.log('bar.log was called');
}
```

Listing 3-57. amd/browserify/node/app.js

```
var foo = require('./foo');
var bar = require('./bar');

foo();
bar.log();
```

Now let's convert this code so that it is an AMD compatible module. On the command line, run the command as shown in Listing 3-58.

Listing 3-58. Command Line Arguments to Convert app.js into an AMD Module

```
browserify app.js -o amdmodule.js
```

This takes app.js and all its dependencies (foo.js and bar.js) and converts them into a single AMD compatible module amdmodule.js in the same folder. As a final step, we simply load this module from our client app.js (Listing 3-59) to show that it works in the browser.

Listing 3-59. amd/browserify/client/app.js

```
define(['../node/amdmodule'], function (amdmodule) {
});
```

Now if we start the server (server.js) and open up the web browser (http://localhost:3000), you will see the console.log messages in the chrome dev tools, as shown in Figure 3-5. We have successfully ported the Node.js code to the browser.

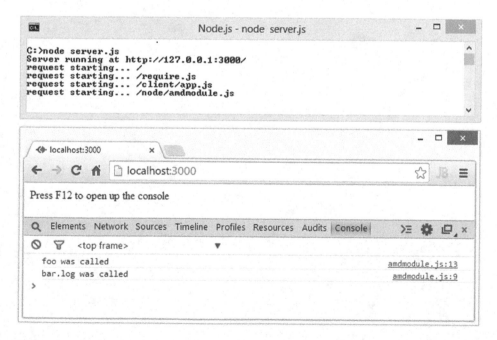

Figure 3-5. *Reusing Node.js/CommonJS code in the browser*

One thing to note is that it is not possible to convert *every* Node.js module into a browser module. Specifically, Node.js modules that depend on features only available on the server (such as the file system) will not work in the browser.

Browserify has a lot of options and is also able to navigate NPM packages (`node_modules`). You can learn more about Browserify online at `http://browserify.org/`.

Summary

In this chapter, we discussed a few important maintainability topics that you should be aware of in order to become a successful Node.js developer. We looked closely at `require`/`module.exports` combinations, giving you a firm understanding of the principles of Node.js modules and its simplicity. Then we discussed a few core built-in Node.js modules. (We will take a look at more of these core modules as we learn about events, streams, and specific areas such as TCP/HTTP.) Finally, we discussed the differences between AMD and CommonJS and how to reuse Node.js code in the browser.

In the next chapter, we will discuss one of the great things about Node.js—its open source ecosystem. There are packages upon packages of open source Node.js projects available, and we will show you how you can take advantage of them using NPM.

CHAPTER 4

∎ ∎ ∎

Node.js Packages

Any application that can be written in JavaScript will eventually be written in JavaScript.

—Atwood's Law, by Jeff Atwood

As we saw in Chapter 3, core Node.js does not ship with a massive list of libraries. There is a good reason for this. Having something shipped as a part of core Node.js has the potential to stifle competition and evolution of ideas. As a result, the core Node.js tries to limit what it contains and relies on the open source community to paint the complete picture. Letting the open source community find the best solution to a problem X is better than prescribing a one-hammer-for-everything solution.

The number of JavaScript developers is much larger than for any other programming language. Also, more and more people are writing more and more libraries to do any given task X in the browser, and all of this work is available for you to use in your applications.

To make it easy to consume third-party JavaScript libraries in your applications, Node.js comes with its own package management system called *Node Package Manager* (NPM). In this chapter, we will discuss how to consume NPM packages in our applications. We will cover a few important ones every Node.js developer should be aware of. We will also use this as a practical opportunity to learn more about how JavaScript works.

Revisiting Node Modules

In the previous chapter, we learned that there are three kinds of Node.js modules: file-based modules, core modules, and external node_modules. We discussed file-based modules and core modules, and now we will look at node_modules. To understand them better, let's take a deeper look at the file system scanning order of the Node.js require function.

- If the module name passed into the require function is prefixed with './' or '../' or '/', then it is assumed to be a file-based module and the file is loaded, as we saw in the Chapter 3. Some sample calls: require('./bar'), require('../bar/bar'), require('/full/path/to/a/node/module/file')

- Otherwise, we look for core modules with the same name, for example, `bar` if the call was require('bar'). If no core module matching this name is found, we look for a node_module called `bar`.

Scanning for node_modules

Let's just look at an example first. If a file /home/ryo/project/foo.js has a require call require('bar'), Node.js scans the file system for node_modules in the following order. The first bar.js that is found is returned.

- /home/ryo/project/**node_modules/bar.js**

- /home/ryo/**node_modules/bar.js**

- /home/**node_modules/bar.js**

- **/node_modules/bar.js**

In other words, Node.js looks for `node_modules/bar.js` in the current folder followed by every parent folder until it reaches the root of the file system tree for the current file or until a bar.js is found. A simple example of this is a module foo.js that loads a module node_modules/bar.js, as shown in Listing 4-1 and Listing 4-2.

Listing 4-1. hello/foo.js

```
var bar = require('bar');
bar(); // hello node_modules!
```

Listing 4-2. hello/node_modules/bar.js

```
module.exports = function () {
    console.log('hello node_modules!');
}
```

As you can see, our module bar.js looks *exactly* the same as it would if we were simply using file-based modules. And that is intentional. The *only* difference between file-based modules and node_modules is *the way in which the file system is scanned* to load the JavaScript file. All other behavior is the same.

Folder-Based Modules

Before we discuss all the advantages of node_modules mechanism, we need to learn one final code organization trick supported by the Node.js require function. It is not uncommon to have a several files working toward a singular goal. It makes sense to organize these files into a single module that can be loaded with a single require call. We discussed organizing such files into a single folder and having an index.js to represent the folder in Chapter 3.

This is such a common scenario that Node.js has explicit support for this mechanism. That is, if a path to the module resolves to a folder (instead of a file), Node.js will look for an index.js file in that folder and return that as the module file. This is demonstrated in a simple example (chapter4/folderbased/indexbased1) where we export two modules bar1.js and bar2.js using an index.js and load the module bar (and implicitly bar/index.js) in a module foo, as shown in Listing 4-3 (run node folderbased/indexbased1/foo.js).

Listing 4-3. Implicit Loading of index.js from a Folder (Code: folderbased/indexbased1)

```
// bar/bar1.js
module.exports = function () {
    console.log('bar1 was called');
}

// bar/bar2.js
module.exports = function () {
    console.log('bar2 was called');
}
```

```
// bar/index.js
exports.bar1 = require('./bar1');
exports.bar2 = require('./bar2');

// foo.js
var bar = require('./bar');
bar.bar1();
bar.bar2();
```

As we stated earlier, the *only* difference between file-based modules and node_modules is the way in which the file system is scanned. So for a call like require('./bar'), the same code for node_modules would be a simple move of the bar folder into node_modules/bar folder and the require call changed from require('./bar') to require('bar').

This example is present in the chapter4/folderbased/indexbased2 folder (run node folderbased/ indexbased2/foo.js). Since the call now resolves to node_modules/bar folder, Node.js looks for node_modules/bar/ index.js and since it is found, that is what is returned for require('bar'). (See Listing 4-4.)

Listing 4-4. Implicit Loading of index.js from a node_modules/module Folder (Code: folderbased/indexbased2)

```
// node_modules/bar/bar1.js
module.exports = function () {
    console.log('bar1 was called');
}

// node_modules/bar/bar2.js
module.exports = function () {
    console.log('bar2 was called');
}

// node_modules/bar/index.js
exports.bar1 = require('./bar1');
exports.bar2 = require('./bar2');

// foo.js
var bar = require('bar'); // look for a node_modules module named bar
bar.bar1();
bar.bar2();
```

The require call semantics look exactly the same for node_modules as they do for core modules (compare require('fs') to require('bar') function call). This is intentional. You get the feeling of expanding the built in Node.js functionality when using node_modules.

Using folder-based code organization when working with node_modules is a common strategy and what you should do whenever possible. In other words, refrain from making top-level JavaScript files in the node_modules folder if all you want is a single file. Then, instead of node_modules/bar.js, use a node_modules/bar/index.js file.

Advantages of node_modules

We now understand that node_modules are the same as file-based modules with just a different file system scanning mechanism used on loading the module JavaScript file. The obvious question at this point is, "What are the advantages?"

Simplify Long File Relative Paths

Say you have a module foo/foo.js that provides a number of utilities that you need to use at a variety of different places in your application. In a section bar/bar.js, you would have a require call require('../foo/foo.js'), and in a section bas/nick/scott.js, you would have a require call like require('../../../foo/foo.js'). At this point, you should ask yourself, "Is this foo module self-contained?" If so, it is a great candidate to move into node_modules/foo/index.js in the root of your project folder. This way you can simplify your calls to be just require('foo') throughout your code.

Increasing Reusability

If you want to share a module foo with another project, you only need to copy node_modules/foo to that project. In fact, if you are working on two similar sub projects, you can move node_modules/foo to a folder that contains both your projects, as shown in Listing 4-5. This makes it easier for you to maintain foo from a single place.

Listing 4-5. Sample Code Organization for Sub Projects Using Shared node_modules

```
projectroot
    |-- node_modules/foo
    |-- subproject1/project1files
    |-- subproject2/project2files
```

Decreasing Side Effects

Because of the way the node_modules are scanned, you can limit the availability of a module to a particular section of your codebase. This allows you to safely do partial upgrades, assuming that your original code organization was as shown in Listing 4-6.

Listing 4-6. Demo Project Using a Module foo

```
projectroot
    |-- node_modules/foo/fooV1Files
    |-- moduleA/moduleAFiles
    |-- moduleB/moduleBFiles
    |-- moduleC/moduleCFiles
```

Now, when you are working on a new module (say moduleD) that needs a new (and backward incompatible) version of module foo, you can simply organize your code as shown in Listing 4-7.

Listing 4-7. Partial Upgrade of Module foo

```
projectroot
    |-- node_modules/foo/fooV1Files
    |-- moduleA/moduleAFiles
    |-- moduleB/moduleBFiles
    |-- moduleC/moduleCFiles
    |-- moduleD
            |-- node_modules/foo/fooV2Files
            |-- moduleDFiles
```

In this way, moduleA, moduleB, and moduleC continue to function as always and you get to use the new version of foo in moduleD.

Overcoming Module Incompatibility

Node.js does not suffer from the module dependency/incompatibility hell that is present in a number of traditional systems. In many traditional module systems, a moduleX cannot work with moduleY because they depend on different (and incompatible) versions of moduleZ. In Node.js, each module can have its own node_modules folder and different versions of moduleZ can coexist. Modules do not *need* to be global in Node.js!

Module Caching and node_modules

You might recall from our discussion in Chapter 3 that require caches the result of a require call after the first time. The reason is the performance boost you get from not needing to load JavaScript and run it from the file system again and again. We said that require returns the same object each time the path resolves *to the same file*.

As we have already shown, node_modules are just a different way of scanning for file-based modules. Therefore, they follow the same module caching rule. If you have two folders where moduleA and moduleB require module foo i.e require('foo'), which is present in some parent folder as shown in Listing 4-8, they get the same object (as exported from node_modules/foo/index.js in the given example).

Listing 4-8. Both Modules Get the Same foo Module

```
projectroot
    |-- node_modules/foo/index.js
    |-- moduleA/a.js
    |-- moduleB/b.js
```

However, consider the code organization as shown in Listing 4-9. Here moduleB's require('foo') call will resolve to moduleB/node_modules/foo/index.js, whereas moduleA's require call will resolve to node_modules/foo/index.js and therefore they do not get the same object.

Listing 4-9. Module A and B Get Different foo Module

```
projectroot
    |-- node_modules/foo/index.js
    |-- moduleA/a.js
    |-- moduleB
        |-- node_modules/foo/index.js
        |-- b.js
```

This is a good thing as we have already seen that it prevents you from going into a dependency problem. But this disconnection is something you should be conscious of.

JSON

NPM uses JSON files for configuring modules. Before we delve deeper into NPM, let's take a look at JSON.

Beginner's Introduction to JSON

JSON is a standard format used to transfer data over the network. It can be considered a subset of JavaScript object literals for most purposes. It basically restricts what JavaScript object literals are considered valid. JSON objects to make it easier to implement the specification and shield users from edge cases they need to worry about. We will take a practical look at JSON in this section.

One of restrictions enforced by the JSON spec is that you must use quotation marks for JavaScript object keys. This allows you to avoid cases where you cannot have JavaScript keywords as keys for an object literal. For example, the JavaScript in Listing 4-10 was a syntax error in ECMA Script 3 (an older version of JavaScript) because for is a JavaScript keyword.

Listing 4-10. Invalid JS in Old Browsers (Pre ECMAScript 5)

```
var foo = { for : 0 }
```

Instead, a valid representation of the same object compatible with all version of JavaScript would be what is shown in Listing 4-11.

Listing 4-11. Valid JS Even in Old Browsers (Pre ECMAScript 5)

```
var foo = { "for" : 0 }
```

Additionally, the JSON spec limits what you can have as a value for a given key to be a safe subset of JavaScript objects. The values can only be a string, number, boolean (true or false), array, null, or another valid JSON object. A JSON object that demonstrates all of these is shown in Listing 4-12.

Listing 4-12. Sample JSON

```
{
    "firstName": "John",
    "lastName": "Smith",
    "isAlive": true,
    "age": 25,
    "height_cm": 167.64,
    "address": {
        "streetAddress": "21 2nd Street",
        "city": "New York",
        "state": "NY",
    },
    "phoneNumbers": [
        { "type": "home", "number": "212 555-1234" },
        { "type": "fax",  "number": "646 555-4567" }
    ],
    "additionalInfo": null
}
```

The firstName value is a string, age is a number, isAlive is a boolean, phoneNumbers is an array of valid JSON objects, additionalInfo is null, and address is another valid JSON object. The reason for this restriction of types is to simplify the protocol. If you need to pass arbitrary JavaScript objects as JSON, you can try and serialize/deserialize them to a string (common for dates) or a number (common for enums).

Another restriction is that the last property must not have an extra comma. Again this is because of old browsers (for example, IE8) being restrictive about what is and isn't a valid JavaScript literal. For example, in Listing 4-13, although the first example is a valid JavaScript object literal in Node.js and modern browsers, it is not valid JSON.

Listing 4-13. Trailing Command after Last Value

```
// Invalid JSON
{
    "foo": "123",
    "bar": "123",
}
// Valid JSON
{
    "foo": "123",
    "bar": "123"
}
```

To reiterate, JSON is pretty much just JavaScript object literals with a few reasonable restrictions that only serve to increase the ease of implementing the specification and that have been instrumental in its popularity as a data transfer protocol.

Loading JSON in Node.js

Since JSON is such an important part of the web, Node.js has fully embraced it as a data format, even locally. You can load a JSON object from the local file system the same way you load a JavaScript module. Every single time within the module loading sequence, if a file.js is *not found*, Node.js looks for a file.json. If it is found, it returns a JavaScript object representing the JSON object. Let's work on a simple example. Create a file config.json with a single key foo and a string value (shown in Listing 4-14).

Listing 4-14. json/filebased/config.js

```
{
    "foo": "this is the value for foo"
}
```

Now, let's load this file as a JavaScript object in app.js and log out the value for the key foo (shown in Listing 4-15).

Listing 4-15. json/filebased/app.js

```
var config = require('./config');
console.log(config.foo); // this is the value for foo
```

This simplicity of loading JSON explains why so many libraries in the Node.js community rely on using a JSON file as a configuration mechanism.

The JSON Global

Data transfer over the wire takes place in the form of bytes. To write a JavaScript object from memory onto the wire or to save to a file, you need a way to convert this object into a JSON string. There is a global object in JavaScript called JSON that provides utility functions for converting a string representation of JSON to JavaScript objects and converting JavaScript objects into a JSON string ready to be sent over the wire or written to the file or anything else you want to do with it. This JSON global is available in Node.js as well all modern browsers.

To convert a JavaScript object to a JSON string, you simply call JSON.stringify passing in the JavaScript object as an argument. This function returns the JSON string representation of the JavaScript object. To convert a JSON string into a JavaScript object, you can use the JSON.parse function, which simply parses the JSON string and returns a JavaScript object matching the information contained in the JSON string, as shown in Listing 4-16 and Listing 4-17.

Listing 4-16. json/convert/app.js

```
var foo = {
    a: 1,
    b: 'a string',
    c: true
};

// convert a JavaScript object to a string
var json = JSON.stringify(foo);
console.log(json);
console.log(typeof json); // string

// convert a JSON string to a JavaScript object
var backToJs = JSON.parse(json);
console.log(backToJs);
console.log(backToJs.a); // 1
```

Listing 4-17. Output from app.js

```
$ node app.js
{"a":1,"b":"a string","c":true}
string
{ a: 1, b: 'a string', c: true }
1
```

This rudimentary understanding of JSON and how it relates to JavaScript object literals will go a long way in making you a successful Node.js developer.

NPM

Now we know how to create reusable modules using node_modules. The next piece of the puzzle answers the question, "How do I get what the community has shared with me?"

The answer: Node Package Manger, lovingly called *NPM*. If you installed Node.js as specified in Chapter 1, it not only added "node" to the command line, but it also added "npm", which is simply a command line tool that integrates with the online NPM registry (www.npmjs.org/). A screenshot of NPM is shown in Figure 4-1.

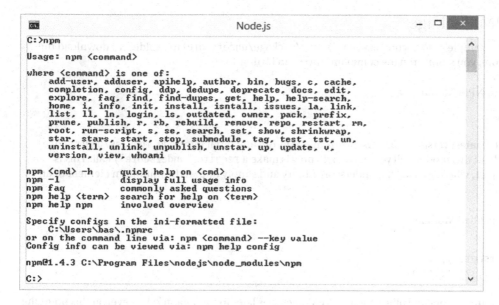

Figure 4-1. At its simplest, NPM is a way to share node_modules with the community

package.json

An integral part of the NPM ecosystem is a simple JSON file called package.json. This file has special meaning for NPM. It is vital to have it set up properly when you want to share your module with the world, but it is just as useful if you are consuming modules from other people. To create a package.json file in the current folder, just run the code in Listing 4-18 on the command line.

Listing 4-18. Initializing a package.json File

```
$ npm init
```

This will ask you a few questions such as the name of the module and its version. I tend to just press enter until the end. This creates a boilerplate package.json in the current folder with the name set to the current folder, version set to 0.0.0, and a few other reasonable defaults as shown in Listing 4-19.

Listing 4-19. A Default package.json

```
{
  "name": "foo",
  "version": "0.0.0",
  "description": "",
  "main": "index.js",
  "scripts": {
    "test": "echo \"Error: no test specified\" && exit 1"
  },
  "author": "",
  "license": "ISC"
}
```

Installing an NPM Package

Let's install a module, for example, underscore (`www.npmjs.org/package/underscore`) to a folder. To download the latest version of underscore, you simply run the command shown in Listing 4-20.

Listing 4-20. Installing an NPM Module

```
$ npm install underscore
```

This will download the latest version of underscore from npmjs.org and put it into `node_modules/underscore` in the current folder. TO load this module, all you need to do now is make a `require('underscore')` call. This is demonstrated in Listing 4-21, where we load the underscore library and simply output the minimum element of an array to the console.

Listing 4-21. Using an Installed Module

```
// npm/install/app.js
var _ = require('underscore');
console.log(_.min([3, 1, 2])); // 1
```

We will take a look at underscore and other popular NPM packages later in this chapter; however, at this point the focus is on the NPM command line tool.

Saving Dependencies

Whenever you run `npm install`, you have an optional command line flag available (`--save`) that tells NPM to write the information about what you installed into package.json, as shown in Listing 4-22.

Listing 4-22. Installing an NPM Module and Updating package.json

```
$ npm install underscore --save
```

If you run install with `--save`, not only will it download `underscore` into node_modules, it will also update dependencies inside package.json to point to the installed version of underscore, as shown in Listing 4-23.

Listing 4-23. Updated Section of package.json

```
"dependencies": {
    "underscore": "^1.6.0"
  }
```

There are quite a few advantages of keeping track of dependencies this way. For one, it is easy to know which published version of a particular library you are using (depend upon), simply by looking at your package.json. The same holds true when you are browsing the source code of other people's modules. Just open up their package.json to see what they are relying on.

Refresh the node_modules Folder

To refresh the node_modules folder from your package.json, you can run the following command:

```
$ npm install
```

This simply looks at your package.json file and downloads a fresh copy of the dependencies specified in your package.json.

Another advantage of using a package.json is that you can now potentially exclude node_modules from your source control mechanism since you can always get a copy from npmjs.org with a simple npm install command.

Listing All Dependencies

To see which packages you have installed, you can run npm ls command, as shown in Listing 4-24.

Listing 4-24. Listing Dependencies

```
$ npm ls
foo@0.0.0
└── underscore@1.6.0
```

Removing a Dependency

Remove a dependency using npm rm. For example, npm rm underscore --save deletes the underscore folder from node_modules locally and modifies the dependencies section of your package.json. This command has an intuitive synonym npm uninstall since the command was npm install for installation.

package.json Online Dependency Tracking

One more advantage of using package.json for dependency tracking is that if at some later point you decide to share your module with the rest of the world (that is, share at npmjs.org), you do not need to ship the dependencies as your users can download them online.

If your package.json is set up properly and they install your module, NPM will automatically download and install the dependencies of your module. To see a simple example, let's install a package (request) that has dependencies, as shown in Listing 4-25.

Listing 4-25. Installing a Module with Lots of Dependencies

```
$ npm install request
npm http GET https://registry.npmjs.org/request
npm http GET https://registry.npmjs.org/tunnel-agent
npm http GET https://registry.npmjs.org/json-stringify-safe
...truncated...
npm http 304 https://registry.npmjs.org/delayed-stream/0.0.5
request@2.34.0 node_modules\request
├── aws-sign2@0.5.0
...truncated...
├── json-stringify-safe@5.0.0
└── form-data@0.1.2 (async@0.2.10, combined-stream@0.0.4)
```

You can see that NPM not only installed request but also brought down a number of other packages that request depends upon. Each of these packages can, in turn, depend on other packages (for example, form-data depends upon async and combined-stream), and they get their own local copy of the packages they depend upon (and will be downloaded into their own node_modules folder, for example, node_modules/request/node_modules/form-data/node_modules/async). As discussed earlier, because of the way the require function works in Node.js, you can safely use sub modules that depend on different version of the same module since they each get their own copy when set up using NPM.

Semantic Versioning

Good Node.js packages/NPM follow semantic versioning, which is an industry standard and should be followed as a good software development practice. Semantics is the study of meaning. *Semantic versioning* means versioning your software in a way that the version numbers have significant meaning. There is much that can be said about semantic versioning, but the following is a simplified but practical explanation for a Node.js developer:

- Put simply, Node.js developers follow a three-digit versioning scheme X.Y.Z where all X, Y, and Z are non-negative integers. X is the major version, Y is the minor, and Z is the patch version.
- Patch versions *must* be incremented if backward compatible fixes are introduced.
- Minor versions *must* be incremented if backward compatible new features are introduced.
- Major versions *must* be incremented if backward *incompatible* fixes/features/changes are introduced.

Keeping these points in mind, you can see that v1.5.0 of a package should be in-place replaceable by v1.6.1 as the new version should be backward compatible (major version 1 is same). This is something that good packages strive for.

However, the reality is that errors are sometimes inevitably introduced with new versions, or the code was used in a manner that the original authors of the package did not predict. In such a case, some breaking change may be introduced unknowingly.

Semantic Versioning in NPM / package.json

NPM and package.json have great support for semantic versioning. You can tell NPM which version of a package you want. For example, the following code installs the exact version 1.0.3 of underscore:

```
$ npm install underscore@1.0.3
```

You can tell NPM that you are okay with all patch versions of 1.0 using a tilde "~":

```
$ npm install underscore@"~1.0.0"
```

Next up, to tell NPM that you are okay with any minor version changes use "^":

```
$ npm install underscore@"^1.0.0"
```

Other version string operators supported include ">=" and ">", which have intuitive mathematical meanings, such as ">=1.4.2". Similarly there are "<=" and "<" , for example, "<1.4.2". There is also a * that can be used at various locations to match any number such as 1.0.* (for example, 1.0.0, 1.0.1, and so on) or 1.* (for example, 1.1.0, 1.3.4, and so on) and simply *, which will get you the latest version *every time*.

You can use these semantic version strings in package.json as well. For example, the following package.json tells NPM that your package is compatible with any minor upgrade on v1.6.0 of underscore:

```
"dependencies": {
  "underscore": "^1.6.0"
}
```

Updating Dependencies

Whenever you use --save flag, the default that NPM uses for updating package.json dependencies section is "^", preceded by the downloaded version. The reason is that you should always try to use the latest version where the major version number hasn't changed. This way, you get any new features plus latest bug fixes for free, and there should not be any breaking changes.

As an example, if run the following command, you get a package.json dependencies section:

```
$ npm install request@1.0.0 -save
```

Following is the default version string added to package.json:

```
"dependencies": {
  "request": "^1.0.0"
}
```

However 1.0.0 is not the latest published version of request. To find the latest online version that is compatible with the current semantic version specified in package.json (in this example ^1.0.0), you can run npm outdated, as shown in Listing 4-26.

Listing 4-26. Check Latest Version of Packages

```
$ npm outdated
npm http GET https://registry.npmjs.org/request
npm http 304 https://registry.npmjs.org/request
Package  Current  Wanted  Latest  Location
request    1.0.0   1.9.9  2.34.0  request
```

You can see that the latest version compatible with ^1.0.0 is ^1.9.9, which is the wanted version based on the semantic string found in our package.json. It also shows you that there is an even more recent version available.

To update these packages to the newest compatible version and save the results into your package.json (to match the version numbers with what is downloaded), you can simply run the following command. Your updated package.json is shown in Listing 4-27.

```
$ npm update -save
```

Listing 4-27. Updated package.json

```
"dependencies": {
  "request": "^1.9.9"
}
```

Having this basic knowledge of package.json and the commands npm install, npm rm, npm update, and the --save NPM flag along with a respect for semantic versioning is mostly all you need to know about managing NPM packages in your project.

Global Node.js Packages

It is really simple to make command line utilities in Node.js. One of the most common motivations for learning Node.js nowadays is the fact that a lot of management utilities for front-end projects are written in Node.js. There are projects to test your web front ends, compile various new programming languages like CoffeeScript and TypeScript into JavaScript and Sass, stylus, and less into CSS, minify your JavaScript and CSS and so on. Popular front-end JavaScript projects such as jQuery, AngularJS, Ember.js, and React depend on Node.js scripts to manage their projects.

The objective of global Node.js packages is to provide command line utilities that you can use from (surprise) the command line. All of the NPM commands we have seen take an optional -g flag to indicate that you are working with global modules.

Remember in Chapter 3 we used a utility Browserify to convert Node.js code into browser AMD compatible code. Browserify is a Node.js package we installed globally (npm install -g browserify). This put *browserify* on the command line, which we used in the previous chapter.

Similarly, you can update global packages (npm update -g package-name), list global packages (npm ls -g), and uninstall packages (npm rm -g package-name). For example, to uninstall Browserify, you would run npm rm -g browserify.

When installing modules globally, NPM does not modify your system configuration. The reason the command line utility suddenly becomes available is because global modules are placed in a location (for example, /usr/local/bin on Mac OSX and the user roaming profile's NPM folder on Windows) where they become available on the command line.

Using require with Global Modules

Modules installed globally are not meant to be used with a require function call in your code, although many packages that support the global flag also support being installed locally in your project (the node_modules folder). If installed locally, that is, without the –g flag, you can use them with the require function as we have already seen. A good and simple example of this is the rimraf module (www.npmjs.org/package/rimraf).

If rimraf is installed globally (npm install -g rimraf), it provides a command line utility that you can use cross platform for recursively and forcefully removing a directory (effectively rm -rf in Unix command line lingo). To remove a directory foo after installing rimraf globally, simply run rimraf foo.

To do the same from your Node.js code, install rimraf locally (npm install rimraf), create an app.js as shown in Listing 4-28, and run it (node app.js).

Listing 4-28. global/rimrafdemo/app.js

```
var rimraf = require('rimraf');
rimraf('./foo', function (err) {
    if (err) console.log('Error occured:', err);
    else console.log('Directory foo deleted!');
})
```

For the sake of completeness, it is worth mentioning that there is a way to load modules from a global location if you set the NODE_PATH environment variable. But this is *strongly* discouraged when consuming modules and you should use dependencies locally (package.json and node_modules).

Package.json and require

Most of package.json we have seen has been for NPM. All it was doing was managing our dependencies and putting them in node_modules. From this point on, require works the way we have already shown. It looks for a JavaScript file/folder in node_modules that matches what we asked require to load, for example, foo in require('foo'). We have already shown that if it resolves to a folder, Node.js tries to load index.js from that folder as the result of the module load.

There is one final thing about the `require` function that you need to know about. You can use package.json to redirect `require` to load a different file from a folder instead of the default (which would look for an index.js). This is done using the `main` property in a package.json. The value of this property is the path to the JavaScript file you want to load. Let's look at an example and create a directory structure, as shown in Listing 4-29.

Listing 4-29. Project Structure for Demo Code chapter4/mainproperty

```
|-- app.js
|-- node_modules
        |-- foo
             |-- package.json
             |-- lib
                   |-- main.js
```

`main.js` is a simple file that logs to the console to indicate it was loaded, as shown in Listing 4-30.

Listing 4-30. mainproperty/node_modules/foo/lib/main.js

```
console.log('foo main.js was loaded');
```

Within the package.json, simply point main to `main.js` in the `lib` folder:

```
{
    "main" : "./lib/main.js"
}
```

This means that if anybody were to `require('foo')`, Node.js would look at package.json, see the `main` property, and run `'./lib/main.js'`. So let's require this module in our `app.js`. If you run it (`node app.js`), you will see that indeed main.js was loaded.

```
require('foo');
```

One thing worth mentioning is that "main" is the *only* property that `require` and hence the node executable cares about. All other properties in package.json are for NPM / npm executable, which is specifically designed for package management.

The advantage of having this "main" property is that it allows library developers complete freedom on how they want to architect their project and keep the structure as clear as they want.

Quite commonly, people will put simple Node.js packages (ones that can go in a file) into a file name that matches the package name `packageName.js` and then create a package.json to point to the file name. For example, this is what `rimraf` does—it has a `rimraf.js` and that is what the `main` property of package.json points to, as shown in Listing 4-31.

Listing 4-31. package.json from the rimraf npm Module Showing the Main Property

```
{
  "name": "rimraf",
  "version": "2.2.7",
  "main": "rimraf.js",

... truncated...
```

Modules Recap

At this point, it might seem that `require` has a lot to do. Indeed it does, but in our honest opinion, it is all kept quite simple and here is a recap to prove that you are already a Node.js modules expert! Assume you `require('something')`. Then the follow is the logic followed by Node.js:

- If `something` is a core module, return it.
- If `something` is a relative path (starts with './' , '../') return that file OR folder.
- If not, look for `node_modules/filename` or `node_modules/foldername` each level up until you find a file OR folder that matches `something`.

When matching a file OR folder:, follow these steps:

- If it matched a file name, return it.
- If it matched a folder name and it has package.json with main, return that file.
- If it matched a folder name and it has an index file, return it.

Of course, the file can be a `file.js` or `file.json` since JSON is first class in Node.js! For JSON, we return the parsed JSON and for JavaScript files we simply execute the file and return 'module.exports'.

That's all there is to it. Having this knowledge allows you to open up and look at thousands of open source Node.js packages available on npmjs.org and Github.

Popular Node.js Packages

Now that we know all the important details of consuming Node.js packages, let's look at a few of the most popular ones.

Underscore

Underscore (`npm install underscore`) is by far the most popular JavaScript library available on NPM. It is the library with the largest number of dependents (other packages that depend on this package).

It is called *underscore* because it creates a global variable '_' when used in the browser. In node, you are free to name the variable returned from `require('underscore')` whatever you want, but it is conventional to still do `var _ = require('underscore')`.

Underscore provides a lot of functional programming support to JavaScript that you find in other languages such as Ruby and Python. Every good JavaScript developer should be familiar with it. Note that bits of functionality of underscore is being added to core JavaScript with new versions, but to work across all browsers and Node.js it is recommended that you use underscore if only for consistency and lesser cognitive load (so you have less stuff to keep in your head at a time).

Let's say we have an array of numbers and we only need the ones that are greater than 100. Doing this in plain old JavaScript would look tedious, as shown in Listing 4-32.

Listing 4-32. popular/underscore/filter/raw.js

```
var foo = [1, 10, 50, 200, 900, 90, 40];

var rawResults = []
for (i = 0; i < foo.length; i++) {
    if (foo[i] > 100) {
        rawResults.push(foo[i]);
    }
}
console.log(rawResults);
```

The same code in underscore is much simpler and neater. The function _.filter takes an array, passes each element of the array to a function (second argument), and returns an array containing all the elements where the second function returns true. This is demonstrated in Listing 4-33.

Listing 4-33. popular/underscore/filter/us.js

```
var foo = [1, 10, 50, 200, 900, 90, 40];

var _ = require('underscore');
var results = _.filter(foo, function (item) { return item > 100 });
console.log(results);
```

Before we continue, we will give a quick introduction to functional programming. Functions in functional programming have well-defined mathematical behavior. If the input is the same, the output will always be the same. This is the mathematical definition of a function and not the programming construct that we as developers commonly associate with the term *function*. As a simple example of a mathematical function, think of addition. If foo and bar are the same, then foo+bar will always be the same. Therefore + is what we call a *pure* function. Similarly, a JavaScript function function add(a,b){return a+b} is a pure function as the output *only* depends on the inputs.

Pure functions are easy to understand, follow along, and therefore maintain. The thing that prevents code from being purely functional is *state*. State is maintained by mutating (modifying) objects. This is what we are doing in the raw example. We are mutating the rawResults array in a loop. This is commonly called an imperative way of coding or thinking. However, in the underscore example, the filter function takes two arguments and, if the arguments are the same, the result will always be the same. Therefore, it is *functional*.

Again, the key motivation for this is maintainability. If you know what filter does, it is immediately obvious from that one line what is being filtered. There is a lot more that can be said about functional programming, but this should have teased you enough to discover more.

Now let's look at other functions in underscore. The _.map function takes an array, calls a function for each element of the array storing the return value as a result, and returns a new array consisting of all the results. It basically maps an input array, through a function, into an output array. For example, let's say we want to multiply each element of an array with 2. We can do that quite simply using _.map as shown in Listing 4-34.

Listing 4-34. popular/underscore/map/app.js

```
// using underscore
var foo = [1, 2, 3, 4];

var _ = require('underscore');
var results = _.map(foo, function (item) { return item * 2 });
console.log(results);
```

Another scenario common in collections is to get all elements *except* those that match a condition. For this, we can use _.reject. An example to get only the odd elements in an array is shown in Listing 4-35.

Listing 4-35. popular/underscore/reject/app.js

```
var _ = require('underscore');
var odds = _.reject([1, 2, 3, 4, 5, 6], function(num){ return num % 2 == 0; });
console.log(odds); // [1, 3, 5]
```

To get the maximum element of an array use _.max, to get the minimum use _.min:

```
var _ = require('underscore');
var numbers = [10, 5, 100, 2, 1000];
console.log(_.min(numbers)); // 2
console.log(_.max(numbers)); // 1000
```

That's sufficient to get you started. To learn more about the functions provided by underscore, have a look at the online documentation at http://underscorejs.org/.

Handling Command Line Arguments

We looked at process.argv in Chapter 3. This is a simple array of all the command line argument passed into the node process. We promised in the previous chapter that once we learn about NPM, we will look at a library that offers better command line handling. Well, here it is. It's called optimist. Because of the sheer number of command line tools published on NPM, this is one of the most downloaded packages out there.

As always, install using npm install optimist. It simply exports an object that contains the parsed command line arguments as the argv property. So instead of using process.argv, you just use require('optimist').argv.

Enough talk. Let's code. Create a JavaScript file that simply logs out the processed arguments, as shown in Listing 4-36.

Listing 4-36. popular/optimist/app1.js

```
var argv = require('optimist').argv;
console.log(argv);
```

If you run this right now, you will notice output similar to that in Listing 4-37.

Listing 4-37. Simple Run of popular/optimist/app1.js

```
$ node app.js
{ _: [],
  '$0': 'node /path/to/your/app.js' }
```

Optimist preserves the first two members of the process.argv array (which are the node executable and the path to your JavaScript file) as '$0'. Since we'd like to keep our output clean for this demo, let's just delete this property so we can log everything else to the console. To do this, modify your code to be what is shown in Listing 4-38.

Listing 4-38. popular/optimist/app.js

```
var argv = require('optimist').argv;
delete argv['$0'];
console.log(argv);
```

Now, if you run the app you get the following output:

```
$ node app.js
{ _: [] }
```

Ahh, much better. The property argv._ is an array of all the command line arguments that are passed in which are not flags. Flags are arguments that begin with a minus '-' sign, for example, '-f'. Let's run app.js and pass in a bunch of arguments, as shown in Listing 4-39.

Listing 4-39. Showing Output When Using Non-Flag Arguments

```
$ node app.js foo bar bas
{ _: [ 'foo', 'bar', 'bas' ] }
```

As a use case, consider a simple scenario of implementing a delete file utility. If wanted, to support taking in multiple files for deletion, all of these files would go in the 'argv._' property.

If we wanted to support flags such as forced delete (-f), optimist supports this completely. Any simple flags you pass in become a property of argv with the value set to true. For example, if you want to check if the flag f was set, just check if argv.f is truthy. Optimist even supports some pretty fancy shortcuts, as shown in Listing 4-40.

Listing 4-40. Showing output when using flags

```
$ node app.js -r -f -s
{ _: [], r: true, f: true, s: true }

$ node app.js -rfs
{ _: [], r: true, f: true, s: true }
```

Optimist also supports flags that take values if, say, you want to accept a timeout flag (-t 100). Optimist supports them similarly to the way it supports simple flags. The property matching the flag name is set on argv (argv.t in this case) and the value is set to the value the user passed (in this case 100), as shown in Listing 4-41.

Listing 4-41. Showing Output When Using Flags with Values

```
$ node app.js -t 100
{ _: [], t: 100 }

$ node app.js -t "la la la la"
{ _: [], t: 'la la la la' }
```

As you can see, you get a lot of processing done for you right out of the box without any configuration. For most purposes where you want to support simple flags, this will be sufficient.

Optimist has lots of other options as well that allow for advanced configuration such as forcing the user to pass in an argument, forcing an argument to be a boolean, listing all the command line arguments supported in the configuration, and providing default argument values. No matter what your command line processing use case, NPM/optimist has you covered and you should definitely explore it further.

Handling Date/Time Using Moment

The built-in JavaScript Date type is fairly limited. It is good enough for simple cases, for example, you can create a date representing the current time with a simple constructor call. There is also a constructor that lets you create dates at the resolution that you want to work on such as year, month, day, hours, minutes, seconds, and milliseconds. One thing to be aware of with JavaScript dates is that the month is 0 index based. So January is 0, February is 1, and so on. You can see a few dates created in Listing 4-42.

Listing 4-42. popular/moment/rawdate.js

```
// Now
var now = new Date();
console.log('now is:', now);

// get sections of time
var milliseconds = now.getMilliseconds();
var seconds = now.getSeconds();
var hours = now.getHours();
var minutes = now.getMinutes();
var date = now.getDate();
var month = now.getMonth();
var year = now.getFullYear();

// detailed constructor for a date
var dateCopy = new Date(year, month, date,
                            hours, minutes, seconds, milliseconds);
console.log('copy is:', dateCopy);

// Other dates
// year, month, date
console.log('1 jan 2014:', new Date(2014, 0, 1));
// year, month, date, hour
console.log('1 jan 2014 9am', new Date(2014, 0, 1, 9));
```

There are lots of features in addition to the basic feature set of JavaScript Date that are provided by moment (npm install moment). At its core, moment provides a function that can be used to wrap a JavaScript date object into a moment object. There are lots of ways to create a moment object. The simplest is to simply pass in a date object. Conversely, to convert a moment object to a JavaScript date, simply call the toDate member function. This is demonstrated in Listing 4-43.

Listing 4-43. popular/moment/wrapping.js

```
var moment = require('moment');

// From date to moment
var wrapped = moment(new Date());
console.log(wrapped);

// From moment to date
var date = wrapped.toDate();
console.log(date);
```

Moment provides reliable string parsing. The result of a parsed string is a wrapped moment object. This is shown in Listing 4-44. To unwrap, we simply call toDate as we already saw in Listing 4-43.

Listing 44. popular/moment/parsing.js

```
var moment = require('moment');

// From string to date
console.log(moment("12-25-1995", "MM-DD-YYYY").toDate());
console.log(moment("2010-10-20 4:30", "YYYY-MM-DD HH:mm").toDate());
```

Another great feature provided by moment is date formatting support (that is, date to a string conversion). A few examples are shown in Listing 4-45.

Listing 4-45. popular/moment/formatting.js

```
var moment = require('moment');

var date = new Date(2010, 1, 14, 15, 25, 50);
var wrapped = moment(date);

// "Sunday, February 14th 2010, 3:25:50 pm"
console.log(wrapped.format('"dddd, MMMM Do YYYY, h:mm:ss a"'));

// "Sun, 3PM"
console.log(wrapped.format("ddd, hA"));
```

There is a lot of power provided by moment.js in terms of formatting. You can even get friendly values like "in 6 hours," "Tomorrow at 9:40 am," and "Last Sunday at 9:40 pm," as shown in Listing 4-46.

Listing 4-46. popular/moment/timeago.js

```
var moment = require('moment');

var a = moment([2007, 0, 15]); // 15 Jan 2007
var b = moment([2007, 0, 16]); // 16 Jan 2007
var c = moment([2007, 1, 15]); // 15 Feb 2007
var d = moment([2008, 0, 15]); // 15 Jan 2008

console.log(a.from(b)); // "a day ago"
console.log(a.from(c)); // "a month ago"
console.log(a.from(d)); // "a year ago"

console.log(b.from(a)); // "in a day"
console.log(c.from(a)); // "in a month"
console.log(d.from(a)); // "in a year"
```

Lots of additional goodies are provided by moment and hopefully you now see the motivation to explore more and have an understanding of how to use them.

Serializing Dates

Since we are discussing dates, let's discuss a good practice to follow when serializing dates for saving to a JSON file or sending JSON over the wire. When we discussed JSON earlier, you might have noticed that Date is not supported as a valid JSON value type. There are various ways for passing dates over the wire, but it is simplest to send them as strings.

What a particular date string means in terms of its actual date value differs based on the local culture (for example, month before date or date before month), so it is best to follow a global standard. The ISO8601 standard specifically relates to how a particular date should be represented as a string.

Various formats are supported by ISO8601, but the one natively supported by JavaScript is something that looks like 2014-05-08T17:35:16Z, where the date and time is expressed in the same string relative to UTC. Since it is always relative to UTC, it is user time zone independent. This is a good thing since the user might not be in the same time zone as the server and UTC is a global time reference.

If we call the toJSON method on a JavaScript date, ISO8601 formatted string is what we get back. Similarly, passing in this string to a JavaScript date constructor gives us a new JavaScript date object, as shown in Listing 4-47.

Listing 4-47. popular/moment/json.js

```
var date = new Date(Date.UTC(2007, 0, 1));

console.log('Original', date);

// To JSON
var jsonString = date.toJSON();
console.log(jsonString); // 2007-01-01T00:00:00.000Z

// From JSON
console.log('Round Tripped',new Date(jsonString));
```

This .toJSON support is carried over in moment as well. If you call .toJSON on a wrapped moment object, you get the same result as you get on the raw date object. This allows you to safely serialize objects that have Date or moment objects as values.

One final thing worth mentioning is that if *any object* (not just Dates) has a toJSON method, it will be called by JSON.stringify when it tries to serialize it to JSON. Hence, we can use it to customize the serialization for *any* JavaScript object if we want to. This is shown in a simple example in Listing 4-48.

Listing 4-48. popular/moment/tojson.js

```
var foo = {};
var bar = { 'foo': foo };

// Uncustomized serialization
console.log(JSON.stringify(bar)); // {"foo":{}}

// Customize serialization
foo.toJSON = function () { return "custom" };
console.log(JSON.stringify(bar)); // {"foo":"custom"}
```

Customizing Console Colors

When working on large Node.js projects, it is not uncommon to end up with quite a few pieces of information getting logged on the console for monitoring purposes. Over time, this simple output begins to look boring and is another place where you will need to manage complexity. Syntax highlighting helps you manage code complexity. The colors package (npm install colors) brings a similar benefit to your console output, making it easier to follow what is going on. It is also one of the most used NPM packages (nearly 50,000 downloads a day).

The API provided by colors is extremely simple. It adds functions to the native JavaScript string so that you can do things such as "some string".red and, if you print this string it, will be colored red on the console. A small sample of the various options used and the output is shown in Listing 4-49.

Listing 4-49. popular/colors/1basic.js

```
// Loading this module modifies String for the entire process
require('colors');

console.log('hello'.green);                    // outputs green text
console.log('world!'.red);                     // outputs red text
console.log('Feeling yellow'.yellow);          // outputs yellow text
console.log('But you look blue'.blue);         // outputs yellow text
console.log('This should cheer you up!'.rainbow); // rainbow
```

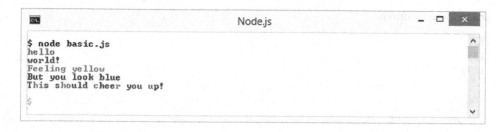

The usage is really simple. Besides the obvious advantage of bringing this power to your fingertips, the reason why we showed you this package was to make a segue into further customizing JavaScript internals. Let's see how this package is actually implemented. Along the way, we will revisit prototypes (a topic we discussed in Chapter 2) and learn about JavaScript property getters and setters.

How Does It Work?

There are two sides of this API:

- how to print colors on the console
- how to modify JavaScript strings and add functions to them

Printing a string in a particular color is something that is supported by most consoles (windows and UNIX) using *ANSI escape codes.* If you print one of these codes, the behavior of the console changes. Create a simple JavaScript file that prints the JavaScript string surrounded by a few of these codes as shown in Listing 4-50. If you run it, you will see a red string logged to the console.

Listing 4-50. popular/colors/2raw.js

```
function getRed(str) {
    // Changes the console foreground to red
    var redCode = '\x1b[31m';

    // Resets the console foreground
    var clearCode = '\x1b[39m';

    return redCode + str + clearCode;
}

console.log(getRed('Hello World!'));
```

This is a sufficient understanding of how we can modify the behavior of the console. It is a simple matter of reading the terminal documentation and finding the color codes to match. The more interesting question for us as JavaScript developers is, "How can I add member functions to all strings?"

In Chapter 2, we discussed how, when you create an object with the new operator, the prototype of the function is copied into the __proto__ member of the created instance. And since it is a reference, if you add a property to the original function prototype, all instances of objects created using this function will get the new property.

Fortunately for us, all the native types in JavaScript (dates, strings, arrays, numbers, and so on) are created from functions that match the name of the type. Consequently, if we add a member to the prototype of these functions, we can successfully extend all instances of these types. Listing 4-51 provides a quick example to demonstrate this principle where we add a property foo to all Arrays, Numbers, and Strings.

Listing 4-51. popular/colors/3prototypeIntro.js

```
Array.prototype.foo = 123;
Number.prototype.foo = 123;
String.prototype.foo = 123;

var arr = [];
var str = '';
var num = 1;

console.log(arr.foo); // 123
console.log(str.foo); // 123
console.log(num.foo); // 123
```

To add a function to strings, add to String.prototyp, as demonstrated in Listing 4-52.

Listing 4-52. popular/colors/4addFunction.js

```
String.prototype.red = function (str) {
    // Changes the console foreground to red
    var redCode = '\x1b[31m';

    // Resets the console foreground
    var clearCode = '\x1b[39m';

    return redCode + this + clearCode;
}

console.log('Hello World!'.red());
```

Notice, however, that in this example we are calling a function on the string, that is, 'Hello World!'.red() whereas when we used colors, we simply did 'Hello World!'.red. That is, with colors, we didn't need to "call()" the member. This is because colors defined red as a *property getter* and not a *function*.

A property getter/setter is simply a way for you to plug into the JavaScript's getter/read value (for example, foo.bar) and setter/set value (for example, foo.bar = 123) semantics. One simple way to add a getter/setter is using the __defineGetter__/__defineSetter__ member functions available on all JavaScript objects. Listing 4-53 gives a simple example to demonstrate this usage.

Listing 4-53. popular/colors/5propertyIntro.js

```
var foo = {};

foo.__defineGetter__('bar', function () {
    console.log('get bar was called!');
});

foo.__defineSetter__('bar', function (val) {
    console.log('set bar was called with value:',val);
});

// get
foo.bar;
// set
foo.bar = 'something';
```

So, finally to add `.red` property on all strings, we only need to add it to `String.prototype` as shown in Listing 4-54.

Listing 4-54. popular/colors/6addProperty.js

```
String.prototype.__defineGetter__('red', function (str) {
    // Changes the console foreground to red
    var redCode = '\x1b[31m';

    // Resets the console foreground
    var clearCode = '\x1b[39m';

    return redCode + this + clearCode;
});

console.log('Hello World!'.red);
```

At the very least, you now have a deeper appreciation of the JavaScript language and can understand its success a bit better. After showing you all this power, we give an obligatory word of caution. As we have said before, global state is bad and unintuitive. So, if you start to add members to these native types (string, number, array, and so on) in an uncontrolled manner (in various different files), it will be difficult for the next person to understand where this functionality is coming from. Reserve this power for modules that are specifically designed with the objective of extending built-in types and be sure to document it! Also be careful not to override any existing or native JavaScript behavior since other libraries might depend on it!

Additional Resources

NPM online registry: http://npmjs.org/
   Semantic versioning the official guide: http://semver.org/
   Semantic versioning parser in NPM: https://github.com/isaacs/node-semver

Summary

In this chapter, we discussed the remaining intricacies of the Node.js module system. Along the way, we presented advantages for why the module system needs to work the way it does. The greatest advantage we feel is not having a dependency hell problem that plagues so many other environments, where module incompatibilities prevent you from using two modules that depend on different versions of a third module.

We showed how NPM works. It is simply a way to manage node_modules based modules shared by the Node.js community. We took a tour of the important command line options offered by NPM to manage the community packages you use.

You also learned about JSON and semantic versioning. Both pieces of information are vital information for all developers (not just Node.js developers).

Finally, we showed a number of important Node.js packages and the lessons that you can learn from them. These should help make you a world-class Node.js and JavaScript developer, and you should not be afraid to pop open the node_modules folder and see what makes a library you like *tick*.

CHAPTER 5

■ ■ ■

Events and Streams

Before we examine specific areas of Node.js development, we need to address a few more core concepts about JavaScript in general and Node.js in particular. Node.js is focused on being the best-performing, simplest way to create server applications. Events and streams play an important role in achieving this goal.

Node.js is single-threaded; we have already discussed advantages of this fact. Due to this evented nature of Node.js, it has first-class support for an event subscription/unsubscription pattern. This pattern is very similar to the way you would handle events using JavaScript in the browser.

Streaming data is one of those areas that fit very naturally in Node.js. Streams are great for improving user experience plus decreasing server resource utilization.

To understand how we can create our own event emitters and streams, we first need to understand JavaScript inheritance.

Classical Inheritance in JavaScript

We saw how prototype works in Chapter 2. JavaScript supports prototypal inheritance. In JavaScript, a member is looked up on the current item (such as item.foo), followed by its prototype (item.__proto__.foo), which is followed by its prototype's prototype (item.__proto__.__proto__.foo), and so on until the prototype itself (for example, item.__proto__.__proto__.__proto__) is null. We have already seen how this can be used to emulate a classical object oriented *class* construct in JavaScript. Now let's look at how it can be used to implement classical object oriented *inheritance*.

Arriving at an Inheritance Pattern

Let's create an Animal class. It has a simple member function called walk. We've already discussed that `this` within a function refers to the newly created object when a function is called with the `new` operator (for example, `new Animal`). We also discussed that the prototype member of the constructor function (Animal.prototype) is referenced by the object prototype (animal.__proto__) because of using the new operator. (See Listing 5-1.)

Listing 5-1. oo/1animal.js

```
function Animal(name) {
    this.name = name;
}
Animal.prototype.walk = function (destination) {
    console.log(this.name, 'is walking to', destination);
};

var animal = new Animal('elephant');
animal.walk('melbourne'); // elephant is walking to melbourne
```

To better understand how the lookup is performed on `animal.walk`, have a look at the diagram in Figure 5-1.

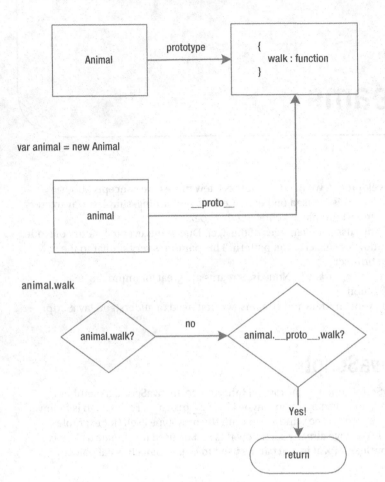

Figure 5-1. *Sample lookup of member from prototype*

Now let's inherit all of the Animal class functionality in a new class, for example, Bird. To do this, we need to do two things:

- Call the Animal constructor from the Bird constructor. This ensures that the properties are set up properly for the Bird object (Animal.name in our example).

- Find a way to make all parent (Animal) prototype members (for example, __proto__.walk) a member of the child (Bird) instance's prototype's prototype. This will allow Bird instances (for example, bird) to have their own functions on their own prototype (bird.__proto__.fly) and the parent members on their prototype's prototype (bird.__proto__.__proto__.walk). This is called *setting up a prototype chain*.

We will begin by fleshing out the Bird class. Based on the algorithm, it will look like the code in Listing 5-2.

Listing 5-2. Building Up to Inheritance

```
function Bird(name){
    // Call the Animal constructor
}
// Setup the prototype chain between Bird and Animal

// Finally create child instance
var bird = new Bird('sparrow');
```

Calling the Parent Constructor

We cannot simply call the parent Animal constructor from Bird. That is because if we do so, then `this` within Animal will not refer to the newly created Bird object (created from new Bird). Hence, we need to force the meaning of this within the Animal function to point to the value of this inside the Bird function. Fortunately, we can force the meaning by using the '.call' member function available on all JavaScript functions (it comes from Function.prototype). Listing 5-3 presents a demonstration of the call member. As usual, the comments explain what is going on.

Listing 5-3. oo/2call.js

```
var foo = {};
var bar = {};

// A function that uses `this`
function func(val) {
    this.val = val;
}

// Force this in func to be foo
func.call(foo, 123);

// Force this in func to be bar
func.call(bar, 456);

// Verify:
console.log(foo.val); // 123
console.log(bar.val); // 456
```

You can see that we forced `this` inside the `func` function to be foo and then bar. Great! Now that we know how to force this, let's use it to call the parent, as shown in Listing 5-4.

Listing 5-4. Calling the Parent Constructor

```
function Bird(name){
    Animal.call(this,name);

    // Any additional initialization code you want
}
// Copy all Animal prototype members to Bird
```

You use this pattern (Parent.call(this, /* additional args */)) every time you need to call a parent constructor. Now you have a firm functional understanding of why this is.

Setting Up the Prototype Chain

We need a mechanism so that when we create a new Bird (such as, bird = new Bird), its prototype chain contains all the parent prototype functions (for example, bird.__proto__.__proto__.walk). This can be done quite simply if we do Bird.prototype.__proto__ = Animal.prototype.

This process works because when we will do bird = new Bird, we will effectively get bird.__proto__.__proto__ = Animal.prototype and that will make the parent prototype members (for example, Animal.prototype.walk) available on the child prototype (bird.__proto__.__proto__.walk), which was the desired result. Listing 5-5 shows a simple code sample.

Listing 5-5. oo/3prototype.js

```
// Animal Base class
function Animal(name) {
    this.name = name;
}
Animal.prototype.walk = function (destination) {
    console.log(this.name, 'is walking to', destination);
};

var animal = new Animal('elephant');
animal.walk('melbourne'); // elephant is walking to melbourne

// Bird Child class
function Bird(name) {
    Animal.call(this, name);
}
Bird.prototype.__proto__ = Animal.prototype;
Bird.prototype.fly = function (destination) {
    console.log(this.name, 'is flying to', destination);
}

var bird = new Bird('sparrow');
bird.walk('sydney'); // sparrow is walking to sydney
bird.fly('melbourne'); // sparrow is flying to melbourne
```

To understand how an inherited member (bird.walk in our example) lookup is performed, take a look at Figure 5-2.

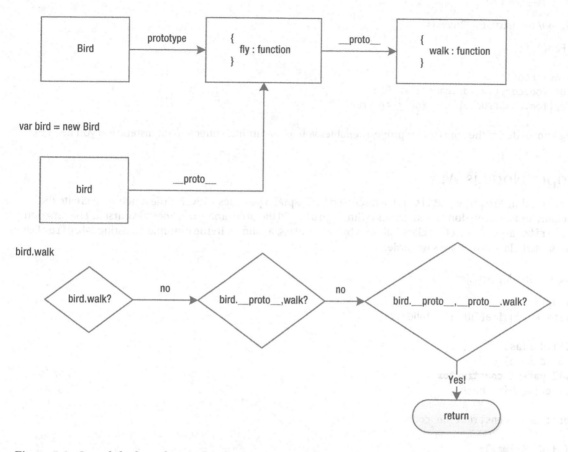

Figure 5-2. *Sample lookup of a member from a prototype chain*

Note that manually modifying the __proto__ property is *not recommended* since it isn't a part of the ECMAScript standard. We will discuss a more standard way of setting the prototype shortly, but the principle shown here makes you an expert of JavaScript prototypal inheritance.

The Constructor Property

By default, every function gets a member called `prototype`, which we have already seen. By default, this member has a constructor property that points to the function itself. Listing 5-6 demonstrates this.

Listing 5-6. oo/4constructor/1basic.js

```
function Foo() { }
console.log(Foo.prototype.constructor === Foo); // true
```

What is the advantage of having this property? After you create an instance using a function (for example, instance = new Foo), you can get access to the constructor using a simple lookup instance.constructor (which is really going to be looking at instance.__proto__.constructor). Listing 5-7 shows this in an example where we use the property name of named functions (function Foo) to log out what created the object.

Listing 5-7. oo/4constructor/2new.js

```
function Foo() { }

var foo = new Foo();
console.log(foo.constructor.name); // Foo
console.log(foo.constructor === Foo); // true
```

Having knowledge of the constructor property enables you to do runtime reflection on instances if you need to.

The Proper Node.js Way

The util core module (require('utils')) we discussed in Chapter 3 provides a lovely little function to create the prototype chain for us so you don't need to mess with `__proto__` (the nonstandard property) yourself. The function is called `inherits` and takes a child class followed by parent class, as shown in the example in Listing 5-8. Bird class extends the Animal class, which we saw earlier.

Listing 5-8. oo/5nodejs/util.js

```
// util function
var inherits = require('util').inherits;

// Bird Child class
function Bird(name) {
    // Call parent constructor
    Animal.call(this, name);

    // Additional construction code
}
inherits(Bird, Animal);

// Additional member functions
Bird.prototype.fly = function (destination) {
    console.log(this.name, 'is flying to', destination);
}

var bird = new Bird('sparrow');
bird.walk('sydney'); // sparrow is walking to sydney
bird.fly('melbourne'); // sparrow is flying to melbourne
```

There are two things of note:

- Call the parent constructor: Animal.call(this, /* any original arguments */)
- Set up the prototype chain: inherits(Bird, Animal);

Simple enough to become second nature, this is all you need to do to inherit classes!

Overriding Functions in Child Classes

To override parent functions but still utilize some of the original functionality, simply do the following:

- Create a function on the child prototype with the same name.

- Call the parent function similar to the way we called the parent constructor, basically using the Parent.prototype.memberfunction.call(this, /*any original args*/) syntax.

Listing 5-9 demonstrates this.

Listing 5-9. oo/6override.js

```
// util function
var inherits = require('util').inherits;

// Base
function Base() { this.message = "message"; };
Base.prototype.foo = function () { return this.message + " base foo" };

// Child
function Child() { Base.call(this); };
inherits(Child, Base);

// Overide parent behaviour in child
Child.prototype.foo = function () {
    // Call base implementation + customize
    return Base.prototype.foo.call(this) + " child foo";
}

// Test:
var child = new Child();
console.log(child.foo()); // message base foo child foo
```

We simply created the child function Child.prototype.foo and called the parent function from within Base.prototype.foo.call(this).

Checking Inheritance Chain

Setting up a prototype chain (__proto__.__proto__) as we have seen has an additional advantage in that it allows you to check if a particular object instance is of a particular class, or its parent class, or its parent's parent class, and so on. This is done using the instanceof operator.

In pseudocode when you do someObj instanceof Func the you use this algorithm:

- Check someObj.__proto__ == Func.prototype and if so return true.

- If not, check someObj.__proto__.__proto__ == Func.prototype and if so return true.

- Repeat moving up the prototype chain.

- If __proto__ is null and we haven't found a match, return false.

From the pseudocode, you can see that it is very similar to how a property lookup is performed. We travel up the prototype chain until we find a __proto__ equal to the Func.prototype. Finding a match is an indication of the new operator being used on the specified Func as the new operator copies prototype to __proto__. A quick demonstration of using instanceof is shown in Listing 5-10.

Listing 5-10. oo/7instanceof.js

```javascript
var inherits = require('util').inherits;

function A() { }
function B() { }; inherits(B, A);
function C() { }

var b = new B();
console.log(b instanceof B); // true because b.__proto__ == B.prototype
console.log(b instanceof A); // true because b.__proto__.__proto__ == A.prototype
console.log(b instanceof C); // false
```

Deeper Understanding of the Internals of util.inherits

You do not *need* to go through this section, but it is worthwhile just so you can sit at the cool kids' table. We said that setting __proto__ manually is not recommended as it is not a part of the standardized JavaScript.

Fortunately, there is a function in JavaScript that can create a blank object with a specified __proto__ already set. The function is called Object.create and the way it works is shown in Listing 5-11.

Listing 5-11. oo/8internals/1check.js

```javascript
var foo = {};
var bar = Object.create(foo);
console.log(bar.__proto__ === foo); // true
```

In this example, we simply verified that the newly created object (that is, bar) has its __proto__ member set to what we passed into Object.create (in other words, foo). It can be used for inheritance as shown in Listing 5-12.

Listing 5-12. oo/8internals/2inherit.js

```javascript
// Animal Base class
function Animal() {
}
Animal.prototype.walk = function () {
    console.log('walking');
};

// Bird Child class
function Bird() {
}
Bird.prototype = Object.create(Animal.prototype);

var bird = new Bird();
bird.walk();
```

Compared to the original non-standard __proto__ mechanism we showed before, here we simply replaced Bird.prototype.__proto__ = Animal.prototype with what is effectively Bird.prototype = { __proto__ : Animal.prototype }.

This mechanism correctly inherits the members from the parent, but it creates one slight problem. When we reassigned Bird.prototype, the constructor information that was there in Bird.prototype.constructor was lost because we reassigned Bird.prototype to a completely new object. To bring the constructor property back, a simple solution is to pass a second parameter to Object.create, which specifies additional properties to add to the object to be created. In Listing 5-13, we specify that the constructor is a property that points to the function itself, which is what the Bird.prototype.constructor was originally (remember that Bird.prototype.constructor === Bird).

Listing 5-13. oo/8internals/3inheritBetter.js

```javascript
// Animal Base class
function Animal() {
}
Animal.prototype.walk = function () {
    console.log('walking');
};

// Bird Child class
function Bird() {
}
Bird.prototype = Object.create(Animal.prototype, {
    constructor: {
        value: Bird,
        enumerable: false,
        writable: true,
        configurable: true
    }
});

var bird = new Bird();
bird.walk();
console.log(bird.constructor === Bird); // true
```

And this is exactly the implementation found in Node.js util module (which is written in JavaScript). The implementation straight from the source is shown in Listing 5-14.

Listing 5-14. Code Retrieved from Node.js source util.js

```javascript
exports.inherits = function(ctor, superCtor) {
  ctor.super_ = superCtor;
  ctor.prototype = Object.create(superCtor.prototype, {
    constructor: {
      value: ctor,
      enumerable: false,
      writable: true,
      configurable: true
    }
  });
};
```

One more thing that the inherits function does is it adds a property super_ to the child class, which points to the parent class. This is simply for convention so that you know that this child function prototype has received members from this super_ class when debugging or writing reflection-based code.

Mastering inheritance is so involved because JavaScript was designed with simple prototypal inheritance. We are simply utilizing the power offered by it to mimic a traditional OO hierarchy.

Node.js Events

We already have a way to execute some code based on some occurrence (event) using callbacks. A more general concept for handling occurrences of significance is events. An event is like a broadcast, while a callback is like a handshake. A component that raises events knows nothing about its clients, while a component that uses callbacks knows a great deal. This makes events ideal for scenarios where the significance of the occurrence is determined by the client. Maybe the client wants to know, maybe it doesn't. Registering multiple clients is also simpler with this even as we will see in this section.

Node.js comes with built-in support for events baked into the core events module. As always, use require('events') to load the module. The events module has one simple class "EventEmitter", which we present next.

EventEmitter class

EventEmitter is a class designed to make it easy to emit events (no surprise there) and subscribe to raised events. Listing 5-15 provides a small code sample where we subscribe to an event and then raise it.

Listing 5-15. events/1basic.js

```
var EventEmitter = require('events').EventEmitter;

var emitter = new EventEmitter();

// Subscribe
emitter.on('foo', function (arg1, arg2) {
    console.log('Foo raised, Args:', arg1, arg2);
});

// Emit
emitter.emit('foo', { a: 123 }, { b: 456 });
```

As shown in the example, you can create a new instance with a simple `new EventEmitter` call. To subscribe to events, you use the `on` function passing in the event name (always a string) followed by an event handling function (also called a *listener*). Finally, we raise an event using the emit function passing in the event name followed by any number of arguments we want passed into the listeners (in Listing 5-15 we used two arguments for demonstration).

Multiple Subscribers

As we mentioned previously, having *built-in support* for multiple subscribers is one of the advantages of using events. Listing 5-16 is a quick sample where we have multiple subscribers for an event.

Listing 5-16. events/2multiple.js

```
var EventEmitter = require('events').EventEmitter;
var emitter = new EventEmitter();

emitter.on('foo', function () {
    console.log('subscriber 1');
});
```

```
emitter.on('foo', function () {
    console.log('subscriber 2');
});
```

```
// Emit
emitter.emit('foo');
```

Another thing to note in this sample is the fact that the listeners are called in the *order that they registered* for the event. This is a nice consequence of the single-threaded nature of Node.js, which makes it easier for you to reason about your code. Additionally, any arguments passed in for the event are *shared* between the various subscribers, as demonstrated in Listing 5-17.

Listing 5-17. events/3shared.js

```
var EventEmitter = require('events').EventEmitter;
var emitter = new EventEmitter();

emitter.on('foo', function (ev) {
    console.log('subscriber 1:', ev);
    ev.handled = true;
});

emitter.on('foo', function (ev) {
    if (ev.handled) {
        console.log('event already handled');
    }
});

// Emit
emitter.emit('foo', { handled: false });
```

In this sample, the first listener modified the passed event argument and the second listener got the modified object. You can potentially use this fact for getting you out of a tricky situation, but I highly caution against it. The reason for showing this sharing of the event arguments is to warn you about the dangers of modifying the event object directly in a listener.

Unsubscribing

The next question to ask is how do we unsubscribe from an event. `EventEmitter` has a `removeListener` function that takes an event name followed by a function object to remove from the listening queue. One thing to note is that you must have a reference to the function you want removed from the listening queue and, therefore, should not use an anonymous (inline) function. This is because two functions in JavaScript are not equal if their bodies are the same, as shown below in Listing 5-18, since these are two different and distinct function objects.

Listing 5-18. Sample to Demonstrate Function Inequality

```
$ node -e "console.log(function(){} == function(){})"
false
```

Listing 5-19 shows how you can unsubscribe a listener.

Listing 5-19. events/4unsubscribe.js

```
var EventEmitter = require('events').EventEmitter;
var emitter = new EventEmitter();

var fooHandler = function () {
    console.log('handler called');

    // Unsubscribe
    emitter.removeListener('foo',fooHandler);
};

emitter.on('foo', fooHandler);

// Emit twice
emitter.emit('foo');
emitter.emit('foo');
```

In this sample, we unsubscribe from the event after it is raised once. As a result, the second event goes unnoticed.

Has This Event Ever Been Raised?

It is a common use case that you don't care about every time an event is raised—just that it is raised once. For this, EventEmitter provides a function `once` that calls the registered listener only once. Listing 5-20 demonstrates its usage.

Listing 5-20. events/5once.js

```
var EventEmitter = require('events').EventEmitter;
var emitter = new EventEmitter();

emitter.once('foo', function () {
    console.log('foo has been raised');
});

// Emit twice
emitter.emit('foo');
emitter.emit('foo');
```

The event listener for foo will only be called once.

Listener Management

There are a few additional utility functions available on the EventEmitter that you need to be aware of to be a Node.js event-handling expert.

EventEmitter has a member function, listeners, that takes an event name and returns all the listeners subscribed to that event. This can be very useful when you are debugging event listeners. Listing 5-21 demonstrates its usage.

Listing 5-21. events/6listeners.js

```
var EventEmitter = require('events').EventEmitter;
var emitter = new EventEmitter();

emitter.on('foo', function a() { });
emitter.on('foo', function b() { });

console.log(emitter.listeners('foo')); // [ [Function: a], [Function: b] ]
```

EventEmitter instances also raise a `newListener` event whenever a new listener is added and `removeListener` whenever a listener is removed, which can help you out in tricky situations such as when you want to track down the instant an event listener is registered/unregistered. It can also be useful for any management you want to do when listeners are added or removed, as shown in Listing 5-22.

Listing 5-22. events/7listenerevents.js

```
var EventEmitter = require('events').EventEmitter;
var emitter = new EventEmitter();

// Listener addition / removal notifications
emitter.on('removeListener', function (eventName, listenerFunction) {
    console.log(eventName, 'listener removed', listenerFunction.name);
});
emitter.on('newListener', function (eventName, listenerFunction) {
    console.log(eventName, 'listener added', listenerFunction.name);
});

function a() { }
function b() { }

// Add
emitter.on('foo', a);
emitter.on('foo', b);

// Remove
emitter.removeListener('foo', a);
emitter.removeListener('foo', b);
```

Note that if you add a `removeListener` after adding a handler for `newListener`, you will get notified about the `removeListener` addition as well, which is why it is conventional to add the removeListener event handler first as we did in this sample.

EventEmitter Memory Leaks

A common source of memory leaks when working with events is subscribing to events in a callback but forgetting to unsubscribe at the end. By default, EventEmitter will tolerate 10 listeners for *each* event type—anymore and it will print a warning to the console. This warning is specifically for your assistance. All you code will continue to function. In other words, more listeners will be added without warning and all listeners will be called when an event is raised, as shown in Listing 5-23.

Listing 5-23. events/8maxEventListeners.js

```javascript
var EventEmitter = require('events').EventEmitter;
var emitter = new EventEmitter();

var listenersCalled = 0;

function someCallback() {
    // Add a listener
    emitter.on('foo', function () { listenersCalled++ });

    // return from callback
}

for (var i = 0; i < 20; i++) {
    someCallback();
}
emitter.emit('foo');
console.log('listeners called:', listenersCalled); // 20
```

The output from the application is shown in Listing 5-24. You can see that despite the warning, all 20 listeners were called when we emitted the event.

Listing 5-24. Running the Max Event Listeners Demo

```
$ node 8maxEventListeners.js
(node) warning: possible EventEmitter memory leak detected. 11 listeners added.
Use emitter.setMaxListeners() to increase limit.
Trace
    at EventEmitter.addListener (events.js:160:15)
    at someCallback (/path/to/8maxEventListeners.js:8:13)
    at Object.<anonymous> (/path/to/8maxEventListeners.js:14:5)
    at Module._compile (module.js:456:26)
    at Object.Module._extensions..js (module.js:474:10)
    at Module.load (module.js:356:32)
    at Function.Module._load (module.js:312:12)
    at Function.Module.runMain (module.js:497:10)
    at startup (node.js:119:16)
    at node.js:902:3
listeners called: 20
```

A common cause of this memory leak is forgetting to unsubscribe for the event when in an error condition of a callback. A simple solution is to create a new event emitter in the callback. This way the event emitter is not shared, and it is disposed along with all of its subscribers when the callback terminates.

Finally, there are cases where having more than 10 listeners is a valid scenario. In such cases, you can increase a limit for this warning using the setMaxListeners member function, as shown in Listing 5-25.

Listing 5-25. events/9setMaxListeners.js

```
var EventEmitter = require('events').EventEmitter;
var emitter = new EventEmitter();

// increase limit to 30
emitter.setMaxListeners(30);

// subscribe 20 times
// No warning will be printed
for (var i = 0; i < 20; i++) {
    emitter.on('foo', function () { });
}
console.log('done');
```

Note that this increases the limit for *all* event types on this event emitter. Also, you can pass in 0 to allow an unlimited number of event listeners to be subscribed without warning.

Node.js tries to be safe by default; memory leaks can weigh heavily when working on a server environment, which is why this warning message exists.

Error Event

An 'error' event is treated as a special *exceptional* case in Node.js. If there is *no* listener for it, then the default action is to print a stack trace and exit the program. Listing 5-26 gives a quick sample to demonstrate this.

Listing 5-26. events/10errorEvent.js

```
var EventEmitter = require('events').EventEmitter;
var emitter = new EventEmitter();

// Emit an error event
// Since there is no listener for this event the process terminates
emitter.emit('error', new Error('Something horrible happened'));

console.log('this line never executes');
```

If you run this code, you will get an output, as shown in Listing 5-27. You should use an Error object if you ever need to raise an error event, as we did in this example. You can also see from the example that the last line containing the console.log never executes as the process terminated.

Listing 5-27. Sample Run of Error Event Sample

```
$ node 10errorEvent.js

events.js:72
        throw er; // Unhandled 'error' event
        ^
Error: Something horrible happened
    at Object.<anonymous> (/path/to/10errorEvent.js:6:23)
    at Module._compile (module.js:456:26)
    at Object.Module._extensions..js (module.js:474:10)
    at Module.load (module.js:356:32)
```

```
    at Function.Module._load (module.js:312:12)
    at Function.Module.runMain (module.js:497:10)
    at startup (node.js:119:16)
    at node.js:902:3
```

Hence, the lesson: Raise the error event only for *exceptional* circumstances that *must* be handled.

Creating Your Own Event Emitters

Now that you are an expert at handling and raising events in Node.js, a lot of open source surface area opens up to you. A number of libraries export classes that inherit from EventEmitter and, therefore, follow the same event handling mechanism. At this stage, it is useful for you to know how you can extend EventEmitter and create a public class that has all of the functionality of EventEmitter baked in.

All you need to do to create your own EventEmitter is call the EventEmitter constructor from your class's constructor and use the util.inherits function to set up the prototype chain. This should be second nature to you considering the amount of discussion we gave this at the start of this chapter. Listing 5-28 is a quick example to demonstrate this.

Listing 5-28. events/11custom.js

```
var EventEmitter = require('events').EventEmitter;
var inherits = require('util').inherits;

// Custom class
function Foo() {
    EventEmitter.call(this);
}
inherits(Foo, EventEmitter);

// Sample member function that raises an event
Foo.prototype.connect = function () {
    this.emit('connected');
}

// Usage
var foo = new Foo();
foo.on('connected', function () {
    console.log('connected raised!');
});
foo.connect();
```

You can see that usage of your class is exactly the same as if it was an EventEmitter. With these two simple lines, you have a fully functional custom event emitter.

Process Events

A number of classes inside core Node.js inherit from EventEmitter. The global process object is also an instance of EventEmitter, as you can see in Listing 5-29.

Listing 5-29. Sample to Demonstrate That Process Is an EventEmitter

```
$ node -e "console.log(process instanceof require('events').EventEmitter)"
true
```

Global Exception Handler

Any global unhandled exceptions can be intercepted by listening on the `uncaughtException` event on process. You should not resume execution outside this event handler because this only happens when your application is in an unstable state. The best strategy is to log the error for your convenience and *exit the process with an error code,* as shown in Listing 5-30.

Listing 5-30. process/1uncaught.js

```
process.on('uncaughtException', function (err) {
    console.log('Caught exception: ', err);
    console.log('Stack:', err.stack);
    process.exit(1);
});

// Intentionally cause an exception, but don't try/catch it.
nonexistentFunc();

console.log('This line will not run.');
```

If you run the code in Listing 5-30, you get a nice error log, as shown in Listing 5-31.

Listing 5-31. Sample Run of an Uncaught Exception

```
$ node 1uncaught.js
Caught exception:  [ReferenceError: nonexistentFunc is not defined]
Stack: ReferenceError: nonexistentFunc is not defined
    at Object.<anonymous> (E:\DRIVE\Google Drive\BEGINNING NODEJS\code\chapter5\
process\1uncaught.js:8:1)
    at Module._compile (module.js:456:26)
    at Object.Module._extensions..js (module.js:474:10)
    at Module.load (module.js:356:32)
    at Function.Module._load (module.js:312:12)
    at Function.Module.runMain (module.js:497:10)
    at startup (node.js:119:16)
    at node.js:902:3
```

The `uncaughtError` event is also raised on a process if any event emitter raises the `**error**` event and there are no listeners subscribed to the event emitter for this event.

Exit

The exit event is emitted when the process is about to exit. There is no way to abort exiting at this point. The event loop is already in teardown so you *cannot* do any *async* operations at this point. (See Listing 5-32.)

Listing 5-32. process/2exit.js

```
process.on('exit', function (code) {
    console.log('Exiting with code:', code);
});

process.exit(1);
```

Note that the event callback is passed in the exit code that the process is exiting with. This event is mostly useful for debugging and logging purposes.

Signals

Node.js process object also supports the UNIX concept of signals, which is a form of inter-process communication. It emulates the most important ones on Windows systems as well. A common scenario that is supported on both Windows and UNIX is when the user tries to interrupt the process using Ctrl+C key combination in the terminal. By default, Node.js will exit the process. However, if you have a listener subscribed to the `SIGINT` (signal interrupt) event, the listener is called and you can choose if you want to exit the process (process.exit) or continue execution. Listing 5-33 provides a small sample where we chose to continue running and exit after five seconds.

Listing 5-33. process/3signals.js

```
setTimeout(function () {
    console.log('5 seconds passed. Exiting');
}, 5000);
console.log('Started. Will exit in 5 seconds');

process.on('SIGINT', function () {
    console.log('Got SIGINT. Ignoring.');
});
```

If you execute this example and press Ctrl+C, you will get a message that we are choosing to ignore this. Finally, the process will exit after five seconds naturally once we don't have any pending tasks (demonstrated in Listing 5-34).

Listing 5-34. Sample Run of Ignoring Ctrl+C Messages Demo

```
$ node 3signals.js
Started. Will exit in 5 seconds
Got SIGINT. Ignoring.
Got SIGINT. Ignoring.
5 seconds passed. Exiting
```

Streams

> *Drop by drop is the water pot filled.*
>
> —Buddha

Streams play an important role in creating performant web applications. To understand what streams bring to the table, consider the simple case of serving a large file (1GB) from a web server. In the absence of streams, it would look like Figure 5-3. The user would have to wait a long time before they get any sign of the file they requested.

This is called *buffering,* and we should try to limit it as much as possible. Besides the obvious bad user experience, it also wastes resources. The complete file needs to be loaded and kept in memory before we start sending it down to the user.

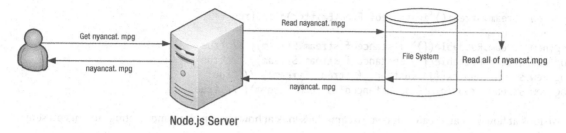

Figure 5-3. *Buffered web response*

The same scenario looks much better when we use streaming. We start reading the file and whenever we have a new chunk of data, we send it down to the client until we reach the end, as shown in Figure 5-4.

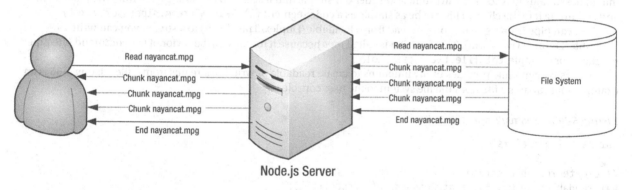

Figure 5-4. *Streaming web response*

This improvement in user experience and better utilization of server resources is the main motivation behind steams.

The most important concepts are that of Readable streams, Writable streams, Duplex streams, and Transform streams. A *readable* stream is one that you can read data from but not write to. A good example of this is process. stdin, which can be used to stream data from the standard input. A *writable* stream is one that you can write to but not read from. A good example is process.stdout, which can be used to stream data to the standard output. A *duplex* stream is one that you can both read from and write to. A good example of this is the network socket. You can write data to the network socket as well as read data from it. A *transform* stream is a special case of a duplex stream where the output of the stream is in some way computed from the input. These are also called *through* streams. A good example of these is encryption and compression streams.

All of the basic building blocks of streams are present in the Node.js core stream module that you load using require('stream'). There are base classes for implementing streams present in this module, aptly called Readable, Writable, Duplex, and Transform.

Streams in Node.js are based on events, which is why it was important to have a firm understanding of events before we could dive into streams. All of these stream classes inherit from a base abstract Stream class (abstract because you should not use it directly), which in turn inherits from EventEmitter (which we saw earlier). This hierarchy is demonstrated in Listing 5-35.

Listing 5-35. streams/1concepts/eventBased.js

```
var stream = require('stream');
var EventEmitter = require('events').EventEmitter;

console.log(new stream.Stream() instanceof EventEmitter); // true

console.log(new stream.Readable({}) instanceof stream.Stream); // true
console.log(new stream.Writable({}) instanceof stream.Stream); // true
console.log(new stream.Duplex({}) instanceof stream.Stream); // true
console.log(new stream.Transform({}) instanceof stream.Stream); // true
```

Before we look at how we can create our own streams, let's look at how we can consume existing streams present in the Node.js library.

Pipe

All the streams support a pipe operation that can be done using the pipe member function. This is one of the things that make streams in Node.js so awesome. Consider our simple initial scenario of loading a file from the file system and streaming it to the client. This can be as simple as a code segment fileSystemStream.pipe(userSocket).

You can pipe from a stream you can read from (Readable/Duplex/Transform) to a stream you can write to (Writable/Duplex/Transform). This function is called *pipe* because it mimics the behavior of the command line pipe operator, for example, cat file.txt | grep lol.

The fs core module provides utility functions to create readable or writable streams from a file. Listing 5-36 is an example that streams a file from the file system to the user console.

Listing 5-36. streams/2pipe/1basic.js

```
var fs = require('fs');

// Create readable stream
var readableStream = fs.createReadStream('./cool.txt');

// Pipe it to stdout
readableStream.pipe(process.stdout);
```

You can also chain multiple streams using pipe. For example, the code in Listing 5-37 creates a read stream from a file, pipes it through a zip transform stream, and then pipes it to a writable file stream. This creates a zip file on the file system.

Listing 5-37. streams/2pipe/2chain.js

```
var fs = require('fs');
var gzip = require('zlib').createGzip();

var inp = fs.createReadStream('cool.txt');
var out = fs.createWriteStream('cool.txt.gz');

// Pipe chain
inp.pipe(gzip).pipe(out);
```

Streams in Node.js are based on events. All that the pipe operation does is subscribe to the relevant events on the source and call the relevant functions on the destination. For most purposes, pipe is all that you need to know about as an API consumer, but it is worth knowing more details when you want to delve deeper into streams.

Consuming Readable Streams

We've said it many times already that streams work based on events. The most important event for a readable stream is 'readable'. This event is raised whenever there is new data to be read from a stream. Once inside the event handler, you can call the read function on the stream to read data from the stream. If this is the end of the stream, the read function returns null, as demonstrated in Listing 5-38.

Listing 5-38. streams/3readable/basic.js

```
process.stdin.on('readable', function () {
    var buf = process.stdin.read();
    if (buf != null) {
        console.log('Got:');
        process.stdout.write(buf.toString());
    }
    else {
        console.log('Read complete!');
    }
});
```

A sample run of this code is shown in Listing 5-39, where we pipe data into process.stdin from the command line.

Listing 5-39. Sample Run of streams/3readable/basic.js

```
$ echo 'foo bar bas' | node basic.js
Got:
'foo bar bas'
Read complete!
```

Writing to Writable Streams

To write to a stream, you simply call write to write some data. When you have finished writing (end of stream), you simply call end. You can also write some data using the end member function if you want, as shown in Listing 5-40.

Listing 5-40. streams/4writable/basic.js

```
var fs = require('fs');
var ws = fs.createWriteStream('message.txt');

ws.write('foo bar ');
ws.end('bas');
```

In this sample, we simply wrote foo bar bas to a writable file stream.

Creating Your Own Stream

Creating your own stream is very similar to how you create your own EventEmitter. For streams you inherit from the relevant base, stream class and implement a few base methods. This is detailed in Table 5-1.

Table 5-1. *Creating Your Own Custom Streams*

Use-case	Class	Method(s) to Implement
Reading only	Readable	_read
Writing only	Writable	_write
Reading and writing	Duplex	_read, _write
Operate on read data and write the result	Transform	_transform, _flush

The inheritance mechanism is the same as we have seen before. That is, you call the base constructor from your class constructor and call utils.inherits after declaring you class.

Creating a Readable Stream

As stated, you simply inherit from Readable class. You implement the _read member in your class, which is called by the stream API internally when someone requests data to be read. If you have data that you want to be passed on (pushed), you call the inherited member function push passing in the data. If you call push(null), this signals the end of the read stream.

Listing 5-41 is a simple example of a readable stream that returns 1-1000. If you run this, you will see all these numbers printed (as we pipe to stdout).

Listing 5-41. streams/5createReadable/counter.js

```
var Readable = require('stream').Readable;
var util = require('util');

function Counter() {
    Readable.call(this);
    this._max = 1000;
    this._index = 1;
}
util.inherits(Counter, Readable);

Counter.prototype._read = function () {
    var i = this._index++;
    if (i > this._max)
        this.push(null);
    else {
        var str = ' ' + i;
        this.push(str);
    }
};
```

```
// Usage, same as any other readable stream
var counter = new Counter();
counter.pipe(process.stdout);
```

As you can see, the underlying Readable class provides most of the stream logic for you.

Creating a Writable Stream

Creating your own writable stream class is similar to how we created a readable stream. You inherit from the Writable class and implement the _write method. The _write method is passed in a chunk that needs processing as its first argument.

Listing 5-42 is a simple writable stream that logs to the console all the data passed in. In this example, we simply pipe from the readable file stream to this writeable stream (Logger).

Listing 5-42. streams/6createWritable/logger.js

```
var Writable = require('stream').Writable;
var util = require('util');

function Logger() {
    Writable.call(this);
}
util.inherits(Logger, Writable);

Logger.prototype._write = function (chunk) {
    console.log(chunk.toString());
};

// Usage, same as any other Writable stream
var logger = new Logger();

var readStream = require('fs').createReadStream('message.txt');
readStream.pipe(logger);
```

Again, for most purposes, the bulk of the functionality is handled internally by the Writable base class.

Summary

Hopefully, this chapter has given you a greater appreciation of JavaScript as a language. There are a few simple ideas that provide a lot of expressive power. We started this chapter providing a crash course on JavaScript prototypal inheritance along with explaining how simple it is to do in Node.js. We then showed how Node.js comes with built-in support for common event-handling paradigms. We also demonstrated how you can create your own event emitter with simple inheritance. Finally, we looked at streams and why you would want to add them to your arsenal. You saw how easy it is to consume and write to streams in Node.js. It's almost as if Node.js was designed for them! We ended the chapter with a discussion on how you can create your own custom streams utilizing the built-in functionality provided by Node.js core base classes.

CHAPTER 6

■ ■ ■

Getting Started with HTTP

Node.js was created specifically to make scalable server-side and networking applications. It ships with battle-tested functionality to handle network connections effectively. This provides the groundwork on which the community can build full-blown application servers.

In this chapter, we will look at the *core* functionality provided by Node.js for creating web applications. We will then review the *connect* middleware framework that allows you to create reusable web server components. Finally, we will take a look at securing your web servers with *HTTPS*.

Basics of Node.js HTTP

Following are the main core networking modules for creating web applications in Node.js:

- net / require('net'): provides the foundation for creating TCP server and clients

- dgram / require('dgram'): provides functionality for creating UDP / Datagram sockets

- http / require('http'): provides a high-performing foundation for an HTTP stack

- https / require('https'): provides an API for creating TLS / SSL clients and servers

We will start by using the http module to create our simple server to serve static files. Creating our web server from scratch will give us a deeper appreciation of the features provided by the community NPM modules that we will explore later.

■ **Note**   We will be using curl to test our web applications to start with. It is available by default on Mac OS X / Linux. You can get curl for windows as a part of Cygwin (www.cygwin.com/).

The http module has a lovely little function, createServer, which takes a callback and returns an HTTP server. On each client request, the callback is passed in two arguments—the incoming request stream and an outgoing server response stream. To start the returned HTTP server, simply call its listen function passing in the port number you want to listen on.

Listing 6-1 provides a simple server) that listens on port 3000 and simply returns "hello client!" on every HTTP request.

Listing 6-1. 1create/1raw.js

```
var http = require('http');

var server = http.createServer(function (request, response) {
    console.log('request starting...');

    // respond
    response.write('hello client!');
    response.end();

});

server.listen(3000);
console.log('Server running at http://127.0.0.1:3000/');
```

To test the server, simply start the server using Node.js, as shown in Listing 6-2.

Listing 6-2. Starting a Server

```
$ node 1raw.js
Server running at http://127.0.0.1:3000/
```

Then test an HTTP connection using curl in a new window, as shown in Listing 6-3. The server sends the data as we expected.

Listing 6-3. Making a Client Request Using curl

```
$ curl http://127.0.0.1:3000
hello client!
```

To exit the server, simply press Ctrl+C in the window where the server was started.

Inspecting Headers

Even at this point, a lot of HTTP logic has been silently taken care of. The actual request sent by curl contained a few important HTTP headers. To see these, let's modify the server to log the headers received in the client request (sent by curl), as shown in Listing 6-4.

Listing 6-4. 1create/2defaultheaders.js

```
var http = require('http');

var server = http.createServer(function (req, res) {
    console.log('request headers...');
    console.log(req.headers);

    // respond
    res.write('hello client!');
    res.end();

}).listen(3000);
console.log('server running on port 3000');
```

Now start the server. We will also ask curl to log out the server response headers using the -i (that is, include protocol headers in output) option, as shown in Listing 6-5.

Listing 6-5. Making a Client Request and Displaying Returned Response Headers

```
$ curl http://127.0.0.1:3000 -i
HTTP/1.1 200 OK
Date: Thu, 22 May 2014 11:57:28 GMT
Connection: keep-alive
Transfer-Encoding: chunked

hello client!
```

The HTTP request headers sent from curl, which are processed by the Node.js HTTP server, are logged on the server console, as shown in Listing 6-6. As you can see, req.headers is a simple JavaScript object literal. You can access any header using req['header-name'].

Listing 6-6. Request Headers Printout on Client Request

```
$ node 2defaultheaders.js
server running on port 3000
request headers...
{ 'user-agent': 'curl/7.30.0',
  host: '127.0.0.1:3000',
  accept: '*/*',
  connection: 'Keep-Alive' }
```

■ **Note**   Wikipedia has good list of HTTP status codes at http://en.wikipedia.org/wiki/List_of_HTTP_status_codes. This includes codes that are not a part of the HTTP/1.1 spec, which are described at http://tools.ietf.org/html/rfc2616.

Using a Debugging Proxy

A great tool to use to help you explore and experiment with HTTP is a web debugging proxy. A debugging proxy is an application that sits between the client and the server, and logs all the requests and responses exchanged between the two. A brief overview of how this exchange is going to take place is shown in Figure 6-1.

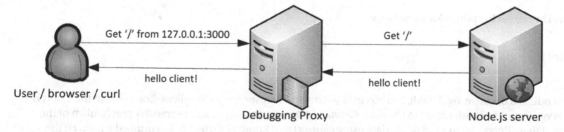

Figure 6-1. A web debugging proxy sits between the client and the server

A very popular and free debugging proxy that is available for Windows as well as Mac OS X is fiddler (www.telerik.com/fiddler), which has a simple one-click installer. (Note: on Mac OS X, you will need to install mono www.mono-project.com/download/ before you can install fiddler). Once you start fiddler, it listens on port 8888 by default. You need to tell the client application to use a proxy to connect to the server. For curl, you can do that using the -x (use the proxy) option. Start the simple server we just created and launch fiddler. Then run the following command (Listing 6-7) to make a client request using fiddler as a proxy.

Listing 6-7. Making a curl Request Specifying a Proxy Server

```
$ curl http://127.0.0.1:3000 -x 127.0.0.1:8888
hello client!
```

Since fiddler is running, it is going to capture the request as well as the response. As you can see from Figure 6-2, the actual data sent from the server in the server response is slightly encoded, as shown again in Listing 6-8.

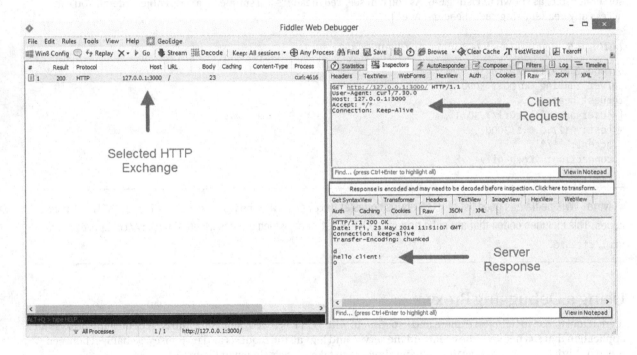

Figure 6-2. *Fiddler showing the complete details of the HTTP client request and server response*

Listing 6-8. The Server Response Message Body

```
d
hello client!
0
```

This encoding is because, by default, Node.js tries to stream the response to the client. You see that the Transfer-Encoding server response header is set to chunked. *Chunked transfer encoding* is a data-transfer mechanism of the HTTP protocol that allows you to send down data using *chunks* (also known as *stream*). In chunked transfers, the size of the transfer (in hexadecimal) is sent right before the chunk itself so the receiver can tell when it has finished receiving the data for that chunk. Node.js sent d (decimal 13) because that is the length of 'hello client!'. The transfer is terminated by sending a chunk of length 0 (hence the trailing 0). All of this was taken care of for you by the built-in Node.js HTTP server.

Key Members of the Response Stream

Beyond the fact that the response implements a writable stream, there are a few other useful methods that you need to be aware of. The response is split into two sections: writing the headers and writing the body. The reason for this is that the body might potentially contain a large chunk of data that needs streaming. The headers specify how this data is going to be presented and needs to be interpreted by the client before such streaming can begin.

As soon as you call response.write or response.end, the HTTP headers that you set up are sent, followed by the portion of body that you want written. After this, you cannot modify the headers anymore. At any point, you can check if the headers are sent using the read-only response.headersSent boolean value.

Setting the Status Code

By default, the status code is going to be 200 OK. As long as the headers are not sent, you can explicitly set the status code using the statusCode response member (for example, to send a 404 NOT FOUND you would use the following code:

```
response.statusCode = 404;
```

Setting Headers

You can explicitly queue any HTTP header in the response using the response.setHeader(name, value) member function. One common header that you need to set is the Content-Type of the response so that the client knows how to interpret the data the server sends in the body. For example, if you are sending down an HTML file to the client, you should set the Content-Type to text/html, which you can with the following code:

```
response.setHeader("Content-Type", "text/html");
```

The formal term for the value of the Content-Type header is *MIME type*. MIME types for a few key content types are shown in Table 6-1.

Table 6-1. Popular MIME Types

Name	MIME type
HyperText Markup Language (HTML)	text/html
Cascading Style Sheets (CSS)	text/css
JavaScript	application/javascript
JavaScript Object Notation (JSON)	application/json
JPEG Image	image/jpeg
Portable Network Graphics (PNG)	image/png

For this and a *lot* more MIME types, there is a simple NPM package called *mime* (npm install mime), which you can use to get the official mime type from a file extension. Listing 6-9 shows how you can use it.

Listing 6-9. Demonstration of Using the MIME NPM Package

```
var mime = require('mime');

mime.lookup('/path/to/file.txt');          // => 'text/plain'
mime.lookup('file.txt');                    // => 'text/plain'
mime.lookup('.TXT');                        // => 'text/plain'
mime.lookup('htm');                         // => 'text/html'
```

Going back to our headers discussion, you can get a header that's queued for sending using the response.getHeader function:

```
var contentType = response.getHeader('content-type');
```

You can remove a header from the queue using the response.removeHeader function:

```
response.removeHeader('Content-Encoding');
```

Send Headers Only

When you want to *explicitly* send the headers (not just queue them) and move the response into *body only* mode, you can call the response.writeHead member function. This function takes the status code along with optional headers that will be added on to any headers you might have already queued using response.setHeader. For example, here is a snippet that sets the status code to 200 and sets the Content-Type header for serving HTML:

```
response.writeHead(200, { 'Content-Type': 'text/html' });
```

Key Members of the Request Stream

The request is also a readable stream. This is useful for cases when the client wants to stream data to the server , for example, file upload. The client HTTP request is also split into a head and body part. We can get useful information about the client request HTTP head. For example, we have already seen the request.headers property, which is simply a read-only map (JavaScript Object Literal) of header names and values (shown in Listing 6-10).

Listing 6-10. Snippet for Demonstrating Reading the Request Headers

```
// Prints something like:
//
// { 'user-agent': 'curl/7.30.0',
//   host: '127.0.0.1:3000',
//   accept: '*/*' }
console.log(request.headers);
```

To check an individual header, you can index this object like you index any other JavaScript object literal:

```
console.log(request.headers['user-agent']); // 'curl/7.30.0'
```

A key piece of information you need when responding to a request is the HTTP method and the URL used by the client when making the request. This information is necessary in order to create **RESTful** web applications. You can get the HTTP method used from the `request.method` read-only property. You can get the URL requested by the client using the `request.url` property. As an example, consider the following client request:

```
GET /resources HTTP/1.1
Accept: */*
```

In this case, `request.method` will be `GET` and `request.url` will be `/resources`.

Creating Your Own File Web Server
Serving Base HTML

Now that we have a deeper understanding of the response stream and MIME types, we can create a simple web server that returns HTML files from a folder. Create a simple HTML file, called `index.html`, that we plan to return on every request to GET '/' on the server, as shown in Listing 6-11.

Listing 6-11. 2server/public/index.html

```
<html>
<head>
    <title>Hello there</title>
</head>
<body>
    You are looking lovely!
</body>
</html>
```

To start with, let's create a few utility functions. It is always better to break out the functionality into separate functions instead of one monolithic block of code. If we receive a request for a url that we do not accept, we should return a 404 (Not Found) HTTP response. Listing 6-12 provides a function that does exactly that.

Listing 6-12. A Utility Function to Return 404 Not Found HTTP Response

```
function send404(response) {
    response.writeHead(404, { 'Content-Type': 'text/plain' });
    response.write('Error 404: Resource not found.');
    response.end();
}
```

If we can satisfy the request, we should return HTTP 200 along with a MIME type for the content. Returning the HTML file is as simple as creating a read file stream and piping it to the response. Listing 6-13 shows the complete server code.

Listing 6-13. Code from 2server/server.js

```
var http = require('http');
var fs = require('fs');

function send404(response) {
    response.writeHead(404, { 'Content-Type': 'text/plain' });
```

121

```
        response.write('Error 404: Resource not found.');
        response.end();
}

var server = http.createServer(function (req, res) {
    if (req.method == 'GET' && req.url == '/') {
        res.writeHead(200, { 'content-type': 'text/html' });
        fs.createReadStream('./public/index.html').pipe(res);
    }
    else {
        send404(res);
    }
}).listen(3000);
console.log('server running on port 3000');
```

If you start the server (run node server.js from chapter6/2server directory) and open your browser at http://localhost:3000, you will see the HTML page we created earlier (Figure 6-3).

Figure 6-3. *Browser showing index.html was successfully returned*

Similarly, if you visit any other URL on localhost you will get a 404 error message (Figure 6-4).

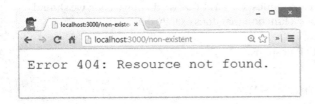

Figure 6-4. *Browser showing an error returned on a nonexistent resource request*

Serving a Directory

That's a good start for a quick handwritten static file server. However, it only serves one file. Let's open it up a bit to serve all the contents of a directory. First off, create a simple client-side JavaScript file that appends to the body after HTML loading is complete, as shown in Listing 6-14. We plan to request this JavaScript file from the server.

Listing 6-14. Code from 3serverjs/public/main.js

```javascript
window.onload = function () {
    document.body.innerHTML += '<strong>Talk JavaScript with me</strong>';
}
```

Let's modify our simple HTML file by adding a script tag in the <head> to load a client-side JavaScript file

```html
<script src="./main.js"></script>
```

Now if we run the same old server, we will get a 404 when our browser parses index.html and tries to load main.js from the server. To support this JavaScript loading, we need to do the following:

- use the path module to resolve the path to the file on the file system based on the request.url property

- see if we have a MIME type registered for the file type requested

- make sure the file exists before we try to read it from the file system

Based on what we already know, we can write the server as shown in Listing 6-15.

Listing 6-15. Code from 3serverjs/server.js

```javascript
var http = require('http');
var fs = require('fs');
var path = require('path');

function send404(response) {
    response.writeHead(404, { 'Content-Type': 'text/plain' });
    response.write('Error 404: Resource not found.');
    response.end();
}

var mimeLookup = {
    '.js': 'application/javascript',
    '.html': 'text/html'
};

var server = http.createServer(function (req, res) {

    if (req.method == 'GET') {

        // resolve file path to filesystem path
        var fileurl;
        if (req.url == '/') fileurl = '/index.html';
        else fileurl = req.url;
        var filepath = path.resolve('./public' + fileurl);

        // lookup mime type
        var fileExt = path.extname(filepath);
        var mimeType = mimeLookup[fileExt];
```

```
        if (!mimeType) {
            send404(res);
            return;
        }

        // see if we have that file
        fs.exists(filepath, function (exists) {

            // if not
            if (!exists) {
                send404(res);
                return;
            };

            // finally stream the file
            res.writeHead(200, { 'content-type': mimeType });
            fs.createReadStream(filepath).pipe(res);
        });
    }
    else {
        send404(res);
    }
}).listen(3000);
console.log('server running on port 3000');
```

Most of the code in the example is self-explanatory and the interesting sections are highlighted. If you open up the browser now and visit localhost:3000, you will see that the HTML was requested and the JavaScript was loaded and ran successfully (Figure 6-5).

Figure 6-5. *Browser showing the client JavaScript was successfully requested and rendered*

There are still quite a lot of features missing from our current implementation. For one, it's not secure against a malicious URL. For example, you can exploit the fact that there is a simple path.resolve in our implementation to request *any* file from the server file system, as demonstrated in Listing 6-16 (here we are requesting the server code from the server).

Listing 6-16. Demonstrating a File System Listing Vulnerability in Our Simple File Server

```
$ curl 127.0.0.1:3000/../server.js
var http = require('http');
var fs = require('fs');
var path = require('path');

...truncated... the rest of server.js
```

Then there is error handling and file caching, both of which are lacking in our implementation. Having the knowledge to build your own Node.js web server from scratch is invaluable, but you don't have to build a web server from scratch. The community has already done it for you, and we will explore those options later.

Introducing Connect

As we have seen, core Node.js modules provide basic but essential features for building your own web applications. There are quite a few web frameworks available on NPM that build on this. A very popular one is connect (npm install connect), which is a middleware framework.

Middleware is basically any software that sits between your application code and some low level API. Connect extends the built-in HTTP server functionality and adds a plug-in framework. The plug-ins act as middleware and, hence, connect is a middleware framework.

Connect has received a recent overhaul (connect 3.0) and now the core connect is just the middleware framework. Each middleware is its own separate NPM module and a part of the larger Connect/ExpressJS ecosystem. We will explore these middlewares in the next chapter. Here we are focused on using connect and authoring our own middlewares.

Creating a Bare-Bones Connect Application

At the heart of connect is the connect function. Calling this function creates the connect dispatcher. The connect dispatcher is simply a function that takes the request/response arguments, meaning that the dispatcher can be used as an argument to http.createServer (which we saw earlier). Listing 6-17 shows the basic connect application.

Listing 6-17. 4connect/1basic.js

```
var connect = require('connect')
    , http = require('http');

// Create a connect dispatcher
var app = connect();

// Register with http
http.createServer(app)
    .listen(3000);
console.log('server running on port 3000');
```

If you run this server, it will return a 404 (Not Found) for every client request. This is the built-in behavior provided by connect. In the absence of some middleware to handle the client request, connect will return a 404. We will create middleware in the next section.

In addition to being a function that can accept a request and response objects, the connect dispatcher has a member function, use, that is used to register a middleware with connect. We will look at this function shortly when we create our own connect middleware.

One utility function is listen. We will internally call http.createServer, register the connect dispatcher with it as we shown previously, (that is, http.createServer(app)), and finally call the created server's listen function. So you can simply do what is shown in Listing 6-18, but it is useful to know that it is still a dispatcher on top of node core http.

Listing 6-18. 4connect/2simpler.js

```
var connect = require('connect');

// Create a connect dispatcher and register with http
var app = connect()
        .listen(3000);
console.log('server running on port 3000');
```

Creating a Connect Middleware

To register a middleware with connect, call the 'use' member method on the connect dispatcher passing in a function that takes three arguments—a request, a response, and a next callback:

- request derives from the Node.js HTTP request class we saw earlier

- response derives from the Node.js HTTP response class we saw earlier

- next allows you to *optionally* pass the control onto the next middleware registered with connect OR inform connect about an error

The simplest no-op (no operation) middleware would be one that does not look at the request, doesn't modify the response, and doesn't simply pass over the control to the next middleware, as shown in Listing 6-19.

Listing 6-19. 5middleware/1noop.js

```
var connect = require('connect');

// Create a connect dispatcher and register with http
var app = connect()
        // register a middleware
        .use(function (req, res, next) { next(); })
        .listen(3000);
console.log('server running on port 3000');
```

Now that we are familiar with the fundamentals of middleware, let's create one that logs the client request's method and url, as shown in Listing 6-20.

Listing 6-20. 5middleware/2logit.js

```
var util = require('util');

// a simple logging middleware
function logit(req, res, next) {
    util.log(util.format('Request recieved: %s, %s', req.method, req.url));
    next();
}

var connect = require('connect');

connect()
    .use(logit)
    .listen(3000);
```

Let's create another middleware that echoes the client request back to the client. Since the client request is a read stream and the response is a write stream, we can simply pipe the two, as shown in Listing 6-21.

Listing 6-21. 5middleware/3echo.js

```
function echo(req, res, next) {
    req.pipe(res);
}

var connect = require('connect');

connect()
    .use(echo)
    .listen(3000);
```

Now if you run this application and make a curl request, the request body (-d, that is, data parameter to curl) will become the response body:

```
$ curl http://127.0.0.1:3000/ -d "hello world!"
hello world!
```

Mounting Middleware by Path Prefix

The use function takes an optional first argument to specify the endpoint for which the specified middleware will be triggered. This is called *mounting* as it is similar to OS disk mounting. For example, say we want to echo only when requests come for '/echo'. For all other requests, we will return the message 'Wassup'. This can be achieved as shown in Listing 6-22.

Listing 6-22. 5middleware/4prefix.js

```
function echo(req, res, next) {
    req.pipe(res);
}

var connect = require('connect');

connect()
    .use('/echo', echo)
    .use(function (req, res) { res.end('Wassup!'); })
    .listen(3000);
```

All requests starting with '/echo' will be handled by the echo middleware, whereas others will be passed to our Wassup! responder. As you can see in Listing 6-23, it behaves as expected.

Listing 6-23. Demonstrating Mounting

```
$ curl http://127.0.0.1:3000/echo -d "hello world!"
hello world!
$ curl http://127.0.0.1:3000/ -d "hello world!"
Wassup!
```

A simple example of needing path prefixes is hosting a static file middleware at a particular prefix (for example, '/public').

Another advantage of mounting is that it allows you to change URLs easily without needing to update the middleware. Your middleware should *not* check for req.url. Assume that it's been mounted where it needs to do its processing.

Using an Object as Middleware

As a middleware author, you have the option to use an object (instead of a simple function) to create a middleware as long as the object has a handle method. For example, the echo middleware as an object would be as shown in Listing 6-24.

Listing 6-24. 5middleware/5object.js

```
var echo = {
    handle: function (req, res, next) {
        req.pipe(res);
    }
};

var connect = require('connect');

connect()
    .use(echo)
    .listen(3000);
```

This allows you to use class instances as middleware as long as they have a handle member function. This is just for convenience and you can safely ignore this for your own creations.

Creating Configurable Middleware

You can use the power of JavaScript closures to create a configurable middleware. For example, in Listing 6-25, we show a middleware that always returns the same message based on how it was configured. The configuration message is captured in a closure by the function that we return.

Listing 6-25. 5middleware/6configurable.js

```
// Configurable middleware creator
function greeter(message) {
    return function (req, res, next) {
        res.end(message);
    };
}

var helloWorldGreeter = greeter('Hello world!');
var heyThereGreeter = greeter('Hey there!');

var connect = require('connect');
connect()
    .use('/hello', helloWorldGreeter)
    .use('/hey', heyThereGreeter)
    .listen(3000);
```

The results are demonstrated in Listing 6-26.

Listing 6-26. Demonstrating Using the Configured Middleware

```
$ curl http://127.0.0.1:3000/hello
Hello world!
$ curl http://127.0.0.1:3000/hey
Hey there!
```

The Power of Chaining

There are many reasons why the chaining of middleware is awesome. For example, it allows middleware to share the functionality of processing requests and responses. You can also use it for providing authorization and authentication. Let's consider a few practical examples.

Sharing Request/Response Information

The request and the response objects passed into each middleware are mutable and shared. You can use this to have a middleware partially process requests for you to make it easier for consumption by a later middleware. As an example, consider a simple middleware that tries to process the body into a JavaScript object if it detects that it is a JSON request, as shown in Listing 6-27.

Listing 6-27. Snippet from 6chain/1parse.js

```
function parseJSON(req, res, next) {
    if (req.headers['content-type'] == 'application/json') {

        // Load all the data
        var readData = '';
        req.on('readable', function () {
            readData += req.read();
        });

        // Try to parse
        req.on('end', function () {
            try {
                req.body = JSON.parse(readData);
            }
            catch (e) { }
            next();
        })
    }
    else {
        next();
    }
}
```

Here is how it functions:

- It simply checks if the client request is of type application/json. If not, it passes the control onto the next middleware.

- Otherwise, it waits for the client request to completely stream to the server and, once done, tries to parse the data using JSON.parse.

  - If it succeeds, req.body is set.

  - Whether the JSON was parsed and req.body was set or not, we still pass the control to the next middleware.

Because of chaining any middleware that comes after our parseJSON, middleware will get access to the parsed JSON object in req.body if the request contains valid JSON. In Listing 6-28, we have a simple connect server with an added middleware that uses the results of parseJSON to tell the client about the value of req.body.foo if valid JSON is found.

Listing 6-28. Snippet from 6chain/1parse.js

```
var connect = require('connect');

connect()
    .use(parseJSON)
    .use(function (req, res) {
        if (req.body) {
            res.end('JSON parsed!, value of foo: '+ req.body.foo);
        }
        else {
            res.end('no JSON detected!');
        }
    })
    .listen(3000);
```

If you test it using curl, you will see the value of the passed JSON object's foo member if present. Otherwise, if you pass an invalid JSON or a non-JSON request, you will get the "no JSON detected" message, as demonstrated in Listing 6-29.

Listing 6-29. Demonstration of the parseJSON middleware in Action

```
$ curl http://127.0.0.1:3000/ -H "content-type: application/json" -d "{\"foo\":123}"
JSON parsed!, value of foo: 123
$ curl http://127.0.0.1:3000/ -H "content-type: application/json" -d "{\"foo\":123,}"
no JSON detected!
```

Chaining Sample: Verifying Requests/Restricting Access

Because we need to explicitly pass control onto the next middleware by calling next, we can optionally stop execution from proceeding at any time by not calling next and terminating the response ourselves (res.end).

Let's implement a *basic access authorization* middleware that returns 401 NOT AUTHORIZED if the client request does not have the correct credentials. Basic authorization is a simple standardized protocol where every client request needs to contain an `Authorization` header. The header needs to be constructed as follows:

- Username and password are combined into a string: "username:password".

- The resulting string literal is then encoded using Base64.

- The authorization method and a space, that is, "Basic" is then put before the encoded string.

An example client header would be `Authorization: Basic QWxhZGRpbjpvcGVuIHNlc2FtZQ==`.

Additionally, to inform the client that it needs to add an `Authorization` header, the server should send a `WWW-Authenticate` header in the response on rejecting a client request. This is fairly simple to do, and we can make a utility function as shown in Listing 6-30.

Listing 6-30. Utility Funciton to Send 401 Unauthorized HTTP Response Requesting a Basic Auth

```
function send401(){
    res.writeHead(401 , {'WWW-Authenticate': 'Basic'});
    res.end();
}
```

In order to decode the client side `Authorization` header, we follow the creation steps backward. In other words, we remove the authorization method by splitting on space, that is, " ", load the second section as Base64, and convert to a simple string. Finally, we split on ":" to get the username/password. In code, this is shown in Listing 6-31.

Listing 6-31. Code Snippet to Read Client Sent Basic Auth Credentials

```
var auth = new Buffer(authHeader.split(' ')[1], 'base64').toString().split(':');
var user = auth[0];
var pass = auth[1];
```

We now have enough information to create the middleware for adding basic access authorization, which is shown in Listing 6-32.

Listing 6-32. Code Segment from 7auth/1auth.js Listing the Auth Middleware

```
function auth(req, res, next) {
    function send401(){
        res.writeHead(401 , {'WWW-Authenticate': 'Basic'});
        res.end();
    }

    var authHeader = req.headers.authorization;
    if (!authHeader) {
        send401();
        return;
    }

    var auth = new Buffer(authHeader.split(' ')[1], 'base64').toString().split(':');
    var user = auth[0];
    var pass = auth[1];
```

```
    if (user == 'foo' && pass == 'bar') {
        next(); // all good
    }
    else {
        send401();
    }
}
```

As a demo, this middleware only accepts username = foo and password = bar at the moment, but we can easily make it configurable if we want to. Notice that we only call next() if the access is authorized so it can be used to provide protection against bad credentials. We demonstrate using this middleware in Listing 6-33.

Listing 6-33. Code Segment from 7auth/1auth.js Demonstrating Using the Auth Middleware

```
var connect = require('connect');

connect()
    .use(auth)
    .use(function (req, res) { res.end('Authorized!'); })
    .listen(3000);
```

Let's test it (start server from 7auth/1auth.js). If you open your browser at http://localhost:3000, you will be greeted with a familiar username/password prompt. Because the middleware responded with a 401 UNAUTHORIZED response along with a WWW-Authenticate header, the browser is asking for your credentials. (See Figure 6-6.)

Figure 6-6. Browser built-in dialog when Basic Auth is requested by a server

If you type in a bad username/password, it will continue to prompt you for the credentials because we will keep returning 401 until a successful authentication attempt is made. In this case, our middleware passes control onto the next middleware, which simply returns the message "Authorized!" as shown in Figure 6-7.

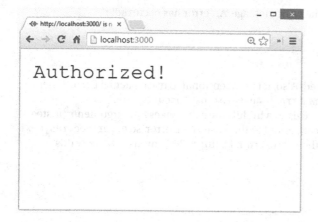

Figure 6-7. Server response when valid credentials are sent by the browser

We can reuse this authentication middleware to restrict specific areas only. (For example, in Listing 6-34 only '/admin' is restricted.) By default, it will fall down to the public handler. Notice that we did not need to change our middleware code at all to achieve this.

Listing 6-34. Code Segement from 7auth/2authArea.js Demonstrating Using Mounting for Admin Area

```
connect()
    .use('/admin', auth)
    .use('/admin', function (req, res) { res.end('Authorized!'); })
    .use(function (req, res) { res.end('Public') })
    .listen(3000);
```

That pretty much sums up the power of a chainable, optionally continuing middleware framework.

Raising a connect Error

One final thing worth mentioning is the fact that you can optionally pass an argument to 'next', which informs connect that an error occurred in your middleware. No other middlewares in the chain are called and the error message is sent to the client request with HTTP status code of 500 INTERNAL SERVER ERROR. Listing 6-35 is a simple example to demonstrate this.

Listing 6-35. 8error/1error.js

```
var connect = require('connect');

connect()
    .use(function (req, res, next) { next('An error has occurred!') })
    .use(function (req, res, next) { res.end('I will never get called'); })
    .listen(3000);
```

If you run this server and make a request, you will get the error message 'An error has occurred!':

```
$ curl http://127.0.0.1:3000
An error has occurred!
```

You can see that the second middleware was never called. Also, it is conventional to use an actual `Error` object instead of the string we used here—in other words, `next(new Error('An error has occurred'))`.

If you want to handle other middleware errors, you can register a middleware that takes four arguments (instead of the three `req,res,next` as we have already seen). The first argument in this case is the error, so `error,req,res,next` are the four arguments. Such a middleware is *only* called if there is an error. Listing 6-36 demonstrates how this functions.

Listing 6-36. 8error/2errorHandler.js

```
var connect = require('connect');

connect()
    .use(function (req, res, next) { next(new Error('Big bad error details')); })
    .use(function (req, res, next) { res.end('I will never get called'); })
    .use(function (err, req, res, next) {
        // Log the error on the server
        console.log('Error handled:', err.message);
        console.log('Stacktrace:', err.stack);
        // inform the client
        res.writeHead(500);
        res.end('Unable to process the request');
    })
    .listen(3000);
```

If you run this server and make a request, you get only the information that we intentionally sent in the response:

```
$ curl http://127.0.0.1:3000
Unable to process the request
```

However, the server log is much more information-rich, as shown in Listing 6-37 (because we used `new Error`).

Listing 6-37. Demonstrating the Server Log from a Middleware Error Handler

```
node 2errorHandler.js
Error handled: Big bad error details
Stacktrace: Error: Big bad error details
    at Object.handle (2errorHandler.js:4:43)
    at next (/node_modules/connect/lib/proto.js:194:15)
... truncated ...
```

Also note that this error handler is called for *all errors* that occur anywhere in the middlewares before this error handler. For example, in Listing 6-48, we intentionally *throw* an error, instead of `next(error)`, and it is still handled correctly.

Listing 6-38. 8error/3throwErrorHandler.js

```
var connect = require('connect');

connect()
    .use(function () { throw new Error('Big bad error details'); })
    .use(function (req, res, next) { res.end('I will never get called'); })
    .use(function (err, req, res, next) {
        console.log('Error handled:', err.message);
        res.writeHead(500);
        res.end('Server error!');
    })
    .listen(3000);
```

This method of error handling actually makes connect much safer to use than raw `http.createServer`, where unhandled errors can crash the server.

Note that the error handler is only called when there is an error. For example, it will never get called in the server shown in Listing 6-39. So you never need to *check* for an error in an error handler—it should always be there if the error handler gets called.

Listing 6-39. 8error/4onlyCalledOnError.js

```
var connect = require('connect');

connect()
    .use(function (req, res, next) { next(); })
    .use(function (err, req, res, next) {
        res.end('Error occured!');
    })
    .use(function (req, res, next) { res.end('No error'); })
    .listen(3000);
```

Finally, it is worth noting that you can optionally call next from your error handler and pass control to any other middleware in the chain.

HTTPS

HTTPS is one of those things that have been difficult to implement in many previous web frameworks. Node.js has first-class support for HTTPS built-ins. Before we show how simple it is to use HTTPS with Node.js, we will provide a quick overview for the beginner.

Asymmetric Cryptography

The fundamental concept that makes HTTPS possible is *public-key encryption* (also called *asymmetric encryption*). For this type of encryption, you need two cryptography keys:

- A public key that *everyone knows*, even possible malicious users
- A private key that *only you know*

And,

- A public key is used for encryption. This means that everyone can talk to you.

- A private key is *needed* for decryption. This means only you can understand what others said!

You can see that it allows everyone to talk to you safely without a chance of eavesdropping. (See Figure 6-8).

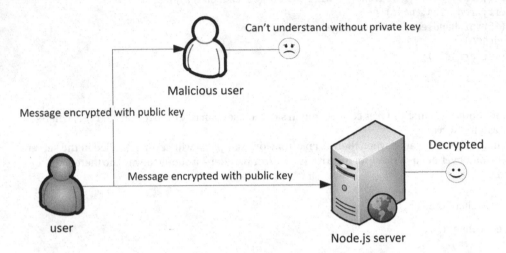

Figure 6-8. *Using a public/private key combination makes it secure for someone to talk to you*

Just for your interest, it is worth mentioning that there are plenty of algorithms to easily compute such key pairs. The strength lies in the fact that is nearly impossible (computationally unfeasible) for a properly generated private key to be determined from its corresponding public key.

Making the Communication Secure Two Ways

So, having a public key shared makes it secure to start a conversation with the server. How can you securely talk back? Simple. The user (the browser basically) generates a pre-master secret on the fly and sends it to the server securely in an encrypted message (encrypted with the server public key). The pre-master secret is used to generate a session key, which is only valid for this session between the client and the server. Now the server and the client can talk to each other if they encrypt the messages with this shared session key.

This is the simplified description of the SSL (or the newer version called TLS) handshake. After the handshake, the actual *standard HTTP* conversation takes place where the entire HTTP message (including headers) is encrypted using a session key. HTTPS is simply HTTP communication over an SSL secured communication channel.

Generating Keys

In this section, we will generate the public/private key pair ourselves. For this, we will use OpenSSL command line tool, which is available on Mac OS X as well as Windows (as a part of Cygwin, which we also needed for curl).

To generate a private key, we specify an encryption algorithm and its complexity. Use the command in Listing 6-40 to generate a 1024 bit RSA key. A sample of the created key.pem file is shown in Listing 6-41.

Listing 6-40. Generating a Private Key

```
$ openssl genrsa 1024 > key.pem
```

Listing 6-41. A Sample Generated Private Key

```
-----BEGIN RSA PRIVATE KEY-----
MIICXQIBAAKBgQDJW6ZZLTawfDyhR8v6/nQMX+PIGtPMO8n7OwRdv1AqqW7a+5Au
... truncated ...
Oj/PimhgOvsDOTDxccytEsLgoldWcx4YLGjzDtoyyaVj
-----END RSA PRIVATE KEY-----
```

Next, we need to generate a corresponding public key, which you can do using the following command:

```
$ openssl req -x509 -new -key key.pem > cert.pem
```

Once you run this command, you will be asked a few questions, such as your country name, all of which have a straightforward answer. This creates a public certificate we can share with world that looks like the code in Listing 6-42.

Listing 6-42. Sample Public Certificate

```
-----BEGIN CERTIFICATE-----
MIIDLjCCApegAwIBAgIJAMdFJbVshZIGMAOGCSqGSIb3DQEBBQUAMG4xCzAJBgNV
... truncated ...
9i+ULx/F6dKgwTLV5L5urT4kIOitM6+QyT+bd1uZ3MXeKaaaJ+dh93aFuFVvxZ3d
t2E=
-----END CERTIFICATE-----
```

Now let's use these keys.

Create an HTTPS Server

Node.js has a core `https` module that you load using `require('https')`. It has a `createServer` function, which behaves exactly the same as `http.createServer` except that it takes an additionally first `'options'` argument that you can use to provide the public/private keys.

Listing 6-43 is the simple HTTP server we saw earlier in this chapter updated to use HTTPS.

Listing 6-43. 9ssl/1basic.js

```javascript
var https = require('https');

var fs = require('fs');
var options = {
    key: fs.readFileSync('./key.pem'),
    cert: fs.readFileSync('./cert.pem')
};

https.createServer(options, function (req, res) {
    res.end('hello client!');
}).listen(3000);
```

As you can see, the listener function is exactly the same—it gets passed a request and response object that we are already familiar with. You can test this using `curl`, as shown in Listing 6-44. The -k argument allows insecure (inse**k**ure)/unverified certificates to work, since we created our certificate ourselves.

Listing 6-44. Testing Our HTTPS Server from curl

```
$ curl https://localhost:3000 -k
hello client!
```

Because the listener function is the same for `http.createServer` and `https.createServer`, using connect with HTTPS is just as simple as using it with HTTP. This is demonstrated in Listing 6-45.

Listing 6-45. 9ssl/2connect.js

```
var https = require('https');

var fs = require('fs');
var options = {
    key: fs.readFileSync('./key.pem'),
    cert: fs.readFileSync('./cert.pem')
};

var connect = require('connect');

// Create a connect dispatcher
var app = connect();

// Register with https
https.createServer(options, app)
    .listen(3000);
```

For public-facing web-sites, you will need to get an SSL certificate from a trusted (one that the user trusts) certification authority (for example, VeriSign, and Thawte). The certificate authority can vouch for the fact that this public key is uniquely secure to *talk to you*. This is because in the absence of such an authority, there can be someone that sits between the client and the server (called Man-in-the-Middle MitM attack) and claim to be the server, sending you *their* public key instead of the *server* public key. This way, MitM can decrypt your message (because they have the corresponding private key), spy on it, and then forward it to the server by re-encrypting it with the server public key.

Use HTTPS by Default

Making a safe web site is easier to ensure if you only use HTTPS and redirect all HTTP traffic to use HTTPS. A lot of web sites do that now. For example, if you visit `http://www.facebook.com`, it will send you a 301 (MOVED PERMANENTLY) HTTP response with the `Location` header set to `https://www.facebook.com`. You can try it yourself; if you open `http://www.facebook.com` in your browser, the address will change to `https://www.facebook.com`. So, whenever possible, just use HTTPS and redirect all HTTP traffic to HTTPS.

Although possible, it is not easy to run HTTP and HTTPS servers on the same port. However, you don't have to. By convention when you request an HTTP web site without specifying a port (for example, **http**://127.0.0.1) the client tries to connect to port 80. However, if you request an HTTPS web site without specifying a port (such as **https**://127.0.0.1), the client tries to connect to port 443 on the server. This allows you run an HTTPS server on port 443 and an HTTP server on port 80 that is simply redirecting client requests to use HTTPS. The code to do this is shown in Listing 6-46.

Listing 6-46. 10redirect/secure.js

```
var https = require('https');

var fs = require('fs');
var options = {
    key: fs.readFileSync('./key.pem'),
    cert: fs.readFileSync('./cert.pem')
};

https.createServer(options, function (req, res) {
    res.end('secure!');
}).listen(443);

// Redirect from http port 80 to https
var http = require('http');
http.createServer(function (req, res) {
    res.writeHead(301, { "Location": "https://" + req.headers['host'] + req.url });
    res.end();
}).listen(80);
```

Now run this server. (On Mac OS X ,you will need to run using sudo—that is, sudo node 10redirect/secure.
js—because only the super user can listen on port 80 and port 443). If you visit http://127.0.0.1 in the browser, you
will notice that the URL changes to https://127.0.0.1 and you get the message "secure!". This is because browsers
know how to handle an HTTP redirect response and do it silently for you. To see the inner workings, you can use curl.
You can see the HTTP and the HTTPS scenarios in Listing 6-47 and Listing 6-48, respectively.

Listing 6-47. Making an HTTPS Request to Our Secure Server

```
$ curl https://127.0.0.1 -k
secure!
```

Listing 6-48. Making an HTTP Request to Our Secure Server Gives Us a Redirect Response

```
$ curl http://127.0.0.1 -i
HTTP/1.1 301 Moved Permanently
Location: https://127.0.0.1/
Date: Sun, 01 Jun 2014 06:15:16 GMT
Connection: keep-alive
Transfer-Encoding: chunked
```

If all your communication takes place over HTTPS, you can use basic HTML input forms to accept client
passwords without worry of interception.

Summary

We started this chapter with a thorough examination of the built-in HTTP functionality found in core Node.js. This close look was necessary because the community frameworks depend on it to provide advanced features, and having a good grasp of the basics will go a long way in making you a successful Node.js developer.

We followed this with a deep dive into the connect middleware framework. Connect allows you to share and create manageable HTTP plug-ins. This helps you manage complexity, which increases your productivity as you can divide and conquer software requirements. Connect is focused on HTTP applications and not very focused on web sites, which is something that ExpressJS (another framework from the connect team) is well-suited for. We will look at ExpressJS later in this book. But know that all of connect middleware is usable with ExpressJS since it has the same middleware convention (that is, the use member function).

Although we wrote about a few middlewares in this chapter, there are a ton of great (tested and secure) middlewares already written by the Node.js community. We will examine those in the next chapter.

Finally, we demonstrated how simple HTTPS is in Node.js. Whenever possible, you should just use HTTPS for all your servers.

Node.js is focused on Application servers. That means you can plug in deeply into HTTP and fully embrace all the innovation that the Web has to offer. In fact, it is not uncommon to find network protocol developers moving to Node.js for prototyping because of its low level access, yet great memory management.

CHAPTER 7

■ ■ ■

Introducing Express

If you are going to make a Node.js web site today, you are probably going to use the Express web application framework.

In the previous chapter, we discussed the core of HTTP/HTTPS functionality provided by Node.js. We also demonstrated how Connect provides a middleware framework on top of a raw `createServer` call. ExpressJS provides everything that Connect provides (the same `use` function we saw in the last chapter as well as a dispatcher) and goes a lot further. It forms the foundation of many web applications that we will explore it in this chapter.

Along the way, we will introduce a few concepts that are relevant on your journey to becoming an HTTP/Node.js expert.

Basics of Express

Express is available on NPM as express (`npm install express`). Let's start with what is common with Connect. Express is from the same team of developers that work on Connect. When you call `require('express')`, you get a function that you can call to create an express app. This app has all of the behavior of the Connect dispatcher that we saw in the previous chapter. For example, it can accept middleware using the 'use' function and can be registered with `http.createServer`, as shown in Listing 7-1.

Listing 7-1. intro/1basic.js

```
var express = require('express'),
    http = require('http');

// Create an express application
var app = express()
            // register a middleware
            .use(function (req, res, next) {
                res.end('hello express!');
            });

// Register with http
http.createServer(app)
    .listen(3000);
```

Having the ability to be registered as a listener with HTTP allows you to use HTTPS if you want to (the same as Connect). Similar to Connect, Express provides a utility `listen` function to register itself with `http`. The simplest Express application can be as simple as Listing 7-2.

Listing 7-2. intro/2simpler.js

```
var express = require('express');

express()
    .use(function (req, res, next) {
        res.end('hello express!');
    })
    .listen(3000);
```

Also error handling works the same as Connect, with an error handling middleware that takes four arguments. AS you can see, all our learning from the previous chapter applies here.

Popular Connect/ExpressJS Middleware

All Connect middleware is Express middleware. However, not all Express middleware is Connect middleware since Express modifies the request and response a bit more for your convenience. For most simple middleware, it is not an issue, but it is a fact that you need to be aware of.

In this section, we will show popular Connect/Express middleware from the core team.

Serving Static Pages

One of the most common things you will want to right away is serve static web-site content. The `serve-static` middleware (`npm install serve-static`) is designed specifically for that. We introduced a similar concept in the previous chapter, but we left the matter unfinished (for example, vulnerable to path-based exploits) because, while the concepts are valuable, you are better off using `serve-static`. (See Listing 7-3.)

Listing 7-3. static/1basic.js

```
var express = require('express');
var serveStatic = require('serve-static');

var app = express()
    .use(serveStatic(__dirname + '/public'))
    .listen(3000);
```

Run this code using node and you get a simple web server serving web pages from the `/public` directory. This little server does quite a few nice things including the following:

- Sets the proper mime type of the response

- Has good HTTP response codes (For example, if you refresh the page and the HTML hasn't changed, you will notice that it sends the response 304 Not Modified, instead of 200 OK. If you request a file that doesn't exist, you get a 404. If the file cannot be accessed for some reason, it sends a 500 Internal Server Error response.)

- By default, does not allow you to get files above the directory you want to serve (not vulnerable to the `../` path bug we had in our simple server from the previous chapter)

- Serves the `index.html` from a directory if the path resolves to a directory

---

■ **Note** By using use '__dirname', we make sure that the path is always relative to the current file instead of the current working directory (CWD). The CWD may be different from the file directory if we run our application from another directory such as from one level up using 'node static/1basic.js' instead of the same directory—that is, 'node 1basic.js'. Relative path names such as './public' resolve relative to the CWD. Using '__dirname', making it independent of the CWD.

You can also pass in additional options as a second argument to the serve-static middleware. For example, to set the index files that it should look for use the index option:

```
app.use(serveStatic(__dirname + '/public', {'index': ['default.html', 'default.htm']}))
```

Express ships with the static middleware as a part of its NPM package. So if you are using Express, you can use express.static, which is an alias to require('serve-static'). Listing 7-4 shows how the example can be rewritten.

Listing 7-4. static/2static.js

```
var express = require('express');

var app = express()
    .use(express.static(__dirname + '/public'))
    .listen(3000);
```

Listing Directory Contents

To list the contents of a directory, there is the serve-index (npm install serve-index) middleware. Since it only lists the contents of the directory, it is conventional to use it in conjunction with the serve-static middleware to actually allow the user to get the file. Listing 7-5 demonstrates its usage.

Listing 7-5. serveindex/basic.js

```
var express = require('express');
var serveIndex = require('serve-index');

var app = express()
    .use(express.static(__dirname + '/public'))
    .use(serveIndex(__dirname + '/public'))
    .listen(3000);
```

By default, it gives a nice directory listing page with a search box as shown in Figure 7-1.

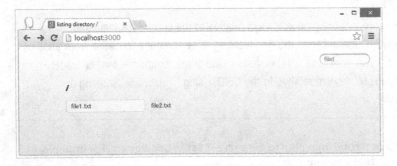

Figure 7-1. *Default directory listing by serve-index middleware*

Notice that we registered `serve-static` before `serve-index` as it gives `serve-static` an opportunity to serve an index file if there is one instead of `serve-index` responding with a directory listing.

Accepting JSON Requests and HTML Form Inputs

Body parsing is the act of parsing a string based *client request body* into a JavaScript object that you can easily consume in your application code. This is a *very* common task in web development, making the `body-parser` middleware (`npm install body-parser`) a must-have in your tool-belt. It simply does the following two things:

- Parses the request body into a JavaScript object if the `content-type` matches JSON (application/JSON) or a user submitted HTML form (the browser sends it as the MIME type application/x-www-form-urlencoded)

- Puts this JavaScript object (if the parse was successful) in `req.body` for easy access in later middleware

Listing 7-6 provides a simple example to respond to the client based on what the `body-parser` middleware has parsed.

Listing 7-6. bodyparser/basic.js

```javascript
var express = require('express');
var bodyParser = require('body-parser');

var app = express()
    .use(bodyParser())
    .use(function (req, res) {
        if (req.body.foo) {
            res.end('Body parsed! Value of foo: ' + req.body.foo);
        }
        else {
            res.end('Body does not have foo!');
        }
    })
    .use(function (err, req, res, next) {
        res.end('Invalid body!');
    })
    .listen(3000);
```

The body-parser sets the `req.body` to an empty object if the request body does not contain any JSON or urlencoded payload. However, if an invalid JSON content is sent by the client, it raises an Express error, which you can handle with an error handling middleware (also shown in Listing 7-7).

We can test it the same way we tested our own JSON middleware in the previous chapter. First, we send a valid JSON payload, and then we send some invalid JSON, as shown in Listing 7-7.

Listing 7-7. Testing bodyparser/basic.js with JSON Content

```
$ curl http://127.0.0.1:3000/ -H "content-type: application/json" -d "{\"foo\":123}"
Body parsed! Value of foo: 123
$ curl http://127.0.0.1:3000/ -H "content-type: application/json" -d "{\"foo\":123,}"
Invalid body!
```

The `body-parser` middleware allows us to use the same code if the client sends an HTML form data (instead of JSON), as shown in Listing 7-8.

Listing 7-8. Testing bodyparser/basic.js with HTML Form Content

```
$ curl http://127.0.0.1:3000/ --data-urlencode "foo=123"
Body parsed! Value of foo: 123
```

We created our own JSON parser in the previous chapter. There were a few issues with our simple implementation. For one, it was susceptible to a malicious client causing a server memory exhaustion by streaming an extraordinarily large chunk of data since we need to load the entire body before we can call `JSON.parse`. By default, `body-parser` will only parse payloads up to a maximum size of 100KB. This is a good default to have. You can specify a different limit by passing in an options argument when creating the middleware, such as `use('/api/v1',bodyParser({limit:'1mb'}))`.

■ **Note** Body-parser internally uses the bytes (`npm install bytes`) NPM package to parse the limit value. It is a simple package that exports a function (`var bytes = require('bytes')`) that allows you to parse common byte strings into byte numbers, such as `bytes('1kb')`, `bytes('2mb')`, `bytes('3gb')`.

Remember that all middleware can be mounted at a specific path and `body-parser` is no exception. So if you want body parsing only for some API endpoint like `"/api/v1"`, you can do `use('/api/v1',bodyParser())`.

Handling Cookies

A *cookie* is some data sent from the web server and stored in the user's web browser. Every time the user's browser makes a request to the web server, the web browser will send back the cookie that it received from the server. Cookies provide a great foundation for creating user sessions.

The Express response object contains a few useful member functions to set client cookies. To set a cookie, call res .cookie(cookieName,value,[options]) function. For example, the code in Listing 7-9 will set a cookie called 'name' to 'foo':

Listing 7-9. cookie/1basic.js

```
var express = require('express');

var app = express()
    .use(function (req, res) {
        res.cookie('name', 'foo');
        res.end('Hello!');
    })
    .listen(3000);
```

If you run this web server, you will see the 'set-cookie' header in the response, as shown in Listing 7-10.

Listing 7-10. Testing cookie/1basic.js with curl

```
$ curl http://127.0.0.1:3000 -i
HTTP/1.1 200 OK
X-Powered-By: Express
Set-Cookie: name=foo; Path=/
Date: Sun, 08 Jun 2014 01:02:23 GMT
Connection: keep-alive
Transfer-Encoding: chunked

Hello!
```

If this response was handled by the browser, then that browser would always send the cookie called 'name' with value 'foo' if the path on the server starts with '/'. The cookie is sent in the 'cookie' header by the client. In Listing 7-11, modify our server to log any cookies sent in the client request.

Listing 7-11. cookie/2show.js

```
var express = require('express');

var app = express()
    .use(function (req, res) {
        console.log('---client request cookies header:\n', req.headers['cookie']);
        res.cookie('name', 'foo');
        res.end('Hello!');
    })
    .listen(3000);
```

If you open http://localhost:3000 in your browser, you will see the cookie logged in the server console:

```
---client request cookies header:
 name=foo
```

While the header is useful, you need something to parse this into a JavaScript object. That's where the **cookie-parser** (npm install cookie-parser) middleware comes in. Put this middleware in your queue and it populates the parsed cookies into the 'req.cookies' object, as shown in Listing 7-12, to demonstrate its usage.

Listing 7-12. cookie/3parsed.js

```javascript
var express = require('express');
var cookieParser = require('cookie-parser');

var app = express()
    .use(cookieParser())
    .use(function (req, res) {
        if (req.cookies.name) {
            console.log('User name:', req.cookies.name);
        }
        else {
            res.cookie('name', 'foo');
        }
        res.end('Hello!');
    })
    .listen(3000);
```

If you run this server, it will log out the value of the name cookie (for example, User name: foo) if it is found in the client request. Otherwise, it will set the cookie. This sample also shows how you can check for the existence of a specific cookie in a client request by simply checking if a particular key is set in the req.cookies object.

You can also clear client cookies in a server response using the Express provided res.clearCookie(cookieName, [options]) member function. For example, the server in Listing 7-13 sets the cookie if it isn't found, and clears it if it is found.

Listing 7-13. cookie/4clear.js

```javascript
var express = require('express');
var cookieParser = require('cookie-parser');

var app = express()
    .use(cookieParser())
    .use('/toggle', function (req, res) {
        if (req.cookies.name) {
            res.clearCookie('name');
            res.end('name cookie cleared! Was:' + req.cookies.name);
        }
        else {
            res.cookie('name', 'foo');
            res.end('name cookie set!');
        }
    })
    .listen(3000);
```

If you visit http://localhost:3000/toggle in your browser, you will get the message "name cookie set!" and "name cookie cleared!" in alternate attempts. We also show you the cookie value sent by the browser (should be "foo") before we clear it.

■ **Note** In case you are curious, the cookie is cleared using the same old `set-cookie` header we saw earlier used to set an initial cookie. However, for clearing, the value is set to empty and expiry set to UNIX epoch, that is, 'Set-Cookie: name=; Path=/; Expires=Thu, 01 Jan 1970 00:00:00 GMT' header in the server response. This tells the browser to delete the cookie.

Preventing Cookie User Modification Using Signing

Since cookies are stored on the client system (and sent in the client request), it is possible for the user to forge a cookie. We can digitally sign a cookie to detect any client cookie forgery. This feature is also provided by the same cookie-parser middleware.

A *digital signature* assures the authenticity of a piece of data. Express cookie signing is done using a *Key-Hash message authentication code (HMAC)*. The HMAC is calculated by taking a secret key (known only to the server) and combining it with a hashing algorithm to calculate a hash for the content of the cookie. Since the secret is only known to the server, the HMAC can only be calculated and verified by the server.

If we create a signed cookie using Express (by providing a secret key), the HMAC value is appended to the value of the cookie we send to the client. So when the client sends the cookie back to us in a request, we can look at the HMAC value in the cookie and compare it with the re-calculated HMAC value to check if it matches the content. If it doesn't match, we know the cookie is bad, and we can discard it. All of this is done for you by the cookie-parser middleware.

You can *set the secret key* for cookie signing by passing it into the cookie-parser middleware creation function—in other words, use(cookieParser('optional secret string')). To *set a signed cookie,* you simply call res.cookie(name,value,{**signed:true**}) (in other words, name and value as normal and passing in an option of signed=true). To *read the signed cookies* sent in the client request, use the req.signedCookies just like you use req.cookies. Using a different property when reading makes it easy for you to know that the cookie signature has been validated. As an example, Listing 7-14 shows our toggle cookie server updated to use signed cookies.

Listing 7-14. cookie/5sign.js

```
var express = require('express');
var cookieParser = require('cookie-parser');

var app = express()
    .use(cookieParser('my super secret sign key'))
    .use('/toggle', function (req, res) {
        if (req.signedCookies.name) {
            res.clearCookie('name');
            res.end('name cookie cleared! Was:' + req.signedCookies.name);
        }
        else {
            res.cookie('name', 'foo', { signed: true });
            res.end('name cookie set!');
        }
    })
    .listen(3000);
```

httpOnly and Secure

By default, the user's browser JavaScript can read the cookie set for the current web page (using `document.cookie`). This makes a cookie vulnerable to cross-side scripting (XSS). That is, if some malicious user manages to inject JavaScript into your web-site content, it allows that JavaScript to read cookies that might contain sensitive information for the currently logged in user and ship it to a malicious web site. To prevent JavaScript access to cookies, you can set `httpOnly` to `true` (`res.cookie(name,value,{`**`httpOnly:true`**`})`). This tells the browser that it should not allow any JavaScript access to this cookie and that it should only be used when communicating with the server.

Additionally, as we showed in the previous chapter, you should use HTTPS on all your public servers. HTTPS ensures that all headers, including the `cookie` header, are encrypted and safe from man in the middle attacks. To ask the browser to never send a particular cookie over HTTP and only use it for HTTPS, you can set the secure flag, that is, `res.cookie(name,value,{`**`secure:true`**`})`.

Based on what you know now, for sensitive cookies you should always use `httpOnly` and `secure` set to `true`. Of course, secure needs an HTTPS server.

Setting a Cookie Expiry

Cookies are great to store persistent bits of information relevant to a particular user, with the user, in their browser. However, in the absence of a cookie expiry time mentioned in the `Set-Cookie` header, the browser clears the cookie after the browser is closed! Such a cookie is commonly called a **browser-session** cookie (since it only valid for current browser session). You should always set the `expiry` if you want cookies to persist over a period of time. You can do that by passing in a `maxAge` option to `setCookie`, which takes the number of milliseconds for which this cookie will be valid and sent in client requests. For example:

```
res.cookie('foo', 'bar', { maxAge: 900000, httpOnly: true })
```

Cookie-Based Sessions

To provide a consistent user experience between different HTTP requests by the same user, it is common to have user *session* information available alongside a client HTTP request. As a simple example, we might want to know if the user has logged in or not.

Cookies provide a nice foundation for small bits of such user-specific information we want to be associated with a client request. However, the API is too low level. For example, the cookie value can only be a string. If you want JavaScript objects, you need to do JSON parsing. This is where the `cookie-session` middleware (`npm install cookie-session`) comes in. It allows you to use a single cookie to store information you feel relevant is for this user session.

When using the `cookie-session` middleware, the user session object is exposed as `req.session`. You can set or update a value using a simple assignment to a member of `req.session`. You can clear a value by deleting a key from `req.session`. By default, the `cookie-session` middleware must be passed at least one secret key, which it uses to ensure the integrity of the session cookie by signing, as we saw earlier. Listing 7-15 gives a simple example to demonstrate using the `cookie-session` middleware.

Listing 7-15. cookiesession/counter.js

```
var express = require('express');
var cookieSession = require('cookie-session');

var app = express()
    .use(cookieSession({
        keys: ['my super secret sign key']
    }))
```

```
    .use('/home', function (req, res) {
        if (req.session.views) {
            req.session.views++;
        }
        else{
            req.session.views = 1;
        }
        res.end('Total views for you: ' + req.session.views);
    })
    .use('/reset',function(req,res){
        delete req.session.views;
        res.end('Cleared all your views');
    })
    .listen(3000);
```

Start this server, open up your browser, and visit `http://localhost:3000/home` to see the counter increment, and `http://localhost:3000/reset` to reset the counter. In addition to clearing a single value from the session as we demonstrated, you can delete the entire user session by setting `req.session` to `null`, in other words, `req.session=null`.

You can pass additional options in the `cookieSession` function (in addition to keys). To specify the cookie name that the session is stored against, you can pass in the `name` option. By default, the cookie name will be `express:sess`. A few other options for cookie are also supported such as `maxage`, `path`, `httpOnly` (true by default),and `signed` (true by default).

Use Cookie-Session Sparingly

Note that cookies need to be sent with *every* client request (if path matches) in the HTTP header so large cookies have a performance impact. There are also limitations on how much information browsers will let you store in cookies (a general guidance for most browsers is 4093 bytes and a maximum of 20 cookies per site). Consequently, it is not feasible to have all the user information become a part of the cookie.

A more powerful session-management strategy is to use a database to store user session information instead of using cookies. In that scenario, you would only store a token in the user cookie and that token would point to session information we can read from our database at the server. You can use the `express-session` middleware (`npm install express-session`) with a database (like Mongo or Redis) for that purpose. We will see an example in Chapter 8.

Compression

Zip compression over the wire is extremely easy to enable in Express- and Connect-based applications, thanks to the compression (`npm install compression`) middleware. Listing 7-16 is a simple server that compresses pages greater than 1kb before sending them to the client.

Listing 7-16. compression/compress.js

```
var express = require('express');
var compression = require('compression');

var app = express()
    .use(compression())
    .use(express.static(__dirname + '/public'))
    .listen(3000);
```

You can test it using `curl` by specifying the `--compressed` command-line flag, as shown in Listing 7-17, to tell the server that you can handle compressed information.

Listing 7-17. Testing compression/compress.js with curl

```
$ curl http://127.0.0.1:3000 -i --compressed
HTTP/1.1 200 OK
...truncated...
Content-Encoding: gzip
Connection: keep-alive
Transfer-Encoding: chunked

<div>Hello compression!</div>
<div>
lalalalalalalalalalalalalalalalalalalalala
... truncated ...
```

Notice that Node.js can still stream the response even when compression is enabled. To specify a threshold different from the default `1kb`, you can use the `threshold` option to specify the number of bytes. For example, `compression({threshold: 512})` will compress responses that are longer than 512 bytes.

Time-out Hanging Requests

It is possible to get in a situation where some middleware fails to end the request *and* fails to call next. For example, this can happen if your database server is down and your middleware is waiting for a response from the database server. In such a case, the client HTTP request will be left hanging, taking up server memory. In these circumstances, you should time-out the client request instead of leaving it hanging.

This is exactly what the connect-timeout (`npm install connect-timeout`) middleware is for, as Listing 7-18 demonstrates.

Listing 7-18. timeout/basic.js

```
var express = require('express');
var timeout = require('connect-timeout');

var app = express()
    .use('/api', timeout(5000),
                function (req, res, next) {
                    // simulate a hanging request by doing nothing
                })
    .listen(3000);
```

If you start this webserver and visit `http://localhost:3000/api`, the request will hang for five seconds, after which the `connect-timeout` middleware kicks in and terminates the request, sending the client a 503 Service Unavailable HTTP response.

You can customize the response of a timeout by adding an error handling middleware and checking if a timeout occurred by checking the `req.timedout` property, as shown in Listing 7-19.

Listing 7-19. timeout/error.js

```
var express = require('express');
var timeout = require('connect-timeout');

var app = express()
    .use('/api', timeout(5000)
            , function (req, res, next) {
                // simulate a hanging request by doing nothing
            }
            , function (error, req, res, next) {
                if (req.timedout) {
                    res.statusCode = 500;
                    res.end('Request timed out');
                }
                else {
                    next(error);
                }
            })
    .listen(3000);
```

Notice that you should not use this middleware at the top level ('/') since you probably want to stream a few responses that might take longer than what you might think upfront.

Be Careful of the Sleeping Middleware

When you use this middleware, you need to be mindful of the case when your hanging middleware suddenly awakens and calls next (for example, a database request took longer than expected but did succeed eventually). In such a case, you should check req.timedout and prevent the middleware from going further as the error handling response has already been sent. This is demonstrated in Listing 7-20, which will crash on the first request.

Listing 7-20. timeout/propogateError.js

```
var express = require('express');
var timeout = require('connect-timeout');

var app = express()
    .use(timeout(5000))
    .use(function (req, res, next) {
        // simulate database action that takes 6s
        setTimeout(function () {
            next();
        }, 6000)
    })
    .use(function (req, res, next) {
        res.end('Done'); // ERROR request already terminated
    })
    .listen(3000);
```

For this, you should use a utility halt function after every middleware in your chain, which is susceptible to hanging, as shown in Listing 7-21.

Listing 7-21. timeout/propogateErrorHandled.js

```
var express = require('express');
var timeout = require('connect-timeout');

var app = express()
    .use(timeout(1000))
    .use(function (req, res, next) {
        // simulate database action that takes 2s
        setTimeout(function () {
            next();
        }, 2000)
    })
    .use(haltOnTimedout)
    .use(function (req, res, next) {
        res.end('Done'); // Will never get called
    })
    .listen(3000);


function haltOnTimedout(req, res, next) {
    if (!req.timedout) next();
}
```

Express Response Object

Express response derives from the standard Node.js server response object we saw in the previous chapter. It also adds quite a few useful utility functions that make your web development experience more fun. In fact, we have already seen the res.cookie/res.clearCookie functions, which were provided by Express.

The response has a function res.status, which has the same effect as setting the res.statusCode except that it is chainable. For example:

```
res.status(200).end('Hello world!');
```

To set individual or *multiple* response headers at once, instead of the good old res.setHeader we saw earlier, you can use the res.set function, as shown in Listing 7-22.

Listing 7-22. Using the set Method

```
res.set('Content-Type', 'text/plain');

res.set({
  'Content-Type': 'text/plain',
  'Content-Length': '123',
  'ETag': '12345'
})
```

Similarly, to get a queued header, in addition to the good on res.getHeader, there is a res.get, which is case-insensitive:

```
res.get('content-Type'); // "text/plain"
```

If all you want to do is set the content-type (a common task), it provides a nice utility res.type(type) function, which can either take the content-type directly or even look up the content type for you based on a file extension or file extension name. For example, all of the following have the same effect:

```
res.type('.html');
res.type('html');
res.type('text/html');
```

Sending a redirect response is quite a common task. Express makes it really easy for you by providing the res.redirect([status], url) function. The url argument can be absolute, relative to site root, relative to current URL, and even relative to the middleware mount point, as shown in Listing 7-23.

Listing 7-23. Using the Redirect Method

```
res.redirect('http://example.com'); // absolute
res.redirect('/login'); // relative to site root
res.redirect('../bar'); // relative to current url
res.redirect('foo/bar'); // relative to middleware mount point

// Status code demo
res.redirect(301, 'http://example.com');
```

The default status code of 302 FOUND is good to have, but you can override it if you want by passing a first number argument.

Simplifying Send

There is one extremely useful function that, once you learn, you can't stop using. Its res.send([body|status], [body]). This is the function that you should use whenever you want to send a non-streaming response. This greatly simplifies a common pattern we have been using up to this point of stating a status and sending a body, as demonstrated in Listing 7-24.

Listing 7-24. Send Saves Lines, Lines Save Kittens

```
// instead of
res.statusCode = 404;
res.end('These are not the droids you are looking for');

// you can do
res.send(404, 'These are not the droids you are looking for');
```

It also allows you to send JavaScript objects as JSON in one go. If you pass in a JavaScript object as the body, it also sets the content-type header to be application/json for you:

```
res.send({ some: 'json' });
```

Finally, you can just send a status code. If it is a known status code, the body will automatically be populated for you. For example, it will read OK in the following example:

```
res.send(200); // OK
```

Express Request Object

Similar to the response, the Express request object derives from the Node.js request object we saw in Chapter 6. Express adds a few nice features that we will explore in this section.

Express simplifies your access to the request headers (req.headers as we saw in the previous chapter) with a req.get function, which allows case in-sensitive lookup, as shown in Listing 7-25.

Listing 7-25. Demonstrating the Get Method

```
req.get('Content-Type'); // "text/plain"
req.get('content-type'); // "text/plain"
req.get('not-present');  // undefined
```

If all you want to do is look up the content-type of the request, you can use the utility req.is(type) function as shown in Listing 7-26, which even does a mime-type inspection for you.

Listing 7-26. Using the Is Method

```
// When Content-Type is application/json
req.is('json');              // true
req.is('application/json');  // true
req.is('application/*');     // true
req.is('html');              // false
```

You can get the client IP address using the req.ip property.

To check if the request came over HTTPS, you can use the req.secure flag, which is true if the request was over HTTPS, and false otherwise.

URL Handling

Express parses the query parameters from the URL into the req.query JavaScript object. Query parameters are great for when you want to return search results. Listing 7-27 provides a sample of how the URL query section gets parsed into a JavaScript object.

Listing 7-27. Demo to Show the Built-in Query Parsing

```
// GET /shoes?order=desc&shoe[color]=blue&shoe[type]=converse
req.query.order     // "desc"
req.query.shoe.color // "blue"
req.query.shoe.type  // "converse"
```

If you just want the path section of the URL (that is, the section before the query), it can be found in req.path:

```
// GET /users?sort=desc
req.path // "/users"
```

When your middleware is mounted, Express tries to make it easier for you to access only the relevant portion of the `req.url`. For example, if you mount your middleware at ''`/api`', for the request '`/api/admin`', `req.url` will only be '`/admin`'. This is demonstrated in Listing 7-28.

Listing 7-28. requestmount/mountUrl.js

```javascript
var express = require('express');

express()
    .use('/home', function (req, res, next) {
        console.log('first:', req.url); // GET /home => "first: /"
        next();
    })
    .use(function (req, res, next) {
        console.log('second:', req.url); // GET /home => "second: /home"
        next();
    })
    .listen(3000);
```

To get the complete original URL you can use the `req.originalUrl` property.

Making Request and Response Cross Visible

Express also assigns the response object to `req.res` and the request object to `res.req`. This makes it possible for you to pass only one of them around (request or response) and, when debugging, get access to the corresponding request or the corresponding response object.

Understanding REST

REST (*Representational State Transfer*) is a term coined by Roy Fielding (one of the principal authors of the HTTP specification) as a general architectural style, specifying constraints on how connected components in a distributed Hypermedia system should behave. Web APIs that adhere to these constraints are called RESTful.

In REST, there are two broad kinds of URLs. URLs that point to collections (such as `http://example.com/resources`), and URLs that point to an individual item in the collection (such as `http://example.com/resources/item5identifier`). In order to be RESTful, you need to adhere to the behavior as shown in Table 7-1 for collection and Table 7-2 for item URLs, based on the kind of URL and the HTTP method used by the client. Also notice the relationship between the collection URL and the item in the collection URL (which is the collection URL + item identifier in the collection).

Table 7-1. *RESTful API HTTP Method Behavior for **collection** URLs*

HTTP method	Behavior
GET	**Get** the summarized details of the members of the collection, including their unique identifiers.
PUT	**Replace** the entire collection with a new collection.
POST	**Add** a new **item** in the collection. It is common to return a unique identifier for the created resource.
DELETE	**Delete** the entire collection

*Table 7-2. RESTful API HTTP Method Behavior for **item** URLs*

HTTP method	Behavior
GET	**Get** the details of the item.
PUT	**Replace** the item.
POST	Would treat the item as a collection and **add** a new **sub-item** in the collection. It is not generally used as you tend to simply replace properties on the item as a whole (in other words, use PUT).
DELETE	**Delete** the item.

It is recommended that you put the new item details in the *body* of the PUT and POST messages. Also worth mentioning is the fact that in HTTP you cannot have a request body in GET and DELETE methods.

Express Application Routes

Because of the importance of HTTP verbs when making good web APIs, Express provides first-class verb + URL based routing support.

Let's start with the basics. You can call app.get / app.put / app.post /app.delete—in other words, app.VERB(path, [callback...], callback)—to register a middleware chain that is only called when the path + HTTP verb in the client request matches. Also you can call app.all to register a middleware that is called whenever the path matches (irrespective of the HTTP verb). Listing 7-29 is a simple demo that drives this point home.

Listing 7-29. approute/1verbs.js

```
var express = require('express');

var app = express();
app.all('/', function (req, res, next) {
    res.write('all\n');
    next();
});
app.get('/', function (req, res, next) {
    res.end('get');
});
app.put('/', function (req, res, next) {
    res.end('put');
});
app.post('/', function (req, res, next) {
    res.end('post');
});
app.delete('/', function (req, res, next) {
    res.end('delete');
});
app.listen(3000);
```

All of these methods form a standard middleware chain where order + calling next matters. If you run this server you will note that the .all middleware is always called followed by the relevant verb middleware. We can test it by using curl and specifying the request (-X) verb to use, as shown in Listing 7-30.

Listing 7-30. Testing approute/1verbs.js Using curl

```
$ curl http://127.0.0.1:3000
all
get
$ curl -X PUT http://127.0.0.1:3000
all
put
$ curl -X POST http://127.0.0.1:3000
all
post
$ curl -X DELETE http://127.0.0.1:3000
all
delete
```

Creating a Route Object

Now specifying the path in each of these routes can be cumbersome (and prone to spelling mistakes). Therefore, Express has a nice little app.route member function to specify the prefix only once, which returns a route object that has the same all/get/put/post/delete functions. All of these are demonstrated in the example in Listing 7-31. The output is exactly the same as we saw in the previous example (Listing 7-20).

Listing 7-31. approute/2route.js

```
var express = require('express');

var app = express();
app.route('/')
    .all(function (req, res, next) {
        res.write('all\n');
        next();
    })
    .get(function (req, res, next) {
        res.end('get');
    })
    .put(function (req, res, next) {
        res.end('put');
    })
    .post(function (req, res, next) {
        res.end('post');
    })
    .delete(function (req, res, next) {
        res.end('delete');
    });
app.listen(3000);
```

A Deeper Look at the Path Option

Unlike the app.use function, which takes a *path* **prefix**, the verb-based routing in ExpressJS matches the *exact path* (not *exact URL* because the query string part is ignored). If you want to match a path prefix you can use the * placeholder to match anything after the prefix. You can also set up a route based on a regular expression. All of these options are demonstrated in Listing 7-32.

Listing 7-32. approute/3path.js

```
var express = require('express');

var app = express();
app.get('/', function (req, res) {
    res.send('nothing passed in!');
});
app.get(/^\/[0-9]+$/, function (req, res) {
    res.send('number!');
});
app.get('/*', function (req, res) {
    res.send('not a number!');
});
app.listen(3000);
```

The first middleware is only called if the path is exactly '/', in which case it sends a response and does not pass control to any other middleware. The number middleware is only called when the number regex matches and, again, it returns a response and doesn't pass the control any further. Finally, we have a catchall middleware. You can test this using curl, as shown in Listing 7-33.

Listing 7-33. Testing approute/3path.js Using curl

```
$ curl http://127.0.0.1:3000/
nothing passed in!
$ curl http://127.0.0.1:3000/123
number!
$ curl http://127.0.0.1:3000/foo
not a number!
```

Parameter-Based Routing

Instead of putting too much filtering logic into your path prefix matching, a much nicer option is to use path parameters. You can specify path parameters using the :parameterName syntax. For example `/user/:userId` will match `/user/123` and populate the userId request parameter for you. Express puts all the parameter values in req.params object. Listing 7-34 demonstrates its usage (along with a sample run shown in Listing 7-35).

Listing 7-34. approute/4param.js

```
var express = require('express');

var app = express();
app.get('/user/:userId', function (req, res) {
    res.send('userId is: ' + req.params['userId']);
});
app.listen(3000);
```

Listing 7-35. testing approute/4param.js using curl

```
$ curl http://127.0.0.1:3000/user/123
userId is: 123
```

In fact, by using the `app.param` function, you can register a middleware to load the relevant information for you. The `app.param` middleware function is called whenever a parameter name matches in a route and is also passed in the parameter value as a fourth argument. This is demonstrated in Listing 7-36.

Listing 7-36. approute/5paramload.js

```
var express = require('express');

var app = express();
app.param('userId', function (req, res, next, userId) {
    res.write('Looking up user: ' + userId + '\n');
    // simulate a user lookup and
    // load it into the request object for later middleware
    req.user = { userId: userId };
    next();
});
app.get('/user/:userId', function (req, res) {
    res.end('user is: ' + JSON.stringify(req.user));
});
app.listen(3000);
```

Run this server and do a simple `curl` request. You can see that the `param` function is called if a route with the specified param matches before any other middleware gets a whack at it. This allows you to create a reusable parameter loading middleware:

```
$ curl http://127.0.0.1:3000/user/123
Looking up user: 123
user is: {"userId":"123"}
```

Express Router Object

An Express router is an isolated instance of middleware + routes. It can be thought of as a "mini" Express application. You can create a router object quite easily using `express.Router()` function.

At its root level, it has the `use`, `all`, `get`, `post`, `put`, `delete`, `param`, and `route` functions, which behave exactly the same as their Express app counterparts that we have already seen.

In addition to all of this, the router object behaves like any other middleware. That is, once you set up a router object, you can register it with an Express using the `app.use` function. And obviously you can mount it at a specify mount point by passing in a first argument to the `app.use` function, as we have already seen before.

To demonstrate the power of this pattern, let's create a simple `Router`, which follows the principles of REST, to create a web API for managing an in-memory collection of arbitrary objects, as shown in Listing 7-37.

Listing 7-37. router/basic.js

```
var express = require('express');
var bodyParser = require('body-parser');

// An in memory collection of items
var items = [];

// Create a router
var router = express.Router();
router.use(bodyParser());
```

```
// Setup the collection routes
router.route('/')
    .get(function (req, res, next) {
        res.send({
            status: 'Items found',
            items: items
        });
    })
    .post(function (req, res, next) {
        items.push(req.body);
        res.send({
            status: 'Item added',
            itemId: items.length - 1
        });
    })
    .put(function (req, res, next) {
        items = req.body;
        res.send({ status: 'Items replaced' });
    })
    .delete(function (req, res, next) {
        items = [];
        res.send({ status: 'Items cleared' });
    });

// Setup the item routes
router.route('/:id')
    .get(function (req, res, next) {
        var id = req.params['id'];
        if (id && items[Number(id)]) {
            res.send({
                status: 'Item found',
                item: items[Number(id)]
            });
        }
        else {
            res.send(404, { status: 'Not found' });
        }
    })
    .all(function (req, res, next) {
        res.send(501, { status: 'Not implemented' });
    });

// Use the router
var app = express()
        .use('/todo', router)
        .listen(3000);
```

Other than the fact that we are creating an Express Router, all of this code is already familiar to you. We create an in-memory collection of object. Then we create a router and ask it to use the body-parser middleware (which we have already seen). We set up a root level '/' route. If you make a GET call, you get all the items in the collection. If you make a POST, we create a new item in the collection and return its index. If you make a PUT request, we replace the collection with whatever you PUT. If you make a DELETE call, we clear the collection.

We also support one item level route to GET the item by id. For any other HTTP verb, we return 501 not implemented.

Note that because of the mount-ability of routers, we can reuse the same router at another point (instead of '/todo'), if we want to. This makes the functionality highly reusable and maintainable.

■ **Note**   Remember how we said that `req.originalUrl` points to the original URL, whereas `req.url` is a stripped-down version based on a mount point. That is exactly what makes registering a router at a mount point possible since it internally only looks at `req.url` and it only gets the portion that is relevant for its routes.

Now let's test it out with `curl` in Listing 7-38.

Listing 7-38.   Testing router/basic.js Using curl

```
$ curl http://127.0.0.1:3000/todo
{"status":"Items found","items":[]}

$ curl http://127.0.0.1:3000/todo -H "content-type: application/json" -d
"{\"description\":\"test\"}"
{"status":"Item added","itemId":0}
$ curl http://127.0.0.1:3000/todo/0
{"status":"Item found","item":{"description":"test"}}
$ curl http://127.0.0.1:3000/todo/
{"status":"Items found","items":[{"description":"test"}]}

$ curl http://127.0.0.1:3000/todo/ -X DELETE
{"status":"Items cleared"}
$ curl http://127.0.0.1:3000/todo/
{"status":"Items found","items":[]}

$ curl http://127.0.0.1:3000/todo -X PUT -H "content-type: application/json" -d
"[{\"description\":\"test\"}]"
{"status":"Items replaced"}
$ curl http://127.0.0.1:3000/todo/
{"status":"Items found","items":[{"description":"test"}]}

$ curl http://127.0.0.1:3000/todo/0 -X DELETE
{"status":"Not implemented"}
```

In this demo,) we get the initial collection and it's empty. Then we add an item (using a POST) and query for that item (`GET /todo/0`), which is returned. Then we query all the items (GET /todo). Next, we delete all the items and query to verify. Then we PUT a new collection and again verify. Finally, we show that you cannot delete individual items since we intentionally blocked out that functionality.

When designing an API, you should be consistent. Most commonly, you will be working with JSON, so make sure you accept valid JSON (`bodyParser` does that for you) and return a JavaScript object in all cases. This includes error conditions so the client always gets JSON. Also, standardized HTTP status codes are your friends.

At this point, it might seem that we are doing a lot of work for a simple API, but bear in mind that in the absence of good API design, your UI + API would be all jumbled together. We will see later in the book how we can develop a nice front-end on top of a clean API that is both easy to maintain and performs better than the *page reloading* web design of the old days.

Additional Resources

Roy Fielding's original mention of REST as a part of his dissertation can be found at www.ics.uci.edu/~fielding/ pubs/dissertation/rest_arch_style.htm.

Summary

In this chapter, we dug deeper into various HTTP concepts. We started by showing popular middleware for a variety of web-related tasks. This includes serving static web pages to working with cookies.

We demonstrated that Express offers the same middleware framework as Connect. Then we dug into a few nice value-added features provided by Express on top of the standard request and response objects.

Finally, we covered the principles of REST. We showed how the Express framework embraces the web and makes creating maintainable RESTful web APIs a breeze.

We didn't cover the view rendering side of Express, which will be covered in Chapter 9, when we discuss front-end design. But, first, let's persist (pun on next chapter).

CHAPTER 8

■ ■ ■

Persisting Data

Data persistence is an important part of any real-world application. In this chapter, we will give a solid data-persistence strategy for the beginner. We will introduce MongoDB as well as associated concepts such as NoSQL, ORMs, and ODM.

Introduction to NoSQL

NoSQL (Not Only SQL) is a term used to encompass the general trend of a new generation of database servers. These servers were created in response to challenges that were not being met by traditional SQL (Structured Query Language) relational database servers (for example, Oracle Database, Microsoft SQL Server, and MySQL). These servers can be placed into four broad categories:

- Document databases (for example, MongoDB)

- Key-value databases (for example, Redis)

- Column-family databases (for example, Cassandra)

- Graph databases (for example, Neo4J)

    Scalability is a key motivation common to all of these. For most purposes, a document database provides the largest feature set with an acceptable/scalable performance. For simple cases where you do not want complicated query requirements, key-value databases provide the best performance.

What Is a Document Database?

A document database is one that works based on the concept of documents. What is a document? A **document** is a *self-contained* piece of information for a particular entity. Listing 8.1 gives a possible JSON document.

Listing 8-1. Sample JSON Document

```
{
    "firstName": "John",
    "lastName": "Smith",
    "isAlive": true,
    "age": 25,
    "height_cm": 167.64,
```

```
    "address": {
        "streetAddress": "21 2nd Street",
        "city": "New York",
        "state": "NY",
    }
}
```

We've chosen to use JSON to represent this document, but other formats such as XML, or even binary formats, can be used. In a relational database, such a document would be stored in two tables, one for persons and another for addresses. In a document database, it's just one document.

What Is a Key-Value Store?

A key-value store is effectively a stripped-down version of a document database. The key is a unique ID to identify a document, and the values are the actual documents. What separates a key-value store from a document database is the query ability of the data. In most key-value stores, you can only query the key. In a document database, you can query by Document *contents* as well. This gives key-value stores an opportunity to optimize for faster key-based lookup, and they can use a more compressed storage for the values.

Redis is an excellent example of a key-value store. It actually keeps the entire database in RAM, with background backups to disk, for lightning fast runtime performance.

Why NoSQL?

There are two reasons to use document databases and key-value stores:

- Scalability
- Ease of development

Scalability Issues with a Relational Design

Before we answer what makes relational databases difficult to scale, let's define a few terms:

- **Availability:** Is the data accessible? That is, can the users read and act on the data.

- **Consistency:** Is there only a single source of truth? If all your data is recorded only once at only a single place, then it is consistent for the purpose of this discussion.

On a single machine, *availability* and *consistency* are strongly tied to each other. If the data is available, it is consistent. A single server serving the data with a simple backup server is sufficient for an average enterprise. Relational servers were born in these situations and didn't have a problem handling the load.

However, on the Web, no single machine can handle all the workload of every single client request. Additionally, you might want to *partition* your servers to be closer to the client's geo-location (for example, American clients vs. Australian clients). To have scalability, you need to partition your data across machines. These partitions need to communicate with each other in order to maintain a *consistent* view of the data. Now let's introduce a third term:

- **Partition tolerance:** The system continues to operate in the face of a communication disruption between the partitions.

Consider the case where we have replicated the data over a network partition: one server in America and another in Australia. When the network between the two is down (communication disruption) and a user in Australia asks to update the data, do we allow it (favor *availability*), or do we deny the request to maintain our *consistency*?

This is the foundation of the *CAP theorem*. Simplified, it can be expressed as the following: *Given that you have a network partition, you need to choose between availability and consistency*. It's not an all-or-nothing choice; it's a sliding scale where you make the choice based on your business requirements.

The CAP theorem is a physical and easily understandable limit. To overcome it, we can try to distribute the data to *remove* the partition from the equation. This can be done quite simply by splitting the data into self-contained units (called shards).

For example, consider the case of a reservation system that handles hotels in America as well as hotels in Australia. Here we can shard the data such that an American server contains only the information about the American hotels and the Australian server contains only the information about Australian hotels. In such a way, each server is self-contained and only handles the requests for data that it contains. For any information about American hotels requested by Australian hotels, we access the American server and vice versa. This brings us back to the good, old, happy single server scenario where availability and consistency were strongly tied to each other. If the American server is down (unavailable) or inaccessible from Australia (network disruption), there is no issue in responding to Australian hotel reservations for Australians. *This partitioning no longer has an availability-consistency choice impact.*

So, what is it about relational databases that makes it hard to scale in terms of the CAP theorem? It is the issue of *consistency boundary*. In a relational database schema, you are encouraged to have relations among the various tables. *Relationships make sharding difficult.*

In a document database, the document is the consistency boundary. It is designed to be self-contained from the get-go and the data easily be sharded.

Beyond sharding, there are other positive performance impacts of a document-oriented database design. In a relational database, to load the information for an entity (for example, People), you need to query the linked tables (for example, the Addresses Table) as well. This is wasteful in terms of query response times. For complex entities, you end up needing multiple queries to load a single entity. In a document-oriented design, complex entities are still just a *single document*. This makes querying and loading documents faster.

Ease of Development

Object-relational mapping is the Vietnam of computer science.

—Ted Neward

Relational databases operate in terms of relations and tables. To use or manipulate the data in a relational database from our applications, we need to convert these "tables" into "objects" and vice versa. This is the process of Object Relational Mapping (ORM). ORM can be a tedious process and can be completely avoided by using a document database. For our example for the person document, it's a simple matter of `JSON.parse`. Of course, document databases provide you with an API to get JavaScript objects returned from the database, so you don't have to do any parsing and don't have to mess with an ORM.

There are real-world reasons to consider a relational database over a NoSQL database, such as complex queries and data analysis. These things can, however, be done using a relational database in parallel with a NoSQL database serving the main data requirements of your web site.

By now, we've hopefully convinced you that there are real technical advantages to document databases on the Web. This means you can enjoy the rest of this chapter more and put in the effort to consider non-relational options in your projects.

Installing MongoDB

The name MongoDB comes from hu**mongo**us. Installing MongoDB is extremely simple. It ships as a simple zip file containing a few binaries that you can extract anywhere on your filesystem. Zipped binaries are available for Windows as well as Mac OS X and Linux systems. It is recommended that you use the 64-bit version of MongoDB as well as a 64-bit OS in production. This allows MongoDB to use all the memory address space offered by a 64-bit OS. The zipped files are available at `www.mongodb.org/downloads`.

Understanding the Binaries

After you download the zip file, extract it into any folder in your filesystem that has enough space. Everything you need is contained in the bin folder inside the zip file you downloaded for your OS. MongoDB is self-contained and doesn't care about its location on the filesystem as long as it has write access. Its ease of installation is one of the reasons for its popularity.

The bin folder contains quite a few binary files. The windows binaries have a .exe extension, but the same ones exist for Mac OS X (for example, mongod.exe for windows vs. mongod for Mac OS X). The most important binaries are the following:

- mongod.exe: This is the **Mongo**DB **D**aemon—that is, the main server binary. This is what you will execute to start your database server.

- mongo.exe: This is a utility REPL provided with the server that can be used for various administrative and code exploration tasks.

Other binaries exist in the bin folder for importing/exporting data, gathering system statistics, and managing other features provided by MongoDB such as sharding and MongoDB's distributed file system (called GridFS). All of these can be ignored when getting started.

To make it easier to follow along, after extracting the zip file, it is best to just put the bin folder into your system path. This will make mongod as well as mongo available from any directory in your command prompt/terminal.

Running Your First Server

MongoDB requires a data directory (called the dbpath in MongoDB literature) to store all the database data. The default dbpath is /data/db (or \data\db in Windows, based on the drive of your current working directory such as C:\data\db). It is always best to just specify an explicit dbpath.

Start by making a db folder that will contain all your MongoDB database data at a place where you have write access:

```
$ mkdir db
```

Now you can start the MongoDB server as shown in Listing 8-2. If everything goes well, you should see the waiting for connections message. Once the server starts, leave the terminal open to keep the server running.

Listing 8-2. Start MongoDB Server with a Specified Database Directory

```
$ mongod --dbpath="./db"
Sun Jun 15 17:05:56.761 [initandlisten] MongoDB starting : pid=6076 port=27017
dbpath=./db 64- ...truncated...
Sun Jun 15 17:05:57.051 [initandlisten] waiting for connections on port 27017
Sun Jun 15 17:05:57.051 [websvr] admin web console waiting for connections on port 28017
```

The MongoDB REPL

The mongo executable is an interactive JavaScript shell interface to MongoDB. You can use it for system administration as well as for testing queries and operations against the database. As soon as you start it, it tries to connect to localhost on the default port (27017).

The mongo REPL provides access to a few global variables and functions that we can use to interact with the database. The most important is the db variable, which is your handle to the current database connection. Once the REPL is started, you can exit at any time by typing in exit. You can get the help of the options available by typing in help. Also, many functions that we will use in the REPL have a 'help' member. Let's spin up the mongo REPL and see what options we have available on db. (See Listing 8-3.)

Listing 8-3. A Sample Session Using Mongo Shell

```
$ mongo
MongoDB shell version: 2.6.1
connecting to: test
> db.help()
DB methods:
        db.adminCommand(nameOrDocument) - switches to 'admin' db, and runs command [ just calls
db.runCommand(...) ]
        db.auth(username, password)
        db.cloneDatabase(fromhost)
        ...truncated...
        db.version() current version of the server
> exit
bye
```

Notice that by default it connects us to the **test** database. Now that you know how to get in and out of the REPL, let's look at a few key MongoDB concepts.

Important MongoDB Concepts

A MongoDB deployment consists of multiple databases. Each database can contain multiple collections. Each collection can contain multiple documents. Hence, it is a hierarchy from database to collections to documents.

A document is effectively a JSON document that we are already familiar with, plus a few niceties. For example, these documents have first-class support for the Date data type (we say in Chapter 4 that JSON spec doesn't allow Date as a valid value and must be serialized to a string). An example document would be the "person document" representing an individual.

A *collection* is simply a name that you give to a *collection of documents*. Storing multiple documents into the same collection *doesn't* enforce any concept of *schema* on the documents. It is up to you to be disciplined about your document semantics. This schema-less-ness makes it possible to do partial upgrades of documents to new schemas in an agile fashion.

Finally, a single MongoDB *server* can contain multiple databases, allowing you to do a logical separation of a *set of collections* in your server. A common use case for using multiple databases is multi-tenancy applications. A multi-tenant application is one that has multiple customers. For each customer, you can have different databases with the same collection names inside each database. This allows you to efficiently use your server resources while still allowing easier development (same collection names) and maintainability (same backup procedures for different databases).

Now that we understand documents, collections, and databases, let's explore them in the mongo REPL. You can specify the database the REPL will use with the 'use' command (for example, use demo will use the demo database). If a demo database doesn't exist, it will be created for you. The variable db refers to the currently active database. To use a collection in the current database, you simply access it using the collection name property on db (for example, db.people will look at the people collection in the current database). Next, you manage individual documents using the collection API. Listing 8-4 provides a simple example where we insert a single person into the people collection, followed by querying all the people from the collection.

Listing 8-4. Working with Databases, Collections, and Documents Using Mongo Shell

```
$ mongo
MongoDB shell version: 2.6.1
connecting to: test
> use demo
switched to db demo
> db.people.insert({name:"John"})
WriteResult({ "nInserted" : 1 })
> db.people.find()
{ "_id" : ObjectId("539ed1d9f7da431c00026e17"), "name" : "John" }
>
```

This example is fairly straightforward, but the interesting bit is that when we query the document back we see that it has a _id field. Let's explore that a bit more.

MongoDB _id field

Every document in MongoDB must have a "_id" field. You are allowed to use any value for _id as long as it is unique in the collection. By default, MongoDB (the provided client driver or the server) will create an ObjectId for you.

Why Not Use a Natural Primary Key?

The fundamental rule of database development is that the primary key *must never change*. For some data models, you might be tempted to find a *natural primary key* (in other words, something that is unique to the entity in nature and does not change over its lifetime.) For example, for a person, you might be tempted to consider the Social Security Number (SSN). But you will be surprised to find how common seemingly *natural primary keys* change. For example, in the United States, you are legally allowed to request a new SSN if, for example, your life is in danger. Similarly, consider the case of the ISBN. If you change the title of the book (seemingly natural thing to request), you will get a new ISBN.

In most cases, you will want to use a surrogate primary key. A surrogate primary key is a key that has no natural meaning to the entity but is used to uniquely identify the entity in the database. The MongoDB generated ObjectId is one such good-quality surrogate key.

More about the ObjectId

Now that we have hopefully convinced you that it is better to use a generated primary key, the question is why an ObjectId? Why not an auto-incrementing number? Because an auto-incrementing number does not scale; it is difficult to manage in a distributed environment as the next number requires knowledge of the last used number. The ObjectId that MongoDB generates uses 12 bytes of storage. This means it takes 24 hexadecimal digits (2 digits per byte) to represent it in a string, as we saw earlier (for example, "539ed1d9f7da431c00026e17"). The 12 bytes of the MongoDB ObjectId are generated as shown in Figure 8-1.

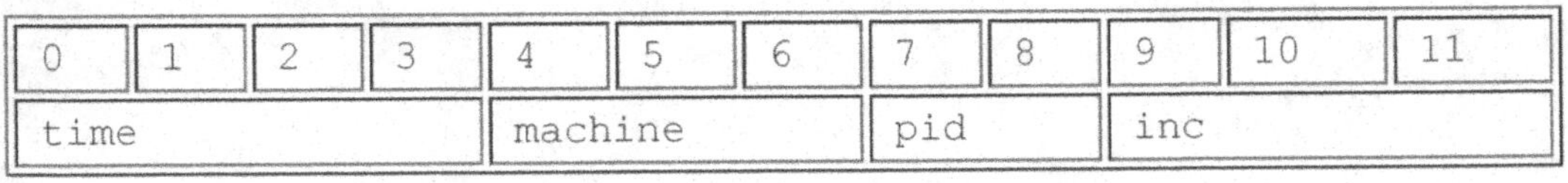

0	1	2	3	4	5	6	7	8	9	10	11
time				machine			pid		inc		

Figure 8-1. *Byte structure of the MongoDB ObjectId*

The first four bytes are the timestamp in seconds since EPOCH. This means that using an ObjectId allows you to sort objects in *roughly* the same order as they are created! We said *roughly* since the clocks of all the machines generating the ObjectId might not be in sync.

The next three bytes are unique to a machine and generally generated using a hash of the machine hostname. This guarantees ObjectId uniqueness per machine.

The next two bytes are taken from the process id (PID) of the ObjectId generating process, making it unique to a single process on a single machine.

To reiterate, the first 9 bytes guarantee uniqueness across machines and processes for a single second. So the last three bytes are an incrementing number that allow for uniqueness within a second for a single process on a single machine. Since each byte has 256 possible values, this means that we can generate 256^3 = 16,777,216 unique ObjectIds *per process in a single second*. As a result, for most cases you don't need to worry about uniqueness.

Let's play with ObjectId a bit in the REPL. You can create a new ObjectId using the new JavaScript operator. Also ObjectId provides a useful API for getting the time at which the ObjectId was created (using the first four bytes of the value, which as we saw contains sufficient information for this). Listing 8-5 demonstrates this.

Listing 8-5. A Sample Session of Exploring ObjectId from Mongo Shell

```
$ mongo --nodb
MongoDB shell version: 2.6.1
> var id = new ObjectId()
> id
ObjectId("53a02d3979d8322ea34c4179")
> id.getTimestamp()
ISODate("2014-06-17T11:57:45Z")
>
```

Note that we can start the shell without its trying to connect to a server using the --nodb flag.

MongoDB Document Format

A MongoDB document is stored internally using BSON (**Binary JSON**). This is the format that the MongoDB client drivers use on the network as well. BSON is effectively a binary way for storing JSON documents.

One key feature offered by BSON is a length prefix. In other words, each value in a document is prefixed by the length of the value. This makes it easier for someone reading the document to skip a field if it is not relevant to the current client request. In JSON, you would need to read the whole field to get to the closing indicator ("}" or " , " or "]") even though you want to skip a field.

A BSON document also contains information about the type of the field value, such as the value of a number, a string, or a Boolean. This aids in parsing as well as performing storage optimizations.

Additionally, BSON provides for additional primitive types not supported by raw JSON such as a UTC Datetime, raw binary, and ObjectId.

MongoDB Using Node.js

Now that we have covered the basics of MongoDB, let's look at using it from our Node.js applications.

The MongoDB team maintains an official Node.js package (npm install mongodb) for communicating to a MongoDB server from Node.js. All the async API provided by MongoDB follows the Node.js convention of the first argument being an Error followed by the actual data if any. Your main connection to a MongoDB server is using the MongoClient class exported from the NPM package. Listing 8-6 is a demo that inserts an object, queries it, and then deletes it.

Listing 8-6. crud/basic.js

```
var MongoClient = require('mongodb').MongoClient;

var demoPerson = { name: 'John', lastName: 'Smith' };
var findKey = { name: 'John' };

MongoClient.connect('mongodb://127.0.0.1:27017/demo', function (err, db) {
    if (err) throw err;
    console.log('Successfully connected');

    var collection = db.collection('people');
    collection.insert(demoPerson, function (err, docs) {
        console.log('Inserted', docs[0]);
        console.log('ID:', demoPerson._id);

        collection.find(findKey).toArray(function (err, results) {
            console.log('Found results:', results);

            collection.remove(findKey, function (err, results) {
                console.log('Deleted person');

                db.close();
            });
        });
    });
});
```

In this demo, we connect to the demo database and then use the people collection. We insert a demo person into the people collection. Notice that the server returns the actual objects inserted. Also note that it modified our memory document with a _id field. We then use the find method to search for any object that has the name: 'John'. Finally, we remove all such objects from the database and disconnect. If you have a MongoDB server running on localhost and you run this application, you will see output similar to Listing 8-7.

Listing 8-7. Sample Run of crud/basic.js

```
$ node basic.js
Successfully connected
Inserted { name: 'John',
  lastName: 'Smith',
  _id: 53a14584e33487a017e6e138 }
ID: 53a14584e33487a017e6e138
Found results: [ { _id: 53a14584e33487a017e6e138,
    name: 'John',
    lastName: 'Smith' } ]
Deleted person
```

That almost takes care of the basics of CRUD's Create/Read/Delete. Update is really powerful in MongoDB and deserves its own section.

Update a Document

The simplest way to update a document is to call the save function of a collection as shown in Listing 8-8.

Listing 8-8. update/1save.js

```
var MongoClient = require('mongodb').MongoClient;

var demoPerson = { name: 'John', lastName: 'Smith' };
var findKey = { name: 'John' };

MongoClient.connect('mongodb://127.0.0.1:27017/demo', function (err, db) {
    if (err) throw err;

    var collection = db.collection('people');

    collection.insert(demoPerson, function (err, docs) {
        demoPerson.lastName = 'Martin';
        collection.save(demoPerson, function (err) {
            console.log('Updated');
            collection.find(findKey).toArray(function (err, results) {
                console.log(results);

                // cleanup
                collection.drop(function () { db.close() });
            });
        });
    });
});
```

You simply update the object and pass it back in to the database. The database looks up the object by _id and sets the new values as specified. The save function replaces the *entire* document. However, most of the time you will not want to replace the *entire* document with a new version. That would be really bad in a distributed, data-intensive environment. Many people might want to modify different fields of the document at about the same time. This is where the collection.update method and the update operators come in.

Update Operators

The collection's update function takes three arguments, an object to match/find the item you want to modify, a second argument that specifies the update operator + property we want to modify in the document, and a final argument which is the callback called once the update has completed.

Let's consider the simple case of a web-site hit counter. Many users might be visiting the same web site at the same time. If we were to read the counter value from the server, increment it on the client, and then send the server the new value, by the time we send it, the original read value might already be out-of-date. Traditionally, database clients would request the database to lock the document, send the value down over the network, receive an updated value, and then request to unlock the document. That would be very slow as network communication takes time.

This is where the update operators come into play. We simply instruct MongoDB to increment whatever the current view count is for a particular document in a *single* client request using the $inc update operator. Once MongoDB receives the request, it locks the document, reads + increments the value, and unlocks the document all on the server. This means that the database server can handle requests almost as fast as it can receive them over the network and no client request needs to wait or retry because of a pending client request. Listing 8-9 is a simple example that demonstrates this.

Listing 8-9. update/2update.js

```
var MongoClient = require('mongodb').MongoClient;

var website = {
    url: 'http://www.google.com',
    visits: 0
};
var findKey = {
    url: 'http://www.google.com'
};

MongoClient.connect('mongodb://127.0.0.1:27017/demo', function (err, db) {
    if (err) throw err;

    var collection = db.collection('websites');

    collection.insert(website, function (err, docs) {

        var done = 0;
        function onDone(err) {
            done++;
            if (done < 4) return;

            collection.find(findKey).toArray(function (err, results) {
                console.log('Visits:', results[0].visits); // 4

                // cleanup
                collection.drop(function () { db.close() });
            });
        }

        var incrementVisits = { '$inc': { 'visits': 1 } };
        collection.update(findKey, incrementVisits, onDone);
        collection.update(findKey, incrementVisits, onDone);
        collection.update(findKey, incrementVisits, onDone);
        collection.update(findKey, incrementVisits, onDone);

    });
});
```

In this example, we demonstrate sending four update requests to the server without waiting for a response. Each request is asking the server to increment the visits count by 1. As you can see, when we fetch the results, after all four requests are complete, the visits count is indeed 4—none of the update requests conflicted with one another.

Lots of other update operators are supported by MongoDB. Operators exist for setting a single field, deleting fields, conditionally updating a field if its current value is greater than or smaller than the value we want, and so on.

Also there are operators for updating sub collections (arrays) inside a document. For example, consider the case of having a simple tags field inside a document that is an array of strings. Multiple users might want to update this array—some will want to add a tag, others would want remove a tag. MongoDB allows you to update the array on the server using $push (to add an item) and $pull (to remove an item) update operators so you don't overwrite the complete array.

Mongoose ODM

As we have seen, MongoDB works with what are effectively simple JSON documents. This means that the business logic that operates on the documents (functions/methods) must live elsewhere. Using an Object Document Mapper (ODM) we can map these simple documents into full-form JavaScript objects (with data + methods for validation and other business logic). The most popular (and supported by MongoDB team) is the Mongoose ODM (npm install mongoose).

Connecting to MongoDB

You can connect to MongoDB using Mongoose in a similar fashion to the native driver that we saw earlier. Listing 8-10 is a simple example straight from the docs.

Listing 8-10. odm/connection.js

```
var mongoose = require('mongoose');

mongoose.connect('mongodb://127.0.0.1:27017/demo');

var db = mongoose.connection;
db.on('error', function (err) { throw err });
db.once('open', function callback() {
    console.log('connected!');
    db.close();
});
```

We connect using the connect member function. Then we get access to the database object using mongoose.connection and wait for the open event to fire, indicating a successful connection. Finally, we close the connection to exit the application.

Mongoose Schema and Model

At the heart of Mongoose is the Schema class. The schema defines all the fields of your document along with their types (for validation purposes) and their behavior during serializing etc.

After you have defined your Schema, you compile it to create a Model function, which is simply a fancy constructor for converting simple Object Literals into JavaScript Objects. These JavaScript objects have the behavior you set up using the Schema. In addition to the ability to create these domain objects, models have static member functions you use to create, query, update, and delete documents from the database.

As an example, consider a simple tank Schema. A tank has a name and a size (small, medium large). We can define a tank Schema quite simply:

```
var tankSchema = new mongoose.Schema({ name: 'string', size: 'string' });
tankSchema.methods.print = function () { console.log('I am', this.name, 'the', this.size); };
```

We also define methods available on the Model instances using the Schema (for example, we specified the print method). Now that we have a Schema, let's make a Model. The Model links the Schema to a database collection and allows you to manage (CRUD) model instances. Creating a Model from a Schema is really simple:

```
// Compile it into a model
var Tank = mongoose.model('Tank', tankSchema);
```

To create instances of the model, you call it like a normal JavaScript constructor passing in the raw document/object literal:

```
var tony = new Tank({ name: 'tony', size: 'small' });
tony.print(); // I am tony the small
```

You can see that the methods we defined in the Schema (such as print) are available on corresponding Model's instances. Additionally, all Model instances have member functions to manage their interaction with the database such as save/remove/update. An example save call is shown in Listing 8-11.

Listing 8-11. Saving/Updating a Mongoose Model Instance

```
var tony = new Tank({ name: 'tony', size: 'small' });
tony.save(function (err) {
  if (err) throw err;

  // saved!
})
```

Additionally, the Model class has static (independent of model instances) member functions to manage all the database documents in the relevant collection. For example, to find a model instance, you can use the findOne static function, as shown in Listing 8-12.

Listing 8-12. Single Item Query Using Mongoose

```
Tank.findOne({ name: 'tony' })
    .exec(function (err, tank) {

    // You get a model instance all setup and ready!
    tank.print();
});
```

Combining all that we have seen, Listing 8-13 provides a complete example that you can run on your own.

Listing 8-13. odm/basic.js

```
var mongoose = require('mongoose');

// Define a schema
var tankSchema = new mongoose.Schema({ name: 'string', size: 'string' });
tankSchema.methods.print = function () { console.log('I am', this.name, 'the', this.size); };

// Compile it into a model
var Tank = mongoose.model('Tank', tankSchema);

mongoose.connect('mongodb://127.0.0.1:27017/demo');
var db = mongoose.connection;
db.once('open', function callback() {
    console.log('connected!');
```

```
// Use the model
var tony = new Tank({ name: 'tony', size: 'small' });
tony.print(); // I am tony the small

tony.save(function (err) {

    Tank.findOne({ name: 'tony' }).exec(function (err, tank) {

        // You get a model instance all setup and ready!
        tank.print();

        db.collection('tanks').drop(function () { db.close();})
    });
});
});
```

One final thing deserving special attention is the fact that the query functions (for example, find, findOne) are chainable. This allows you to build advanced queries by adding function calls. The final query is sent to the server after you call the exec function. For example, using a hypothetical Person model, the code in Listing 8-14 searches for the first 10 people in LA with the last name Ghost, aged between 17 and 66.

Listing 8-14. Sample to Demonstrate Complex Queries

```
Person
.find({ city: 'LA' })
.where('name.last').equals('Ghost')
.where('age').gt(17).lt(66)
.limit(10)
.exec(callback);
```

Using a MongoDB as a Distributed Session Store

In Chapter 7, we saw how we can use cookies to store user session information by using the cookie-session middleware. However, we pointed out that using a cookie for storing *all* your session information is a bad idea since the cookie needs to come from the client with each request and you are limited by the size of a cookie.

Ideally, you should aim for your web applications to be as stateless as possible. However, for certain kinds of applications, large bits of information in user sessions might be what you need. This is where the express-session middleware (npm install express-session) comes in.

By default, express-session middleware will use an in-memory store to maintain the user session information. The cookie sent to the client will only point to the key inside this server memory store. Consider the following server in Listing 8-15, which is based on the cookie-session server we saw in Chapter 7. All that we have done is replace the cookie-session middleware with the express-session middleware.

Listing 8-15. session/inmemory.js

```
var express = require('express');
var expressSession = require('express-session');

var app = express()
    .use(expressSession({
        secret: 'my super secret sign key'
    }))
```

```
    .use('/home', function (req, res) {
        if (req.session.views) {
            req.session.views++;
        }
        else {
            req.session.views = 1;
        }
        res.end('Total views for you: ' + req.session.views);
    })
    .use('/reset', function (req, res) {
        delete req.session.views;
        res.end('Cleared all your views');
    })
    .listen(3000);
```

If you open up your browser and visit http://localhost:3000/home, you will see that it behaves as expected—each time you refresh the page, your views increment. However, if you restart the Node.js server and again refresh the browser, the count goes back to 1. This is because the server memory was cleared on restart. The user cookie only contains the key to the session value inside the server memory, not the actual session values. Good for network performance (cookie is lightweight), bad for scalability as the session value is restricted to a single process on a single server.

This is where the store config option of the express-session middleware comes in. Stores are available for various databases, but since we are discussing MongoDB, let's use that. The MongoDB session store is provided by the connect-mongo (npm install connect-mongo) NPM package. Using it is really simple—you get a reference to the MongoStore class and create a store instance passing the connection configuration for the database you want to connect to. Listing 8-16 provides the complete example with the changed portions highlighted.

Listing 8-16. session/distributed.js

```
var express = require('express');
var expressSession = require('express-session');

var MongoStore = require('connect-mongo')(expressSession);
var sessionStore = new MongoStore({
    host: '127.0.0.1',
    port: '27017',
    db: 'session',
});

var app = express()
    .use(expressSession({
        secret: 'my super secret sign key',
        store: sessionStore
    }))
    .use('/home', function (req, res) {
        if (req.session.views) {
            req.session.views++;
        }
        else {
            req.session.views = 1;
        }
    }
```

```
        res.end('Total views for you: ' + req.session.views);
    })
    .use('/reset', function (req, res) {
        delete req.session.views;
        res.end('Cleared all your views');
    })
    .listen(3000);
```

Make sure you have MongoDB running locally and start this Node.js server. If you visit http://localhost:3000/home now, you will get the same behavior as before except, this time, you can restart your server safely and, if the user reloads the page, the last view count is preserved. The great thing here is that there might potentially be many Node.js servers talking to a MongoDB farm and the user behavior will be the same irrespective of which Node.js server handles the request.

Lesson: Use cookie-session for when you want to store only small bits of information in the user session. Use express-session with a backing store when your session information is heavy.

Managing MongoDB

When you are starting out with MongoDB, it can be intimidating to work with just a REPL like mongo. Eventually, it's useful for quick lookups, but for the beginner better GUI tools can be a lifesaver. For managing a production server, the MongoDB team itself offers a hosted MongoDB Management Service (MMS).

For development time, we would like to recommend the Robomongo desktop application (http://robomongo.org/). It's an open source application, under active development, and they provide installers for Windows (.msi) as well as Mac OS X (.dmg).

Once installed, you simply start the software, connect to a MongoDB server, and you can see the databases, collections, and documents as shown in Figure 8-2. One great thing about the application is that it integrates the mongo shell into its GUI so all your terminal skills are relevant here as well.

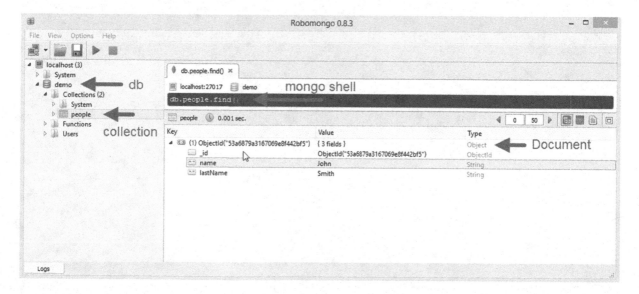

Figure 8-2. *Screenshot of Robomongo with the important sections highlighted*

Additional Resources

Multi-tenancy in MongoDB: `http://support.mongohq.com/use-cases/multi-tenant.html`

BSON language specification: `http://bsonspec.org/`

MongoDB ObjectId: `http://api.mongodb.org/java/current/org/bson/types/ObjectId.html`

MongoDB Update operators: `http://docs.mongodb.org/manual/reference/operator/update/`

Mongoose ODM: `http://mongoosejs.com/`

MongoDB management service: `www.mongodb.com/mongodb-management-service`

Summary

In this chapter, we looked at the motivation for using a document database. Then we examined MongoDB, explained the important concepts, and demonstrated the supported ways of utilizing MongoDB from our Node.js applications.

There is lot more that can be said about MongoDB, Mongoose, and Querying/Indexing, but what we have covered here should be enough for you to be able to comfortably explore the API on your own.

CHAPTER 9

■ ■ ■

Front-End Basics

In the previous chapters, we have discussed how you can create web servers, web services, and APIs. We have also shown how to persist your data in a database. Now we will explore the front end. In this chapter, we will delve into the concept of Single Page Applications (SPA) and create one using AngularJS. Our front end will communicate with a simple Express web service that will store our data in a MongoDB database.

As usual, before we embark on this journey, we will explain all the important concepts in this area and provide justifications for our technology choices so that you have a deep appreciation of the underlying principles.

What Is a SPA?

In a SPA, all the essential code of your application (the HTML/CSS/JavaScript) is loaded upfront in the first request to the web server. A common example given for a SPA is the Gmail (www.gmail.com) web site from Google.

As you navigate from page to page in a traditional web site, the complete page is reloaded, as illustrated in Figure 9-1.

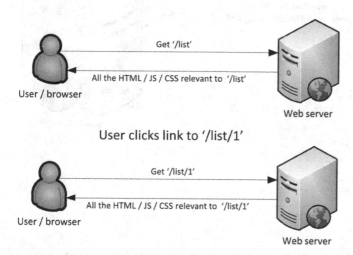

Figure 9-1. Traditional web-site experience

This is a decent experience for web sites, but not a good one for web applications. In a SPA, once you request a web page, the server returns the main template (commonly called `index.html`) along with the necessary client-side JavaScript and CSS. Once this initial load is complete, all that the user interaction with the web site does is load more *data* from the server using client-side XHRs (`XMLHttpRequest`). This data is then rendered on the client by JavaScript using the already downloaded HTML/CSS, as illustrated in Figure 9-2, making it more of a desktop application experience for the user.

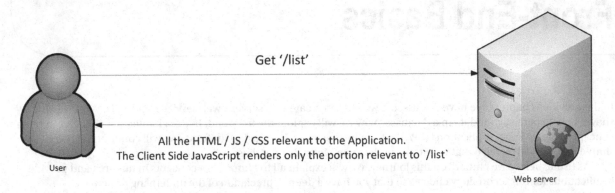

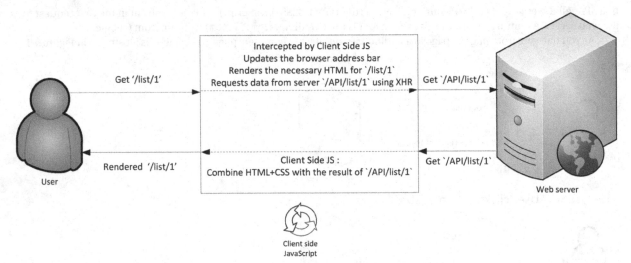

Figure 9-2. *Single Page Application user experience*

You can write all of this code yourself; however, there are technical challenges (for example, how to combine the server returned data with the HTML to show a rendered page) that have already been solved by SPA frameworks. We will be using one such SPA framework: AngularJS.

> ■ **Note**   XMLHttpRequest (XHR) is a global class available in all modern browsers that allows you to make HTTP requests using JavaScript. The name is XMLHttpRequest to ensure that all browsers follow the same name for this class. The name has *XML* in it because that was the original intended data format for making HTTP requests, but it is not relevant anymore as it can be used to make HTTP requests in any format. In fact, most people just use the JSON format now.

Why AngularJS?

There are lots of good-quality, community-driven, single-page application frameworks out there such as AngularJS, EmberJS, ReactJS, KnockoutJS, and BackboneJS, but by far the greatest community interest has been around AngularJS, which was created at Google. This is visible by the Google search trend for these frameworks shown in Figure 9-3.

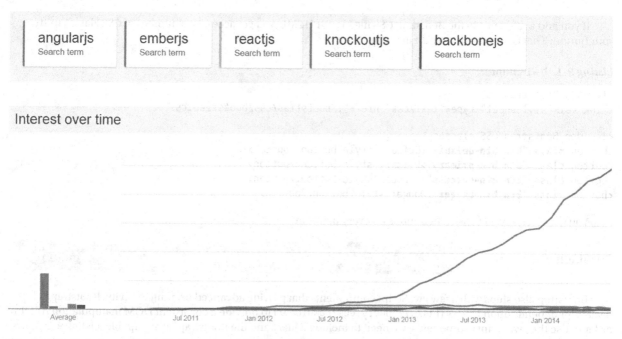

Figure 9-3. *Google search trends for various SPA/data-binding frameworks*

The main reason for its popularity is the fact that it is from a team at Google, it is simple, and it has feature richness:

- Data-Binding/Templating: allows you to update the DOM (the rendered HTML) based on changes to the underlying JavaScript objects

- URL Handling/Routing: handles the browsers address bar to give a fluid navigation experience to the user by loading and rendering templates as required

- Dependency Injection: gives you clear guidance on organizing your client-side JavaScript for enhanced workflow in teams and easing testability

We will look at how AngularJS works as we use its features in this chapter, but for now you have a few reasons to be excited about AngularJS. AngularJS can be downloaded from https://angularjs.org/.

Introduction to Twitter Bootstrap

We will be using Twitter Bootstrap to design/style the front end of our application. HTML/CSS gives you the foundation to design a UI. You can design anything you want from scratch, but again you are probably better off using stuff that other people have already created for you. Twitter Bootstrap is from a team of designers at `twitter.com`. You can download Bootstrap from `http://getbootstrap.com/`.

At its core, Bootstrap is basically a bunch of CSS classes that allow you to quickly customize the way the rendered HTML looks. For example, consider a simple HTML page with a single button:

```
<button>I am a button</button>
```

By default, it looks like the following on Windows:

I am a button

If you add a reference to the Bootstrap CSS file in your HTML, you get access to a number of CSS classes to style your button. That is exactly what we do in Listing 9-1.

Listing 9-1. bs/bs.html

```
<!-- Add Bootstrap CSS -->
<link rel="stylesheet" type="text/css" href="./bootstrap/css/bootstrap.css">

<!-- Use Bootstrap CSS classes -->
<button class="btn btn-default">Default style button</button>
<button class="btn btn-primary">Primary style button</button>
<button class="btn btn-success">Success style button</button>
<button class="btn btn-danger">Danger style button</button>
```

You get nicely styled consistent buttons on every platform:

Default style button   Primary style button   Success style button   Danger style button

Bootstrap also ships with a few JavaScript components that provide advanced user interactivity. Bootstrap JavaScript depends upon JQuery (`http://jquery.com/download/`) to provide a consistent DOM manipulation API. In order to use the JavaScript components, we need to include JQuery and the Bootstrap JavaScript file. Listing 9-2 shows how you can use Bootstrap tool tips.

Listing 9-2. bs/bsjs.html

```
<!-- Add JQuery + Bootstrap JS + CSS-->
<script src="./jquery/jquery.js"></script>
<script src="./bootstrap/js/bootstrap.js"></script>
<link rel="stylesheet" type="text/css" href="./bootstrap/css/bootstrap.css">

<!-- Use a button with a nice tooltip shown at the bottom -->
<button class="btn btn-default"
        data-toggle="tooltip" data-placement="bottom" title="Nice little tooltip message">
    Hover over me to see the tooltip
</button>
```

```
<!-- on page loaded initialize the tooltip plugin -->
<script>
$(function(){ // on document ready
    $('button').tooltip(); // add tooltip to all buttons
});
</script>
```

Things of interest in this code sample are the usage of the $ variable, which is provided by JQuery to register a callback that will be called once the HTML document has been rendered by the browser (on document ready). Then in the callback, we use $ to select all button tags using $('button') and then call the bootstrap tool-tip plug-in to initialize it based on the element's attributes (data-toggle, data-placement, and title). If you run this application and hover over the button, you will see a nice tool tip containing the contents of the title attribute:

We will be using Bootstrap to give an easy-on-the-eyes look to our UI. Bootstrap also has a few full-page layouts to get you started on your project, which you can download from http://getbootstrap.com/getting-started/.

■ **Note**　JQuery is by far the most popular JavaScript library at the moment. It provides a consistent API to access the Document Object Model (DOM) across all browsers. The DOM is basically the API provided by the browser to interact with the rendered HTML using JavaScript. The DOM API has traditionally suffered from inconsistencies among browsers as different vendors introduced different features to compete with one another. JQuery takes care of these inconsistencies to provide a unified API along with value added features such as an awesome DOM query API (similar to CSS selectors).

Set Up a Simple AngularJS Application

The first step to make our single-page app is to create an Express server to serve the client-side JavaScript HTML and CSS, as shown in Listing 9-3. This is a trivial task to achieve with the knowledge we already have (Chapter 7).

Listing 9-3. angularstart/app.js

```
var express = require('express');

var app = express()
    .use(express.static(__dirname + '/public'))
    .listen(3000);
```

This serves HTML from the public folder. Now we will create a vendor folder inside our public folder to contain our JQuery, AngularJS, and Bootstrap files, as shown in Listing 9-4. Finally, we have a simple index.html file.

Listing 9-4. angularstart/public/index.html

```html
<html ng-app="demo">
<head>
    <title>Sample App</title>

    <!-- Add JQuery + Bootstrap JS / CSS + AngularJS-->
    <script src="./vendor/jquery/jquery.js"></script>
    <script src="./vendor/bootstrap/js/bootstrap.js"></script>
    <link rel="stylesheet" type="text/css" href="./vendor/bootstrap/css/bootstrap.css">
    <script src="./vendor/angular/angular.js"></script>
    <script src="./vendor/angular/angular-route.js"></script>

    <!-- Our Script -->
    <script>
        var demoApp = angular.module('demo', []);
        demoApp.controller('MainController', ['$scope', function ($scope) {
            $scope.vm = {
                name: "foo",
                clearName: function () {
                    this.name = ""
                }
            };
        }]);
    </script>
</head>
<body ng-controller="MainController">
    <!-- Our HTML -->
    <label>Type your name:</label>
    <input type="text" ng-model="vm.name" />
    <button class="btn btn-danger" ng-click="vm.clearName()">Clear Name</button>
</body>
</html>
```

The important parts of this file are highlighted. To keep things simple, we will be keeping our entire client-side script in one location. (We will use a simple single script tag for this in the future instead of its being inline, as shown here). Also, our entire HTML will be inside the body tag at one location. We will flesh these sections out as we go along. If you run this Express server right now and visit http://localhost:3000, you will see a simple AngularJS application. If you type your name in the input box, the div below it updates in real time, as shown in Figure 9-4. Also, you can press the clear name button to clear the name.

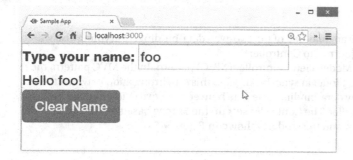

Figure 9-4. *Angularstart sample running in the browser*

Now let's examine our HTML page a bit more. The important sections are the following:

- The Angular **directives** inside our HTML ng-app/ng-controller/ng-model.

- The main Angular **module** created in our JavaScript called demo. Also used in the ng-app directive, this glues the JS module to the HTML.

- The main Angular **controller** in our JS called MainController. The ng-controller directive glues the JS controller to the HTML.

- The $scope injected into the controller by Angular. The scope is the two-way data-binding glue between the HTML and the controller.

Now that you have an overview of a simple and functional Angular application, let's look at what modules, directives, controller, and scope mean in AngularJS.

Modules in AngularJS

Modules in AngularJS allow you to contain and manage all the controllers, directives, and so on. You can associate a particular module to manage a section of HTML using the ng-app directive (which is what we did). We also used the module to register the MainController with Angular (demoApp.controller). Modules are simply a container for easier management purposes.

Directives in AngularJS

Directives are basically segments of code that you want Angular to execute (to provide behavior) when Angular finds a matching string in the HTML. For example, in our application we ask Angular to run the ng-app directive using the ng-app HTML attribute on our html tag (<html ng-app="demo">). Similarly, we triggered the ng-controller and ng-model directives.

It is conventional to namespace directives with a prefix. Directives that come with Angular use the ng- prefix, making it easier to observe in the HTML that this tag has a directive on it. If a beginner sees ng-app, he or she gets a clue that it's an Angular directive and some custom behavior will be applied.

It is extremely easy to create your own directives and an integral part of serious AngularJS application development. But for now we will stick with the directives that come with Angular, which can carry you a long way.

Controller and $scope

Controllers are the heart and soul of AngularJS. These are one-half of the two-way data-binding. Everything else we have seen (modules, directives) can be considered a journey to Controllers.

Controllers are called controllers because of the Model-View-Controller (MVC) pattern. In the MVC pattern, the Controller is responsible for keeping the View and the Model in sync. In Angular, this synchronization between the View and the Model is done by Angular using two-way data-binding. The glue between the two (View and the Model) is the Angular $scope, which gets passed to the Controller. The Controller sets up the $scope based on our application logic. The synchronization of $scope between the view and the model is shown in Figure 9-5.

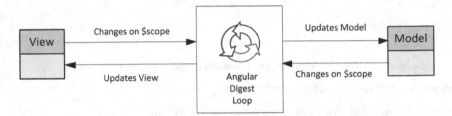

Figure 9-5. *Demonstration of $scope being the glue between View and Model*

Since this model in the Controller is really for the View, it is commonly called the **ViewModel**, or vm for short, as we have called it in our example. Also note that the $scope gets injected into the Controller by Angular. We explicitly ask for the $scope by specifying it in the array members. The relevant segment shown again:

```
demoApp.controller('MainController', ['$scope', function ($scope) {
```

The initial array members (only '$scope' in this example) drive what gets passed as the arguments to the final array member, which is our Controller function. This is one form of *dependency injection* supported by Angular. We will see more of Angular's dependency injection in other examples in this chapter.

We use the $scope from our HTML using directives. In our case, the following HTML's ng-model keeps the input element in sync with the vm.name property:

```
<input type="text" ng-model="vm.name" />
```

Similarly, we can call a function on our controller upon a user click using the ng-click directive:

```
<button class="btn btn-danger" ng-click="vm.clearName()">Clear Name</button>
```

Creating a Simple To-Do List Application

The great thing about Angular is that it is extremely simple to create and design a front end entirely separate from any server code. Then you can wire it up to the back end once it is ready, which is exactly what we will do here. Now that we have a basic understanding of the fact that $scope is the glue between the View and the Model, we will come up with a simple JavaScript model for a to-do list and design a front end for it. Our entire Model (vm) JavaScript is shown in Listing 9-5.

Listing 9-5. todostart/public/main.js

```javascript
var demoApp = angular.module('demo', []);
demoApp.controller('MainController', ['$scope', 'guidService', function ($scope, guidService) {

    // Setup a view model
    var vm = {};

    vm.list = [
        { _id: guidService.createGuid(), details: 'Demo First Item' },
        { _id: guidService.createGuid(), details: 'Demo Second Item' }
    ];

    vm.addItem = function () {
        // TODO: send to server then,
        vm.list.push({
            _id: guidService.createGuid(),
            details: vm.newItemDetails
        });
        vm.newItemDetails = '';
    };

    vm.removeItem = function (itemToRemove) {
        // TODO: delete from the server then
        vm.list = vm.list.filter(function (item) { return item._id !== itemToRemove._id; });
    };

    // For new items:
    vm.newItemDetails = '';

    // expose the vm using the $scope
    $scope.vm = vm;
}]);


demoApp.service('guidService', function () {
    return {
        createGuid: function () {
            return 'xxxxxxxx-xxxx-4xxx-yxxx-xxxxxxxxxxxx'.replace(/[xy]/g, function (c) {
                var r = Math.random() * 16 | 0, v = c == 'x' ? r : (r & 0x3 | 0x8);
                return v.toString(16);
            });
        }
    };
});
```

In Chapter 8, we demonstrated that it is always best to create an immutable unique id for each item that is going to go in the database (natural vs. surrogate primary key discussion). Here we are creating such a unique id on the client using a createGuid function. This function could have been kept inside the Controller, but we chose to make it as a reusable Angular Service called guidService. An Angular service is simply a function that Angular calls once to get an object. It then passes this object to any other Service, Controller, and so on, that asks for it by key (here the key is 'guidService').

In our Controller, we specify 'guidService' as a member of the dependency injection array:

```
demoApp.controller('MainController', ['$scope', 'guidService', function ($scope, guidService) {
```

Angular will look for and pass in the value that was returned from our guidService Service registration function. Here the value has only one member (the createGuid function) that we use in our Controller (guidService. createGuid). The createGuid function itself is a pretty standard function for creating globally unique identifiers (GUIDs) from JavaScript using a randomization algorithm.

With creating and consuming Angular services out of the way, we can see that the rest of the MainController function itself is extremely simple. It is used to manage a list of items (vm.list)—adding to the list (vm.addItem) and deleting from the list (vm.removeItem)—and a simple member that allows us to potentially get user-entered details from a data-bound field in the view (vm.newItemDetails). Now we can design a simple Angular + Bootstrap HTML user interface on top of this. Our HTML is shown in Listing 9-6.

Listing 9-6. todostart/public/index.html

```html
<body ng-controller="MainController">
    <!-- Our HTML -->
    <div class="container">
        <h1>List</h1>

        <!-- Existing items rows -->
        <div class="row">
            <div ng-repeat="item in vm.list track by item._id" style="padding:10px">
                <button class="btn btn-danger" ng-click="vm.removeItem(item)">x</button>
                {{item.details}}
            </div>
        </div>

        <!-- New Item row -->
        <div class="row">
            <form role="form">
                <div class="form-group">
                    <label for="newItemDetails">New Item Details:</label>
                    <input type="text" class="form-control"
                            placeholder="Details of new todo item"
                            ng-model="vm.newItemDetails">
                </div>
                <button type="submit" class="btn btn-primary"
                        ng-click="vm.addItem()"
                        ng-disabled="!vm.newItemDetails">Add</button>
            </form>
        </div>
    </div>
</body>
```

We have a bunch of HTML tags that have Bootstrap specific classes (for example, container, row, form-group, btn, btn-primary, btn-danger, and so on). These give the application a decent look—a designer would customize these classes (and create a few more using CSS) to make the application look nicer, but even in its current state it is not half bad. (See Figure 9-6.)

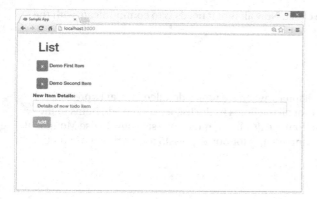

Figure 9-6. *todostart sample running in the browser*

What is more impressive is the fact that it is fully functional! Clicking the x buttons deletes the item from the list. By typing in some new item details, we enable the Add button, which by pressing adds the item to the list. All of this is thanks to the directives that come with Angular, which are talking to the View Model (vm) you have already seen. The list of items in the HTML is generated with an ng-repeat directive shown again in Listing 9-7.

Listing 9-7. snippet from todostart/public/index.html

```
<div ng-repeat="item in vm.list track by item._id" style="padding:10px">
    <button class="btn btn-danger" ng-click="vm.removeItem(item)">x</button>
    {{item.details}}
</div>
```

The ng-repeat directive takes the DOM element it is specified on and clones it for each element in the list (vm.list). As an optimization, we tell it that item uniqueness is determined by the _id property (track by), which helps Angular associate the DOM element with the item in the list. The ng-repeat directive also creates a new item in scope (item in vm.list) within the repeated element (we called it item) that you can further bind to ({{item. details}}) and use in other directives (for example, we have an ng-click wired to remove the item by passing to the vm.removeItem function). Now let's examine the Add Item HTML shown again in Listing 9-8.

Listing 9-8. Snippet from todostart/public/index.html

```
<form role="form">
    <div class="form-group">
        <label for="newItemDetails">New Item Details:</label>
        <input type="text" class="form-control"
                placeholder="Details of new todo item"
                ng-model="vm.newItemDetails">
    </div>
        <button type="submit" class="btn btn-primary"
                ng-click="vm.addItem()"
                ng-disabled="!vm.newItemDetails">Add</button>
</form>
```

We have the simple input wired up to vm.newItemDetails using an ng-model and the Add button wired up to vm.addItem function using an ng-click directive. We also disable the Add button using the ng-disabled directive if the current vm.newItemDetails are falsy (remember empty strings are falsy in JavaScript).

And that's it! We have a fully functional to-do list on the client. Now all that it needs is to communicate with the server in order to persist and load the information.

Creating a REST API

We already have experience with creating a REST API from Chapter 7 when we took a detailed look at ExpressJS. All our REST API needs to do for our simple application is a GET for all the items in the list, a POST to add items to the list (it should return the ID), and a DELETE to delete an item from the list. In Chapter 8, we saw how to use MongoDB. Combining our knowledge of the two, Listing 9-9 provides a simple setup for our ExpressJS router-based API that persists the data to MongoDB.

Listing 9-9. todocomplete/app.js

```javascript
var express = require('express');
var bodyParser = require('body-parser');

// The express app
var app = express();

// Create a mongodb connection
// and only start express listening once the connection is okay
var MongoClient = require('mongodb').MongoClient;
var db, itemsCollection;
MongoClient.connect('mongodb://127.0.0.1:27017/demo', function (err, database) {
    if (err) throw err;

    // Connected!
    db = database;
    itemsCollection = db.collection('items');

    app.listen(3000);
    console.log('Listening on port 3000');
});

// Create a router that can accept JSON
var router = express.Router();
router.use(bodyParser.json());

// Setup the collection routes
router.route('/')
    .get(function (req, res, next) {
        itemsCollection.find().toArray(function (err, docs) {
            res.send({
                status: 'Items found',
                items: docs
            });
        });
    })
    .post(function (req, res, next) {
        var item = req.body;
        itemsCollection.insert(item, function (err, docs) {
```

```
            res.send({
                status: 'Item added',
                itemId: item._id
            });
        });
    })

// Setup the item routes
router.route('/:id')
    .delete(function (req, res, next) {
        var id = req.params['id'];
        var lookup = { _id: new mongodb.ObjectID(id) };
        itemsCollection.remove(lookup, function (err, results) {
            res.send({ status: 'Item cleared' });
        });
    });

app.use(express.static(__dirname + '/public'))
    .use('/todo', router);
```

The important part of integrating MongoDB with Express is that we only start the Express Server once we have verified that our connection with MongoDB is okay. We also store a reference to the items collection that will contain our to-do items.

The rest of the code is pretty self-explanatory and there is nothing here that you do not already know. We have collection-level routes for GET (get the list) and POST (adds an item to the list and returns its ID) as well as an item route to delete individual items. At this point, you can use curl to test your API as we did in Chapter 7. Now let's complete our front end so that it talks to the back end.

Wire Up the Front End with the REST API

Talking to a REST service from Angular couldn't be easier. Angular comes with a $http service, which wraps the browser's XMLHttpRequest object so that it works with the Angular digest loop. It also makes the API consistent across browsers and makes it easier to work with by using promises. Promises are a topic we will discuss in detail in the next chapter, but we will give a brief overview here after you have seen the code.

You can get access to the $http service the same way you got access to our own custom guidService, which we saw earlier. To access the REST API, we will create our own custom Angular service that will use the Angular's built-in $http service to communicate with the server. The complete client-side JavaScript including the controller is shown in Listing 9-10.

Listing 9-10. todocomplete/public/main.js

```
var demoApp = angular.module('demo', []);
demoApp.controller('MainController', ['$scope', 'todoWebService', function ($scope, todoWebService)
{

    // Setup a view model
    var vm = {};

    vm.list = [];
```

```javascript
    // Start the initial load of lists
    todoWebService.getItems().then(function (response) {
        vm.list = response.data.items;
    });

    vm.addItem = function () {
        var item = {
            details: vm.newItemDetails
        };

        // Clear it from the UI
        vm.newItemDetails = '';

        // Send the request to the server and add the item once done
        todoWebService.addItem(item).then(function (response) {
            vm.list.push({
                _id: response.data.itemId,
                details: item.details
            });
        });
    };

    vm.removeItem = function (itemToRemove) {
        // Remove it from the list and send the server request
        vm.list = vm.list.filter(function (item) { return item._id !== itemToRemove._id; });
        todoWebService.removeItem(itemToRemove);
    };

    // For new items:
    vm.newItemDetails = '';

    // expose the vm using the $scope
    $scope.vm = vm;
}]);

demoApp.service('todoWebService', ['$http', function ($http) {
    var root = '/todo';
    return {
        getItems: function () {
            return $http.get(root);
        },
        addItem: function (item) {
            return $http.post(root, item);
        },
        removeItem: function (item) {
            return $http.delete(root + '/' + item._id);
        }
    }
}]);
```

Again the code is actually quite manageable. We dropped any error checking or UI notifications to keep it simple. First, notice our custom Angular service called `todoWebService`. The logic inside it is extremely self-explanatory. It just has a few functions to get, add, and remove items. It uses the Angular's `$http` service to make get, post, and delete HTTP requests against our REST API endpoint (in other words, `'/todo'`) on the same server as the one that served our HTML. It is worth mentioning that each of the methods of `$http` return a promise, and therefore `getItems`/`addItem`/`removeItem` all return promises as well.

We use our `todoWebService` in our `MainController`, which is mostly unchanged since the last time we saw it. All that's changed is that it now makes server calls at the right time using `todoWebService`. We mentioned that the members of the `todoWebService` return promises. For the purpose of this application, it is sufficient to know that a promise has a `then` member function, which is called once the promise is resolved. Here is one way to think of them for now: Instead of passing in a callback directly, you pass it to the `then` member function of the promise. For example, consider the initial load repeated in Listing 9-11.

Listing 9-11. Snippet from todocomplete/public/main.js

```
// Start the initial load of lists
todoWebService.getItems().then(function (response) {
    vm.list = response.data.items;
});
```

The browser does not block the UI/JavaScript thread when it sends this network request to GET the list. It instead takes a callback that will get called once the GET response is received from the server. A promise simply provides a neater way to provide the callback. The key motivation for promises is chain-ability and better error handling offered by promises, a topic we will discuss in detail in the next chapter.

And that's it. We have completed an end-to-end to-do list application. If you have MongoDB running, start up the Node.js server and visit your local host. (See Figure 9-7.)

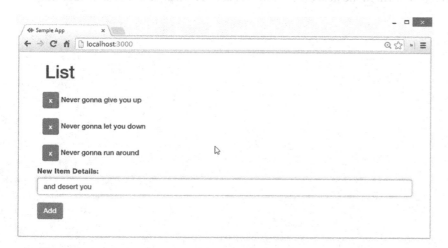

Figure 9-7. *todocomplete sample running in the browser*

Now let's take a step back and look at our application architecture. We could potentially develop such an application in a distributed team quite easily. The front-end JavaScript guru can create your controller, the CSS ninja can design your HTML, and the back-end JavaScript expert can author your REST API. Finally, we wire them up and your shinny application is ready. This is one of the advantages of using a good SPA framework such as AngularJS combined with a REST API.

Next Steps

There is a lot more that can be said about AngularJS. For example, we only used the built-in directives, such as `ng-click`, but you can author your own to create powerful web components. Also we only saw the basic usage of dependency injection (DI) in Angular. The main motivation for DI in Angular is testability. To learn more about testability, it is best to check out the angular-seed project provided by the AngularJS team `https://github.com/angular/angular-seed`. The angular-seed project also contains guidance for how to split your client-side project into multiple JavaScript files for maintainability.

Additional Resources

Twitter Bootstrap: `http://getbootstrap.com/`
   AngularJS: `http://angularjs.org/`
   Angular Seed: `https://github.com/angular/angular-seed`

Summary

In this chapter, we looked at how consuming web services can be done quite easily with a mature framework like AngularJS. We made an effort to be clear about what the code does. We focused on guiding you through the code so that you know exactly what is going on. This will allow you to explore larger code bases with a deep understanding and greater confidence.

We also tried to justify our use of the libraries in this chapter. Along the way, we explained what is meant by SPA and why you should care. After the introduction in this chapter, you should be confident to explore more JQuery, Bootstrap, and AngularJS on your own. In the next chapter, we will take a look at promises and other ways to simplify callbacks.

CHAPTER 10

■ ■ ■

Simplifying Callbacks

The evented/asynchronous nature of Node.js means that it is possible to end up with deeply nested callbacks. There are various strategies in JavaScript that help reduce the callback nesting. In this chapter, we will explore these patterns. These help maintain readability, but more importantly these strategies will help decrease the likelihood of bugs creeping up on you. I promise.

The Callback Hell

Note that as we explore this section, it might seem like the situation is dire. Don't worry. When we look at promises in the next section, you will find the pot of gold at the end of the rainbow.

An obvious issue with callbacks is the *increased indentation*. This has been affectionately called the callback *pyramid of doom*. Consider the simple case in Listing 10-1 where we have three async functions that we need to call (for example, these might be database search, select, and save item).

Listing 10-1. pyramid/indented.js

```
function first(data, cb) {
    console.log('Executing first');
    setTimeout(cb, 1000, data);
}

function second(data, cb) {
    console.log('Executing second');
    setTimeout(cb, 1000, data);
}

function third(data, cb) {
    console.log('Executing third');
    setTimeout(cb, 1000, data);
}

first('data', function (text1) {
    second(text1, function (text2) {
        third(text2, function (text3) {
            console.log('done:', text3); // indented
        });
    });
});
```

As you can see, it isn't particularly easy on the eyes. A simple fix is to name the handlers so that you can compose them without having to place them inline, as shown in Listing 10-2.

Listing 10-2. pyramid/simplify.js

```
function first(data, cb) {
    console.log('Executing first');
    setTimeout(cb, 1000, data);
}

function second(data, cb) {
    console.log('Executing second');
    setTimeout(cb, 1000, data);
}

function third(data, cb) {
    console.log('Executing third');
    setTimeout(cb, 1000, data);
}

// Named handlers
function handleThird(text3) {
    console.log('done:', text3); // no indent!
}

function handleSecond(text2) {
    third(text2, handleThird);
}

function handleFirst(text1) {
    second(text1, handleSecond);
}

// Start the chain
first('data', handleFirst);
```

This takes care of the pyramid problem. Note that we have the handlers in reverse (`third`, `second`, `first`) because it is good to declare functions before using them.

However, besides the obvious indentation problem that we have fixed, there are real technical issues with using callbacks for control flow compared to simple synchronous programming. For one, it confuses the input with the output—that is, we are using a callback function, which is an input, to actually return the value, which would be an output in a synchronous function.

Also, it doesn't work well with control flow primitives (if, else, for, and while). Additionally, error handling can be hard to get right. Let's examine these issues a bit more to allow the concepts to sink in.

If/else in an Async World

If you conditionally need to do an async operation in a function, you must make sure that the whole function is asynchronous. Listing 10-3 is a simple example to demonstrate this complexity.

Listing 10-3. ifelse/bad.js

```
// WARNING! DO NOT USE!
function maybeSync(arg, cb) {
    if (arg) { // We already have data
        // BAD! Do not call synchronously!
        cb('cached data');
    }
    else { // We need to load data
        // simulate a db load
        setTimeout(function () {
            cb('loaded data')
        }, 500);
    }
}
// Without the intimate details of maybeSync
//    its difficult to determine if
//       - foo is called first
//       OR
//       - bar is called first

maybeSync(true, function (data) {
    foo();
});
bar();

function foo() { console.log('foo') }
function bar() { console.log('bar') }
```

Without looking at the code of maybeSync function, it is impossible for a developer to know if foo will be called first or bar will be called first. In fact, in our example foo will be called immediately, whereas an async developer would assume that bar will be called first and foo will be called at *some later point* like any other async operation. The reason why this is not the behavior here is because maybeSync was poorly written and called the callback immediately based on some condition. The proper way is to use the process.nextTick function (as we saw in Chapter 3) to schedule the callback for the next tick of the event loop. Listing 10-4 shows the maybeSync function fixed up (renamed to alwaysAsync).

Listing 10-4. ifelse/good.js

```
function alwaysAsync(arg, cb) {
    if (arg) { // We already have data
        // setup call for next tick
        process.nextTick(function () {
            cb('cached data');
        });
    }
```

```
    else { // We need to load data
        // simulate a db load
        setTimeout(function () {
            cb('loaded data')
        }, 500);
    }
}

alwaysAsync(true, function (data) {
    foo();
});
bar();

function foo() { console.log('foo') }
function bar() { console.log('bar') }
```

Simple lesson: If a function takes a callback, it's async and it should never call the callback directly—process. nextTick is your friend.

Also worth mentioning, for browser-based code you can use setImmediate (if available) or setTimeout.

Loops in an Async World

Consider the simple case of fetching two items via HTTP requests and using the data contained in them. One simple way to approach this is shown in Listing 10-5.

Listing 10-5. loop/simple.js

```
// an async function to load an item
function loadItem(id, cb) {
    setTimeout(function () {
        cb(null, { id: id });
    }, 500);
}

// functions to manage loading
var loadedItems = [];
function itemsLoaded() {
    console.log('Do something with:', loadedItems);
}
function itemLoaded(err, item) {
    loadedItems.push(item);
    if (loadedItems.length == 2) {
        itemsLoaded();
    }
}

// calls to load
loadItem(1, itemLoaded);
loadItem(2, itemLoaded);
```

Here we simply maintain an array (loadedItems) to store items as they come down and then run the itemsLoaded function once we have all the items. There are libraries to make such control flow operations much simpler. The most prominent of these is async (npm install async). The same example rewritten using async is shown in Listing 10-6.

Listing 10-6. loop/async.js

```
// an async function to load an item
function loadItem(id, cb) {
    setTimeout(function () {
        cb(null, { id: id });
    }, 500);
}

// when all items loaded
function itemsLoaded(err, loadedItems) {
    console.log('Do something with:', loadedItems);
}

// load in parallel
var async = require('async');
async.parallel([
    function (cb) {
        loadItem(1, cb);
    },
    function (cb) {
        loadItem(2, cb);
    }
], itemsLoaded)
```

As you can see, we no longer need to maintain a list of completed/fetched items manually. The async.parallel function takes an array of functions as its first argument. Each of the functions is passed a callback that you are supposed to call in the standard node style—in othr words, error argument first followed by actual return values. Our loadItem function already calls its callback correctly so we just hand it the async's callback. Finally, async will call the function passed in as the second argument (itemsLoaded) once all the individual functions in the array have called their callbacks. The behavior we get is exactly the same as what we had done manually in the previous example.

Also note that async supports error aggregation between individual items that we get for free in this example (although we don't have a chance of error here). There are other control flow primitives (such as a serial control flow) supported by async as well if you need them.

The lesson here is that being asynchronous does make control flow more involved than simple synchronous programming, although not prohibitively so. Now let's look at the biggest issue with callbacks.

Error Handling

The worst issue with using callbacks for async tasks is the complexity in error handling. Let's look at a concrete example to solidify the concept. Consider the simple case of authoring an async version of loading JSON from a file. A synchronous version for such a task is shown in Listing 10-7.

Listing 10-7. errors/sync.js

```
var fs = require('fs');

function loadJSONSync(filename) {
    return JSON.parse(fs.readFileSync(filename));
}

// good json file
console.log(loadJSONSync('good.json'));

// non-existent json file
try {
    console.log(loadJSONSync('absent.json'));
}
catch (err) {
    console.log('absent.json error', err.message);
}

// invalid json file
try {
    console.log(loadJSONSync('bad.json'));
}
catch (err) {
    console.log('bad.json error', err.message);
}
```

There are three behaviors of this simple loadJSONSync function: a valid return value, a file system error, or a JSON.parse error. We handle the errors with a simple try/catch as you are used to when doing synchronous programming in other languages. The obvious performance disadvantage is that while the file is being read from the filesystem, no other JavaScript can execute. Now let's make a good async version of such a function. A decent initial attempt with a trivial error checking logic is shown in Listing 10-8.

Listing 10-8. Snippet from errors/asyncsimple.js

```
var fs = require('fs');

function loadJSON(filename, cb) {
    fs.readFile(filename, function (err, data) {
        if (err) cb(err);
        else cb(null, JSON.parse(data));
    });
}
```

Simple enough—it takes a callback and passes any filesystem errors to the callback. If there are no filesystem errors, it returns the JSON.parse result. A few points to keep in mind when working with async functions based on callbacks are the following:

1. Never call the callback twice.

2. Never throw an error.

This simple function, however, fails to accommodate for the second point. In fact, JSON.parse throws an error if it is passed bad JSON, the callback never gets called, and the application crashes, as demonstrated in Listing 10-9.

Listing 10-9. Snippet from errors/asyncsimple.js

```
// load invalid json
loadJSON('bad.json', function (err, data) {
    // NEVER GETS CALLED!
    if (err) console.log('bad.json error', err.message);
    else console.log(data);
});
```

A naïve attempt at fixing this would be to wrap the JSON.parse in a try/catch as shown in Listing 10-10.

Listing 10-10. errors/asyncbadcatch.js

```
var fs = require('fs');

function loadJSON(filename, cb) {
    fs.readFile(filename, function (err, data) {
        if (err) {
            cb(err);
        }
        else {
            try {
                cb(null, JSON.parse(data));
            }
            catch (err) {
                cb(err);
            }
        }
    });
}

// load invalid json
loadJSON('bad.json', function (err, data) {
    if (err) console.log('bad.json error', err.message);
    else console.log(data);
});
```

However, there is a subtle bug in this code. If the callback (cb), and not JSON.parse, throws an error, the catch executes and we call the callback again since we wrapped it in a try/catch. In other words, the callback gets called twice! This is demonstrated in Listing 10-11. A sample execution presented in Listing 10-12.

Listing 10-11. errors/asyncbadcatchdemo.js

```js
var fs = require('fs');

function loadJSON(filename, cb) {
    fs.readFile(filename, function (err, data) {
        if (err) {
            cb(err);
        }
        else {
            try {
                cb(null, JSON.parse(data));
            }
            catch (err) {
                cb(err);
            }
        }
    });
}

// a good file but a bad callback ... gets called again!
loadJSON('good.json', function (err, data) {
    console.log('our callback called');

    if (err) console.log('Error:', err.message);
    else {
        // lets simulate an error by trying to access a property on an undefined variable
        var foo;
        console.log(foo.bar);
    }
});
```

Listing 10-12. Sample Run of errors/asyncbadcatchdemo.js

```
$ node asyncbadcatchdemo.js
our callback called
our callback called
Error: Cannot read property 'bar' of undefined
```

The reason why the callback is called twice is because our loadJSON function wrongfully wrapped the callback in a try block. There is a simple lesson to remember here.

Simple lesson: Contain all your synchronous code in a try/catch, *except* when you call the callback.

Following this simple lesson, we have a fully functional async version of loadJSON, as shown in Listing 10-13.

Listing 10-13. errors/asyncfinal.js

```
var fs = require('fs');

function loadJSON(filename, cb) {
    fs.readFile(filename, function (err, data) {
        if (err) return cb(err);
        try {
            var parsed = JSON.parse(data);
        }
        catch (err) {
            return cb(err);
        }
        return cb(null, parsed);
    });
}
```

The only time we call the callback is outside any try/catch. Everything else in wrapped is a try/catch. Also we return on any call to the callback.

Admittedly, this is not hard to follow once you've done it a few times, but nonetheless it's a lot of boiler plate code to write simply for good error handling. Now let's look at a better way to tackle asynchronous JavaScript using promises.

Introduction to Promises

Before we see how promises greatly simplify asynchronous JavaScript, we need to have a good understanding of how a Promise behaves. Promises are soon (when ECMAScript 6 is finalized) going to be a part of standard JavaScript runtime. Until then, we need to use a third-party library. By far, the most popular one is Q (npm install q), which is what we will use here. Utility functions surrounding promises are different in individual libraries, but Promise instances from all the good libraries are compatible with one another because they all follow the "Promises/A+" specification. This spec is what is going to be a part of ECMAScript 6 as well so your knowledge is future-secure. Throughout this section, we will explain the concept followed by pointing out the Promise advantage over callbacks.

Create a Promise

We will look at the code before explaining promises in detail. Let's start with creating a promise, Q style. In Listing 10-14, we create a promise, subscribe to its completion using the promise.then member function, and finally resolve the promise.

Listing 10-14. promiseintro/create.js

```javascript
var Q = require('q');

var deferred = Q.defer();
var promise = deferred.promise;

promise.then(function (val) {
    console.log('done with:', val);
});

deferred.resolve('final value'); // done with: final value
```

There is a lot more to the then function, and we will look at it in detail in the next section. Our focus with this example is on creating a promise. Q.defer() provides you with an object (a deferred) that

1. contains the promise (deferred.promise), and

2. contains functions to resolve (deferred.resolve) or reject (deferred.reject) the mentioned promise.

There is a good reason for this separation between the promise and the thing that controls the promise (which is deferred object). It allows you to give anybody the promise and still control when and how it gets resolved, as shown in Listing 10-15.

Listing 10-15. promiseintro/seperate.js

```javascript
var Q = require('q');

function getPromise() {
    var deferred = Q.defer();

    // Resolve the promise after a second
    setTimeout(function () {
        deferred.resolve('final value');
    }, 1000);

    return deferred.promise;
}

var promise = getPromise();

promise.then(function (val) {
    console.log('done with:', val);
});
```

So now we know how to create a promise. One immediate benefit of using promises is that the function inputs and outputs are clearly defined.

Promise advantage: Instead of using a callback (which is an input) to provide the output, we return the promise, which can be used to subscribe for the output at your convenience.

Now let's take a look at the promise states (resolved, rejected, and pending).

Promise States

A promise can only be one of three states: Pending, Fulfilled, or Rejected. There is a state transition diagram between them, as shown in Figure 10-1.

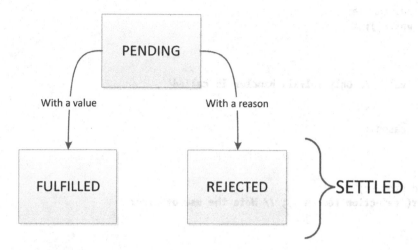

Figure 10-1. *Promsie states and fates*

The promise can only transition from one state to another based on these arrows. For example, it is not possible for a fulfilled promise to become rejected. Additionally, the value it is fulfilled to or the reason it is rejected with cannot change. Also shown in the diagram, if the promise is fulfilled or rejected, we say it has settled.

Promise advantage: Since a promise's transition into fulfilled or rejected is immutable, all individual onFulfilled / onRejected handlers will only be called once. Promises don't have the *called again* problem of callbacks.

You can transition a promise manually using the deferred object we saw earlier. But, most commonly (almost always), some function will give you a promise and from that point on you use the then function to create and fulfill or reject promises.

The Then and Catch Basics

The then member function is the heart of the promise API. At its most basic level, you can use it to subscribe to a promise settled result. It takes two functions (called the onFulfilled and the onRejected handlers), which are called based on the final state of the promise (fulfilled or rejected). However, we recommend only passing in the onFulfilled handler to the then function.

Similar to the then function on a promise, there is the catch function. The catch function only takes the onRejected handler. Therefore, it is conventional to only have the onFulfilled handler in the then function followed by a catch function with the onRejected handler. These two functions are shown in Listing 10-16.

Listing 10-16. thencatch/settle.js

```
var Q = require('q');

var willFulfillDeferred = Q.defer();
var willFulfill = willFulfillDeferred.promise;
willFulfillDeferred.resolve('final value');

willFulfill
    .then(function (val) {
        console.log('success with', val); // Only fulfill handler is called
    })
    .catch(function (reason) {
        console.log('failed with', reason);
    });

var willRejectDeferred = Q.defer();
var willReject = willRejectDeferred.promise;
willRejectDeferred.reject(new Error('rejection reason')); // Note the use of Error

willReject
    .then(function (val) {
        console.log('success with', val);
    })
    .catch(function (reason) {
        console.log('failed with', reason); // Only reject handler is called
    });
```

Note that it is conventional to reject a promise with an `Error` object since it provides you with a stack-trace. This is similar to the recommendation to use `Error` when passing an error argument to a callback. Also the `then`/`catch` pattern should remind you of the `try`/`catch` pattern from synchronous programming.

Also worth mentioning is the fact that `catch(function(){})` is just sugar for `then(null,function(){})`. So the behavior of `catch` will be very similar to that of `then` in many respects.

Note that, as shown in Listing 10-16, it doesn't matter whether the promise is already settled when we call the `then`/`catch` methods. The handlers will be called *if and when* the promise is settled (which might already have happened, as in our example).

You can create an already fulfilled promise using the `` `when` `` member function as shown in Listing 10-17.

Listing 10-17. thencatch/fulfilled.js

```
var Q = require('q');

Q.when(null).then(function (val) {
    console.log(val == null);  // true
});

Q.when('kung foo').then(function (val) {
    console.log(val);  // kung foo
});

console.log('I will print first because *then* is always async!');
```

When you are using Q.when to start a promise chain (we will look at promise chains next), it is common to use when(null). Otherwise, you can create a resolved promise with any value (for example, kung foo). Note that as shown in this example, the then callbacks (onFulfilled/onRejected) execute asynchronously after the synchronous code is executed.

Promise advantage: Promises do not suffer from the *maybe sync* problem of callbacks. If you want to return an immediate promise, just return a resolved promise using Q.when and any then that the user registers is bound to be called asynchronously.

Similar to the when function, there is a Q.reject function that creates an already rejected promise, as shown in Listing 10-18. You might want to return a rejected promise from your function in case you detect an error in some input argument.

Listing 10-18. thencatch/rejected.js

```
var Q = require('q');

Q.reject(new Error('denied')).catch(function (err) {
    console.log(err.message); // denied
});
```

Chain-ability of Then

The chain-ability of promises is *their most important feature*. Once you have a promise, you use the then function to create a chain of fulfilled or rejected promises.

The most important behavior is that the value returned from the onFulfilled handler (or the onRejected handler) is wrapped in a new promise. This new promise is returned from the then function, which allows you to chain promises one after another. This is shown in Listing 10-19.

Listing 10-19. chainability/chain.js

```
var Q = require('q');

Q.when(null)
    .then(function () {
        return 'kung foo';
    })
    .then(function (val) {
        console.log(val); // kung foo
        return Q.when('panda');
    })
    .then(function (val) {
        console.log(val); // panda
        // Nothing returned
    })
    .then(function (val) {
        console.log(val == undefined); // true
    });
```

Note that if you return a promise from the then handler (for example, we return the promise resolved to a panda in our second then function), the next then handler will wait for the promise to settle (resolve or rejected) before calling the appropriate handler.

If at any point there is an uncaught exception or the handler returns a promise that is (or will be) rejected, then no further onFulfilled handlers are called. The chain continues until some onRejected handler is found, at which point the chain is reset and continues based on the value returned from the onRejected handler, as shown in Listing 10-20.

Listing 10-20. chainability/chainWithError.js

```javascript
var Q = require('q');

Q.when(null)
    .then(function () {
        throw new Error('panda'); // uncaught exception
    })
    .then(function (val) {
        console.log('!!!!!!', val); // I will never get called
    })
    .catch(function (reason) {
        console.log('Someone threw a', reason.message);
        return 'all good';
    })
    .then(function (val) {
        console.log(val); // all good
        return Q.reject(new Error('taco'));
    })
    .then(function (val) {
        console.log('!!!!!', val); // I will never get called
    })
    .catch(function (reason) {
        console.log('Someone threw a', reason.message);
    });
```

In this example, whenever there is an error or a rejected promise, no further onFulfilled handlers are called (which we are registering using the then function) until some onRejected handler (registered using the catch function) handles the error.

Promise advantage: Uncaught exceptions inside onFulfilled/onRejected handlers do not blow the application. Instead, they result in the promise in the chain to be rejected, which you can handle gracefully with a final onRejected handler.

Most commonly, your promise chain will look like the one in Listing 10-21. Notice how similar it is to the try/catch semantics of synchronous programming.

Listing 10-21. chainability/demoChain.js snippet

```javascript
somePromise
    .then(function (val) { /* do something */ })
    .then(function (val) { /* do something */ })
    .then(function (val) { /* do something */ })
    .then(function (val) { /* do something */ })
    .then(function (val) { /* do something */ })
    .catch(function (reason) { /* handle the error */ });
```

Converting Callbacks to Promises

In this section, we'll see how to interoperate Promises with classical Node.js async pattern. With this knowledge, we will revisit the loadJSON example to see how much simpler it is.

Interfacing with nodeback

Now that you can partially appreciate the Promise API, the immediate concern will most likely be interoperability with node callback style functions (lovingly called *nodeback*). A nodeback is simply a function that

- takes n number of arguments, the last of which is a callback, and

- the callback is called with (error) or (null, value) or (null, value1, value2,...).

This is the style of functions in the core Node.js modules as well as dependable community-written modules. Converting nodeback-style functions to promises is a simple task of calling Q.nbind, which takes a nodeback-style function, wraps it, and returns a new function that does the following:

- Takes the same first n-1 arguments as the nodeback function (that is, all the arguments excluding the callback argument) and silently passes them to the nodeback function along with an internal callback function

- Returns a promise that is

  - rejected if the internal callback is called by the nodeback function with a non-null error argument (in other words, the (error) case),

  - resolved to a value if the callback is called by the nodeback function like (null, value), and

  - resolved to an array [value1, value2,...] if the callback is called by the nodeback function like (null, value1,value2,...).

In Listing 10-22, we show a practical example of converting nodeback-style functions into ones that work with promises.

Listing 10-22. interop/nodeback.js

```
function data(delay, cb) {
    setTimeout(function () {
        cb(null, 'data');
    }, delay);
}

function error(delay, cb) {
    setTimeout(function () {
        cb(new Error('error'));
    }, delay);
}

// Callback style
data(1000, function (err, data) { console.log(data); });
error(1000, function (err, data) { console.log(err.message); });
```

```
// Convert to promises
var Q = require('q');
var dataAsync = Q.nbind(data);
var errorAsync = Q.nbind(error);

// Usage
dataAsync(1000)
    .then(function (data) { console.log(data); });

errorAsync(1000)
    .then(function (data) { })
    .catch(function (err) { console.log(err.message); });
```

The example illustrates the simplicity of this conversion. In fact, you can even do it inline and call it, for example, Q.nbind(data)(1000). Note our convention of using the -Async postfix to denote converted nodeback functions that return promises. This is a play on the -Sync postfix used by core node for synchronous versions of nodeback functions. You will find other examples of this in the community.

Now let's revisit our loadJSON example and rewrite an async version that uses promises. All that we need to do is read the file contents as a promise, then parse them as JSON, and we are done. This is illustrated in Listing 10-23.

Listing 10-23. interop/ loadJSONAsync.js

```
var Q = require('q');
var fs = require('fs');
var readFileAsync = Q.nbind(fs.readFile);

function loadJSONAsync(filename) {
    return readFileAsync(filename)
                .then(function (res) {
                    return JSON.parse(res);
                });
}

// good json file
loadJSONAsync('good.json')
    .then(function (val) { console.log(val); })
    .catch(function (err) {
        console.log('good.json error', err.message); // never called
    })
// non-existent json file
    .then(function () {
        return loadJSONAsync('absent.json');
    })
    .then(function (val) { console.log(val); }) // never called
    .catch(function (err) {
        console.log('absent.json error', err.message);
    })
```

```
// invalid json file
    .then(function () {
        return loadJSONAsync('bad.json');
    })
    .then(function (val) { console.log(val); }) // never called
    .catch(function (err) {
        console.log('bad.json error', err.message);
    });
```

Note that due to the chain-ability of promises, we didn't need to do any error handling inside our loadJSONAsync function as any errors (whether from the fs.readFile callback or thrown by JSON.parse) would get pushed out to the first catch (onRejected handler). In the previous example, in addition to the simpler error handling, note that we have a long list of async calls chained without any indentation issues.

Promise advantage: Promises save you from an unneeded pyramid of doom.

Now you know how easy it is to convert simple nodeback functions into ones that return promises with a simple call to Q.nbind. The only other thing to be aware of when using Q.nbind to convert functions is that member functions of an instance might depend on this to be the correct calling context as we saw in Chapter 2. This calling context can simply be passed as a second argument to Q.nbind, as demonstrated in Listing 10-24, where we pass foo as a second argument to Q.nbind to ensure the correct this.

Listing 10-24. interop/context.js

```
var foo = {
    bar: 123,
    bas: function (cb) {
        cb(null, this.bar);
    }
};

var Q = require('q');
var basAsync = Q.nbind(foo.bas, foo);

basAsync().then(function (val) {
    console.log(val); // 123;
});
```

Converting Non-nodeback Callback Functions

Many functions in the browser (for example, setTimeout) do not follow the nodeback convention of error being the first argument. These functions were ported as is to Node.js for ease of code reusability. To convert these (and other functions that might not follow the nodeback interface) to return promises, you can use the deferred API (deferred.resolve/deferred.reject) that we are already familiar with. For example, in Listing 10-25 we have a simple promise based sleepAsync function created from setTimeout.

213

Listing 10-25. interop/sleep.js

```
var Q = require('q');
function sleepAsync(ms) {
    var deferred = Q.defer();
    setTimeout(function () {
        deferred.resolve();
    }, ms);
    return deferred.promise;
}

console.time('sleep');
sleepAsync(1000).then(function () {
    console.timeEnd('sleep'); // around 1000ms
});
```

Providing a Promise + nodeback Interface

Now that we have covered how to convert nodeback- and callback-based functions into ones that return promises, it is worthwhile considering the reverse scenario to make it easier for people who are not familiar with promises to use your API with callbacks. Callbacks are, after all, simple enough for any beginner to grasp.

Q promises provide a simple function, promise.nodeify(callback), where if the callback is a function, it assumes it's a nodeback and calls it with (error) if the promise gets rejected or calls it with (null, resolvedValue) if the promise gets fulfilled. Otherwise, promise.nodeify simply returns the promise.

As an example, we can convert our promise based loadJSONAsync to support both promises as well as the nodeback convention as shown with usage in Listing 10-26.

Listing 10-26. interop/dual.js

```
var Q = require('q');
var fs = require('fs');
var readFileAsync = Q.nbind(fs.readFile);

function loadJSONAsync(filename, callback) {
    return readFileAsync(filename)
                .then(JSON.parse)
                .nodeify(callback);
}

// Use as a promise
loadJSONAsync('good.json').then(function (val) {
    console.log(val);
});

// Use with a callback
loadJSONAsync('good.json', function (err, val) {
    console.log(val);
});
```

Note that we didn't need any of the convoluted error handling inside our loadJSONAsync function that we had for the pure callback code and we still managed to support nodeback thanks to promises. This also allows you to partially and incrementally update portions of your application to use promises.

Promise advantage: You can seamlessly support promises + nodeback and still get all the benefits (like simpler error checking) of promises *inside your API*.

Further Notes on the Promise API

Now that we have covered the most bang-for-buck area of promises, it is worth mentioning a few surrounding areas so that you can claim to be a true Promise expert.

Promises Supports Other Promises as a Value

Anywhere you see a value being passed into a promise, you can actually pass in another promise and the next onFulfilled/onRejected handler (depending upon how things go) will be called with the final settled value.

We already saw this happen when we returned a promise from our onFulfilled / onRejected handlers during the discussion on chaining then. The next onFulfilled / onRejected handler in the chain got the final settled value of the promise. The same is true for Q.when and deferred.resolve, as shown in Listing 10-27, and any other time you try to pass a promise as a value for resolution.

Listing 10-27. further/thenable.js

```
var Q = require('Q');

Q.when(Q.when('foo')).then(function (val) {
    console.log(val); // foo
});

var def = Q.defer();
def.resolve(Q.when('foo'));
def.promise.then(function (val) {
    console.log(val); // foo
});

Q.when(null).then(function () {
    return Q.when('foo');
})
.then(function (val) {
    console.log(val); // foo
});
```

This behavior is extremely useful since you can just pass the value if you have it or a promise to the value if you need to make an async request to load it inside your chain.

Ungracefully Terminating a Promise Chain (Intentionally)

As we saw earlier, uncaught exceptions in the onFulfilled / onRejected handlers only result in the next promise in the chain to be rejected, but they do not throw an error in the application main loop. This is great since it allows you to return the promise from your function and cascade the error to the handler that can reliably see why the promise failed. Consider the simple example in Listing 10-28.

Listing 10-28. further/gracefulcatch.js

```
var Q = require('q');

function iAsync() {
    return Q.when(null).then(function () {
        var foo;
        // Simulate an uncaught exception because of a programming error
        foo.bar; // access a member on an undefined variable
    });
}

iAsync()
    .then(function () { }) // not called
    .catch(function (err) { console.log(err.message); });
```

However, when at the root level of your application where you are not returning this promise to anyone, a simple catch (onRejected handler) is not sufficient. If there is a bug in in our own onRejected handler, no one will get notified. Listing 10-29 provides an example where our catch callback itself has an error and there is no notification at runtime. This is because all that happened was the next promise got rejected and no one cared.

Listing 10-29. further/badcatch.js

```
var Q = require('q');

function iAsync() {
    return Q.when(null).then(function () {
        var foo; foo.bar; // Programming error. Will get caught since we return the chain
    });
}

iAsync()
    .catch(function (err) {
        var foo; foo.bar; // Uncaught exception, rejects the next promise
    });
    // But no one is listening to the returned promise
```

In this case, you just want the error to be thrown into the main event loop if the final promise is rejected. This is what the promise.done method is for. It throws an error into the main event loop if the last promise is rejected, as demonstrated in Listing 10-30.

Listing 10-30. further/done.js

```
iAsync()
    .catch(function (err) {
        var foo; foo.bar; // Uncaught exception, rejects the next promise
    })
    .done(); // Since previous promise is rejected throws the rejected value as an error
```

Here you will get an error on the console and the application will exit. This will help you fix possible errors in your code (in your catch of all places!) instead of them getting silently ignored.

Promise Library Compatibility

The behavior of 'then' is what is most important in a promise. How you create promises inside your library is secondary. In fact, the Promises/A+ spec only dictates the behavior of the then function (and the onFulfilled / onRejected handlers) since that is all that is needed for promises from one library to interoperate with another. In Listing 10-31, we show a demonstration of seamlessly using promises between bluebird and Q.

Listing 10-31. further/librarycompat.js

```
var Q = require('q');
var BlueBird = require('bluebird');

new BlueBird(function (resolve) { // A bluebird promise
    resolve('foo');
})
    .then(function (val) {
        console.log(val); // foo
        return Q.when('bar'); // A q promise
    })
    .then(function (val) {
        console.log(val); // bar
    });
```

This means that if you are using a Node.js library that returns promises, you can use then with Q or some other library that you like, or even native promises once ES6 is finalized.

Inspecting the State of Promises

Q promises provide a few useful utility functions to see the state of promises. You can use the promise.
isFulfilled()/ promise.isRejected()/ promise.isPending()to determine the *current* state of a promise. There is
also a utility inspect method, promise.inspect, which returns a snapshot of the current state. This is demonstrated in
Listing 10-32.

Listing 10-32. further/inspect.js

```
var Q = require('q');

var p1 = Q.defer().promise; // pending
var p2 = Q.when('fulfill'); // fulfilled
var p3 = var p3 = Q.reject(new Error('reject')); // rejected

process.nextTick(function () {
    console.log(p1.isPending()); // true
    console.log(p2.isFulfilled()); // true
    console.log(p3.isRejected()); // true

    console.log(p1.inspect()); // { state: 'pending' }
    console.log(p2.inspect()); // { state: 'fulfilled', value: 'fulfill' }
    console.log(p3.inspect()); // { state: 'rejected', reason: [Error: reject] }
});
```

Parallel Flow Control

We have seen how trivial doing a serial sequence of async tasks is with promises. It is simply a matter of chaining
then calls.

However, you might potentially want to run a series of async tasks and then do something with the results of all of
these tasks. Q (as well as most other promise libraries) provides a static all (that is, Q.all) member function that you
can use to wait for n number of promises to complete. This is demonstrated in Listing 10-33, where we start a number
of async tasks and then continue once they are complete.

Listing 10-33. further/parallel.js

```
var Q = require('q');

// an async function to load an item
var loadItem = Q.nbind(function (id, cb) {
    setTimeout(function () {
        cb(null, { id: id });
    }, 500);
});

Q.all([loadItem(1), loadItem(2)])
    .then(function (items) {
        console.log('Items:', items); // Items: [ { id: 1 }, { id: 2 } ]
    })
    .catch(function (reason) { console.log(reason) });
```

The promise return by Q.all will resolve to an array containing all the resolved values of the individual promises, as shown in Listing 10-33. If any individual promise is rejected, the complete promise is rejected with the same reason. (At this point, you can inspect the promises if you want to know *exactly* which promise went rouge.) This example also shows the simplicity of using promises to simplify your callback logic quickly (Q.all) and effortlessly (we still used a nodeback function, just wrapped it in a Q.nbind).

Generators

I am sure that at this point you will agree that promises are a great way to simplify callbacks. But we can actually even do better, almost making asynchronous programming a first-class member of the language. As a thought experiment, imagine the following: a way to tell the JavaScript runtime to pause the executing of code on the await keyword used on a promise and resume *only* once (and if) the promise returned from the function is settled. (See Listing 10-34).

Listing 10-34. generators/thought.js snippet

```
// Not actual code. A thought experiment
async function foo() {
    try {
        var val = await getMeAPromise();
        console.log(val);
    }
    catch(err){
        console.log('Error: ',err.message);
    }
}
```

When the promise settles, execution continues if it was fulfilled. Then await will return the value. If it's rejected, an error will be thrown synchronously, which we can catch. This suddenly (and magically) makes asynchronous programming as easy as synchronous programming. Three things are needed:

- Ability to *pause function execution*

- Ability to *return a value inside* the function

- Ability to *throw an exception inside* the function

The good news is this magic is very real and possible to *try* today. The syntax will be *slightly different* because the technology we will be using wasn't designed *only* for this. It is possible because of JavaScript generators, a technology coming with ECMAScript 6, which you can use today. To use it today, you will need two things, both of which will become unnecessary once ECMAScript 6 is finalized:

- An unstable build of Node.js. Currently this means some version of the form v0.1, for example v0.11.13. You can download prebuilt binaries/installer for Windows as well as Mac OS X from http://nodejs.org/dist and install them as we did in Chapter 1.

- Run your Node.js executable with the `--harmony` flag. For example, to run a file app.js you would do the following:

```
$ node --harmony app.js
```

Motivation for Generators

The main motivation for adding generators to JavaScript is the ability to do lazy evaluation during iteration. A simple example is the desire to return an infinite list from a function. This is demonstrated in Listing 10-35.

Listing 10-35. generators/infiniteSequence.js

```javascript
function* infiniteSequence(){
    var i = 0;
    while(true){
        yield i++;
    }
}

var iterator = infiniteSequence();
while (true){
    console.log(iterator.next()); // { value: xxxx, done: false }
}
```

You signify that a function is going to return an iterator by using function* (instead of function) and, instead of the return keyword, you yield a result. Each time you yield, control leaves the generator back to the iterator. Each time iterator.next is called, the generator function is resumed from the last yield. If you run this simple example, you will see an infinite list of numbers being returned (yielded) from the iterator. This example shows the motivation of adding generators to the language.

Power of Generators in JavaScript

Generators are much more powerful in JavaScript than in many other languages. First, let's look at an example that sheds light on their behavior a bit more (Listing 10-36). Listing 10-37 is a sample run of the application.

Listing 10-36. generators/outside.js

```javascript
function* generator(){
    console.log('Execution started');
    yield 0;
    console.log('Execution resumed');
    yield 1;
    console.log('Execution resumed');
}

var iterator = generator();
console.log('Starting iteration');
console.log(iterator.next()); // { value: 0, done: false }
console.log(iterator.next()); // { value: 1, done: false }
console.log(iterator.next()); // { value: undefined, done: true }
```

Listing 10-37. Sample Execution of generators/outside.js

```
$ node --harmony outside.js
Starting iteration
Execution started
{ value: 0, done: false }
Execution resumed
{ value: 1, done: false }
Execution resumed
{ value: undefined, done: true }
```

As demonstrated in the example, simply calling the generator does not execute it. It just returns the iterator. The first time you call next on the iterator is when execution starts and only continues until the yield keyword is evaluated, at which point iterator.next returns the value passed to the yield keyword. Each time you call iterator.next, the function body resumes execution until we finally arrive at the end of the function body, at which point the iterator.next returns an object with done set to true. This behavior is exactly what makes generating something like an infinite Fibonacci sequence in a lazy way possible.

Our communication using the generator has been mostly one-way with the generator returning values for the iterator. One extremely powerful feature of generators in JavaScript is that they allow two-way communications! Given an iterator, you can call iterator.next(someValue) and that value will be returned *inside* the generator function by the yield keyword. Listing 10-38 a simple example to demonstrate this where we inject the value bar.

Listing 10-38. generators/insideValue.js

```
function* generator(){
    var bar = yield 'foo';
    console.log(bar); // bar!
}

var iterator = generator();
// Start execution till we get first yield value
var foo = iterator.next();
console.log(foo.value); // foo
// Resume execution injecting bar
var nextThing = iterator.next('bar');
```

Similarly, we can even throw an exception inside the generator using the iterator.throw(errorObject) function, as shown in Listing 10-39.

Listing 10-39. generators/insideThrow.js

```
function* generator(){
    try{
        yield 'foo';
    }
    catch(err){
        console.log(err.message); // bar!
    }
}
```

```
var iterator = generator();
// Start execution till we get first yield value
var foo = iterator.next();
console.log(foo.value); // foo
// Resume execution throwing an exception 'bar'
var nextThing = iterator.throw(new Error('bar'));
```

We already know that yield allows us to pause the function execution. Now we also know that we have a way to return a value inside the function for the yield keyword and even throw an exception. As discussed in the beginning of this section, that is all we needed for some form of async/await semantics! In fact, Q ships with a function Q.spawn that wraps all this complexity of waiting for promises to settle, passing in resolved values, and throwing exceptions on promise rejection.

Promises and Generators

Generators combined with promises allow you to do near synchronous style programming with all the performance benefits of Asynchronous JavaScript. The key ingredients are generator functions (function *) that yield on promises (yield promise) wrapped in Q.spawn function call. Let's look at an example. Listing 10-40 shows the two cases (fulfilled and rejected) of yielding a promise inside a generator wrapped in Q.spawn.

Listing 10-40. spawn/basics.js

```
var Q = require('q');

Q.spawn(function* (){
    // fulfilled
    var foo = yield Q.when('foo');
    console.log(foo); // foo

    // rejected
    try{
        yield Q.reject(new Error('bar'));
    }
    catch(err){
        console.log(err.message); // bar
    }
});
```

If the promise is rejected, a synchronous error is thrown inside the generator. Otherwise, the value of the promise is returned from the yield call.

Q also has the Q.async function, which takes a generator function and wraps it up into a function, which, when called, would return a promise that is

- resolved to the final return value of the generator, and

- rejected if there is an uncaught error in the generator or the last value is a rejected promise.

In Listing 10-41, we demonstrate using `Q.async` to author a promise consuming + promise returning function.

Listing 10-41. spawn/async.js

```javascript
var Q = require('q');

// an async function to load an item
var loadItem = Q.nbind(function (id, cb) {
    setTimeout(function () {
        cb(null, { id: id });
    }, 500); // simulate delay
});

// An async function to load items
var loadItems = Q.async(function* (ids){
    var items = [];
    for (var i = 0; i < ids.length; i++) {
        items.push(yield loadItem(ids[i]));
    }
    return items;
});

Q.spawn(function* (){
    console.log(yield loadItems([1,2,3]));
});
```

`Q.async` allows you to author APIs using generators so you can use near synchronous style of development and simply return a promise, which in turn can be used by other people in their own generators.

■ **Note** When you are running in the root level of your application, use `Q.spawn` (this is similar to using the `promise.done` function). When you are authoring a function, that is, writing code to return a result, just wrap the function in `Q.async`.

The Future

There is already an ECMAScript 7 recommendation to make `async` / `await` first-class usable keywords of the language, which provide very light sugar to do a transformation similar to what we have demonstrated. That is, ECMAScript 7 might potentially do the rewrite in Listing 10-42 silently inside the JavaScript VM:

Listing 10-42. Proposed Future Syntax Using Generators Internally

```javascript
async function <name>?<argumentlist><body>

=>

function <name>?<argumentlist>{ return spawn(function*() <body>); }
```

How it pans out is yet to be seen, but it looks *promising*. Note that the final syntax may be significantly different (for example, no async keyword usage), but the behavior seems to be mostly settled.

Promise advantage: You are more prepared to handle the future language changes coming to JavaScript if you use promises.

Additional Resources

Async (npm install async) documentation: www.npmjs.org/package/async

Promises/A+ specification: http://promises-aplus.github.io/promises-spec/

A description of Promise states and fates: https://github.com/domenic/promises-unwrapping/blob/master/docs/states-and-fates.md

ECMAScript ES7 async/await: https://github.com/lukehoban/ecmascript-asyncawait

Summary

In this chapter, we looked at all the areas you need to be careful about when writing high-quality callback style code. Once you start using promises, the lessons of writing good callback-based functions might not be as relevant in your code but will still help you debug other people's code.

After demonstrating that callbacks can get tricky, we provided promises as an alternative that can greatly simplify the flow of your code. We discussed the behavior of a Promise chain and demonstrated how it simplifies error handling and allows your asynchronous code to follow a natural sequential pattern. We also demonstrated how easy it is to convert existing nodeback-style functions to return promises and how to make your promise returning and consuming functions still support nodeback so you can incrementally update your APIs and applications.

Finally, we discussed generators that offer exciting opportunities for JavaScript code innovation. We combined generators with promises to get the best benefits of synchronous programming—in other words, simplified error handling, error bubbling, and function execution to your highly performing asynchronous code.

CHAPTER 11

Debugging

Everyone knows that debugging is twice as hard as writing a program in the first place.

—Brian Kernighan

When undertaking a production application, it is important to have good debugging tools in your tool belt. This can save you plenty of hair pulling and head scratching. In this chapter, we will look at the most basic of debugging assistance tools along with high-powered IDEs and tricks of the trade.

The Console Object

The simplest form of debugging is simple logging. The console is a global object available in Node.js. It is intentionally designed to mimic the behavior of a web browser's console object. We have been using console.log function since the beginning of this book. Now we will take a more in-depth look at this and other member functions of console.

Simple Logging

The simplest behavior of console.log is that it will take any number of arguments and call util.inspect (from the Node.js core util module) on each of these, separated by a space *and* followed by a new line. This is shown on the following Node.js REPL session:

```
> console.log(1,2,3); console.log(4,5,6);
1 2 3
4 5 6
```

The underlying util.inspect function is quite powerful, and it does some nice printing for arbitrary objects out of the box. For example, we can log arbitrary JavaScript objects:

```
> console.log({ life: 42 }, { foo: 'I pitty the foo' }, [1, 0]);
{ life: 42 } { foo: 'I pitty the foo' } [ 1, 0 ]
```

We can customize what is printed by util.inspect for a particular object by adding an `inspect` function to the object, as shown in Listing 11-1.

Listing 11-1. console/inspect.js

```
var foo = {
    bar: 123,
    inspect: function () {
        return 'Bar is ' + this.bar;
    }
};

// Inspect
console.log(foo); // Logs: "Bar is 123"
```

Additionally, *if* the first argument to console.log is a string *and* it contains one of the placeholders, these placeholders are replaced (with formatting) from the remaining arguments to console.log. The following placeholders are supported (same as util.format function):

- %s - String

- %d - Number (both integer and float)

- %j - JSON

A single percent sign ('%') in the absence of a category (s/d/j) does not consume an argument. However, you can always double up the percent sign ('%%') to prevent it from looking at the next character (which may or may not be one of s/d/j) and print a single %. Placeholder-based formatting is demonstrated in Listing 11-2.

Listing 11-2. console/placeholder.js

```
// %d and %s
var name = 'nate';
var money = 33;
console.log('%s has %d dollars', name, money); // nate has 33 dollars

// %j
var foo = {
    answer: 42
};
console.log(foo); // { answer: 42 }
console.log('%j', foo); // {"answer":42}

// %
console.log('% %%'); // % %
console.log('%d', 1); // 1
console.log('%%d', 1); // %d 1
```

Simple Benchmark

Quite commonly, you would like to know the duration of some piece of code. There are two functions, console.time and console.timeEnd, that can be used to instrument your code quickly and painlessly so you don't waste time looking at the wrong place. They simply take a label and on console.timeEnd print out the label + the duration since the last moment `console.time` was called with the same label. In the absence of a label, undefined will get used so you can use that as well for quick throwaway tests. Usage of these functions is demonstrated in Listing 11-3.

Listing 11-3. console/time.js

```
console.time();
setTimeout(function () {
    console.timeEnd(); // undefined: 501ms
}, 500);

console.time('first');
setTimeout(function () {
    console.timeEnd('first'); // first: 1001ms
}, 1000);

console.time('second');
setTimeout(function () {
    console.timeEnd('second'); // second: 2004ms
}, 2000);
```

A Quick Way to Get the Call Stack

You might want to get the stack trace to see why a particular function is being called and by whom. You can get a quick printout of the call stack using the `console.trace` function, which optionally takes a label to display for the particular stack trace, as shown in Listing 11-4.

Listing 11-4. console/trace.js

```
function foo() {
    console.trace('trace at foo');

    // Execution continues
    console.log('Stack trace printed');
}

function bar() {
    foo();
}

bar();
```

A sample output is shown in Listing 11-5. You can see that using `console.trace` has no impact on the execution flow. It simply logs the stack trace.

Listing 11-5. Sample Run of console/trace.js

```
$ node trace.js
Trace: trace at foo
    at foo (.\code\Chapter 11\console\trace.js:2:13)
    at bar (.\code\Chapter 11\console\trace.js:9:5)
    at Object.<anonymous> (.\code\Chapter 11\console\trace.js:12:1)
    ... truncated ...
    at node.js:807:3
Stack trace printed
```

If you want the reference to the stack trace that you can pass around, you can use the `stack` property of the `Error` object. This will be the stack trace at the point where the `Error` object created, as demonstrated in Listing 11-6. A sample execution of the code is presented in Listing 11-7.

Listing 11-6. console/stack.js

```
function foo() {
    var stack = new Error('trace at foo').stack;
    console.log(stack);

    // Execution continues
    console.log('Stack trace printed');
}
function bar() {
    foo();
}
bar();
```

Listing 11-7. Sample Run of console/stack.js

```
$ node stack.js
Error: trace at foo
    at foo (.\code\Chapter 11\console\stack.js:2:17)
    at bar (.\code\Chapter 11\console\stack.js:9:5)
    at Object.<anonymous> (.\code\Chapter 11\console\stack.js:11:1)
    ... truncated ...
    at node.js:807:3
Stack trace printed
```

Again, simply newing up an `Error` object to get the stack has no impact on the program flow.

Print to stderr

The `console.log` function outputs to the program's `stdout` stream. The `console.error` function has the same behavior as `console.log` except that it prints to `stderr`.

You should use `stderr` for error messages. If you think of the program as a function, then this function always returns object with two values, `stdout` and `stderr`. This makes `stdout` clear of any error messages and safe to pipe between applications. For example, consider the simple script shown in Listing 11-8.

Listing 11-8. console/stderr.js

```
console.log('Good output');
console.error('Error message');
```

If we were to redirect this application's output to a file, only `stdout` is sent to the file and `stderr` is sent to the terminal, as shown in Listing 11-9.

Listing 11-9. Sample Runs of console/stderr.js to Show stderr Behavior on redirect

```
$ node stderr.js
Good output
Error message

$ node stderr.js > good.txt
Error message

$ cat good.txt
Good output
```

There are two advantages here. Because of the use of the error stream (stderr), we know that an error occurred despite the redirect. Secondly, only good output is sent to the file. Such a file might be consumed by some other application, and it doesn't need to handle or filter our error messages from the output.

The Debugger Statement

All Node.js debuggers that we will look at in this chapter support the debugger statement. If the application is being actively debugged (has a debugger attached), then this statement will cause a breakpoint to occur on this line. In the absence of any debugger, it has absolutely no effect and is ignored completely by the JavaScript runtime. For example, the following code prints hello world and debugger has no effect:

```
console.log('hello');
debugger;
console.log('world');
```

The debugger statement is a part of the standard JavaScript specification and works in the web-browser debug tools as well.

Node's Built-in Debugger

A quick debugging strategy is to insert a debugger statement in your code where you want to break (and debug) and then start your node application by passing in the debug argument to node:

```
$ node debug yourscript.js
```

■ **Note** You pass arguments to node by mentioning them after node but before your script name. We already saw a usage of this in the previous chapter where we using the --harmony flag. Such arguments do not become a part of `process.argv` and therefore do not pollute your argument processing logic inside your code. These are simply processed by node internally.

Using the debug argument will do the following:

- Start your application
- Pause before executing the first line of your JavaScript
- Give you a shell to control you application flow

The debugger shell has a bunch of commands, but since we are focused on quick debugging in this section, all you need to know are the following:

- Control flow

    - c continue execution

    - n next step (this is step *over* if you are familiar with traditional debuggers)

    - restart restarts the script

- Observe state

    - watch(expression:string) adds a watch

    - unwatch(expression:string) removes a watch

    - repl open the Node.js REPL with current context. Press Ctrl+C to exit the REPL.

    - bt backtrace, prints the call-stack

Let's look at a simple workflow. Assume we have the following piece of code that we want to debug. To prepare for debugging, we have already placed a debugger statement where we want to debug.

```
for (var index = 0; index < 10; index++) {
    var message = 'Loop ' + index;
    debugger;
    console.log(message);
}
```

In Listing 11-10, we launch this application in debug mode, add to watch a few variables we would like to observe (message and index), and then continue (c) to start it. The application will automatically break when the debugger statement is activated and print out the watched expressions. Then we continue until the next time a debugger statement occurs and again message and index print out. Finally, we quit the application/debugger.

Listing 11-10. Sample Debug Session of Debugging debugger/inspect.js

```
$ node debug inspect.js
< Debugger listening on port 5858
connecting to port 5858... ok
break in \code\chapter 11\debugger\inspect.js:1
> 1 for (var index = 0; index < 10; index++) {
  2     var message = 'Loop ' + index;
  3     debugger;
debug> watch('message')
debug> watch('index')
debug> c
break in \code\chapter 11\debugger\inspect.js:3
Watchers:
  0: message = "Loop 0"
  1: index = 0
```

```
 1 for (var index = 0; index < 10; index++) {
 2     var message = 'Loop ' + index;
> 3     debugger;
 4     console.log(message);
 5 }
debug> c
< Loop 0
break in \code\chapter 11\debugger\inspect.js:3
Watchers:
 0: message = "Loop 1"
 1: index = 1

 1 for (var index = 0; index < 10; index++) {
 2     var message = 'Loop ' + index;
> 3     debugger;
 4     console.log(message);
 5 }
debug> quit
```

The built-in debugger is not feature-heavy, but it's worthwhile for you to know that it's there if you need it. More importantly, it is written entirely in JavaScript (check additional resources at the end of this chapter for source code link) and basically communicates with V8 debugger using TCP, so it can lead you to some fun code exploration. This debugger is provided with Node.js to be a proof of concept so that the community can build on it, and it has.

Node-inspector

If all you need is a quick way to debug a Node.js application, we highly recommend node-inspector. Node-inspector is a tool dedicated solely to debugging Node.js applications. It is built on top of the chrome developer tools platform, so if you are used to debugging browser applications using chrome, you will feel right at home with it. First, you need to install it, which is easily done using npm install -g node-inspector.

To debug a script using node-inspector, you simply use node-debug instead of node. For example, to debug inspect.js, we would use the command node-debug inspect.js, as shown in Figure 11-1.

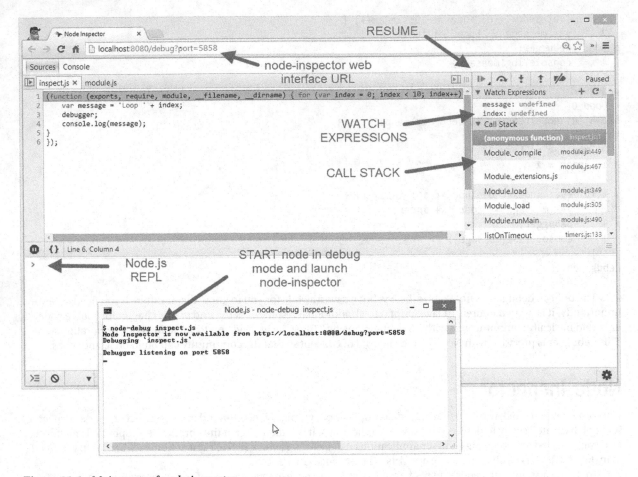

***Figure 11-1.** Main parts of node-inspector*

Running the application with `node-debug` will do the following:

- Start you application

- Pause at the first line

- Open up node-inspector in your default web browser (we highly recommend chrome)

The main portions of `node-inspector` are shown in Figure 11-1. Once you press the resume button (shown in Figure 11-1), the application will start until it hits a breakpoint (or a debugger statement).

You can double-click any item in the call stack to observe the state of various variables at the point before the function call was made. This is shown in Figure 11-2 to Figure 11-4 where we are debugging the code shown in Listing 11-11 and we inspect the state of the `index` variable at `foo` (Figure 11-2), `bar` (Figure 11-3), and the root (Figure 11-4) of the module.

Listing 11-11. debugger/stack.js

```javascript
function foo(index) {
    index++;
    debugger;
    console.log(index);
}
function bar(index) {
    index++;
    foo(index);
}
var index = 0
bar(0);
```

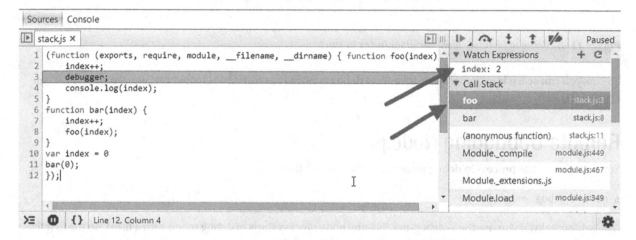

Figure 11-2. *Value of (module level variable)* ***index*** *in foo*

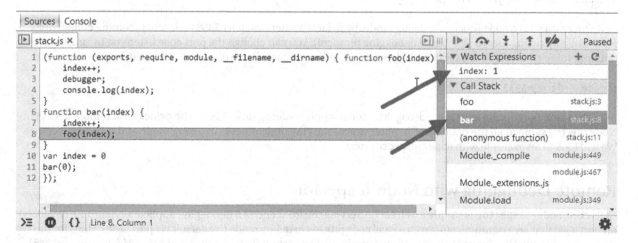

Figure 11-3. *Value of (module level variable)* ***index*** *in bar*

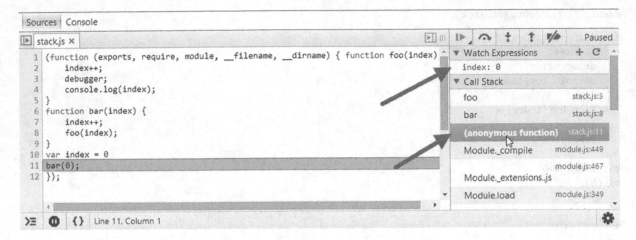

```
Sources | Console
▷ stack.js ×                                                          ▷| III   I▷  ⌒  ↓  ↑  I/►   Paused
 1 (function (exports, require, module, __filename, __dirname) { function foo(index)  ▼ Watch Expressions      + C
 2     index++;                                                                          index: 0
 3     debugger;                                                                        ▼ Call Stack
 4     console.log(index);                                                                foo                  stack.js:3
 5 }                                                                                      bar                  stack.js:8
 6 function bar(index) {                                                                  (anonymous function)  stack.js:11
 7     index++;                                                                           Module._compile      module.js:449
 8     foo(index);                                                                                             module.js:467
 9 }                                                                                      Module._extensions..js
10 var index = 0                                                                          Module.load          module.js:349
11 bar(0);
12 });
▷≡  ⓪  {}  Line 11, Column 1                                                                                        ⚙
```

Figure 11-4. *Value of (module level variable)* ***index*** *at start*

As you can see, it is extremely user-friendly to debug applications with node-inspector, and we encourage you give it a try.

Remote Debugging Node.js

You can start a node process in debug mode using the --debug flag:

```
$ node --debug yourfile.js
```

Additionally, if you use the --debug-brk flag, the node process starts in debug mode with a break on the first line waiting for a debugger to connect before it executes any JavaScript:

```
$ node --debug-brk yourfile.js
```

Once you start a node process in debug mode, by default it listens on port 5858 to accept incoming connections for debugging (using the V8 TCP based debugging protocol). You can change the port node listens on by passing an optional value to –debug. For example, the following node process will listen on port 3333 for a debugger to connect.

```
$ node --debug=3333 yourfile.js
```

The same port option exits for --debug-brk (for example, --debug-brk=3333). The principle of remote debugging Node.js is the same in all the debuggers. In other words, start the node process in debug mode and then connect to it. We will look at an example with node-inspector next.

Remote Debugging with Node-inspector

At its core, node-inspector is simply a web server serving the front end of a debugging application (chrome dev tools) on port 8080 that are communicating with a local node process in debug mode (by default via port 5858). Hints for this are provided in the URL for node-inspector we saw in the last section (http://localhost:8080/debug?port=5858).

Let's create a simple web application and see how we can debug it remotely. Listing 11-12 provides the code for a simple HTTP server same as we had in Chapter 6. Also shown is the output you get (Listing 11-13) when you start the server with the --debug flag.

Listing 11-12. debugger/server.js

```
var http = require('http');

var server = http.createServer(function (request, response) {
    console.log('request starting...');

    // respond
    response.write('hello client!');
    response.end();

});

server.listen(3000);
console.log('Server running at http://127.0.0.1:3000/');
```

Listing 11-13. Starting debugger/server.js in Debug Mode Ready for Remote Debugging

```
$ node --debug server.js
Debugger listening on port 5858
Server running at http://127.0.0.1:3000/
```

In the absence of an attached debugger, the --debug flag has almost no effect (only affects the performance a bit and allows remote control). So you can test the web server like you normally would (visit http://127.0.0.1:3000/ in the browser or use curl). Now let's launch node-inspector with a simple command, as shown in Listing 11-14. Also shown is the output as a result of the command.

Listing 11-14. Launching Node-inspector on Its Own for Remote Debugging

```
$ node-inspector
Node Inspector v0.7.4
Visit http://127.0.0.1:8080/debug?port=5858 to start debugging.
```

This automatically starts the node-inspector's HTTP server to serve the debug tools UI on localhost:8080. Now as soon as you open your browser of choice at `http://127.0.0.1:8080/debug?port=5858`, node-inspector will try to connect to the node V8 debugger on port 5858 *on the same machine* that is running the node-inspector server. This means that you just need to run node-inspector on the same machine as the debug mode (--debug) node process and you can visit `http://yourmachine:8080/debug?port=5858` from anywhere to debug it. The page returned from the node-inspector server is shown in Figure 11-5. This is a page you are already familiar with from node-debug.

Figure 11-5. *Inserting a breakpoint on a line*

Also we clicked the sidebar to place a breakpoint in our server code at the point before we send the response to the client. Now as soon as somebody visits yourmachine:3000, the callback to createServer is called and the breakpoint will be activated, at which point you can inspect various variables. An example where we examine the incoming request by hovering over the request variable is shown is Figure 11-6.

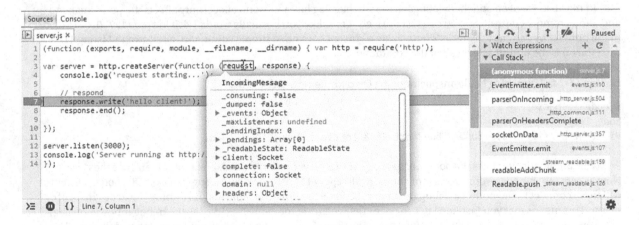

Figure 11-6. *Observing variables on hover when paused*

Note that the node-debug command we looked at in the previous section provided by node-inspector is simply an alias to the following:

- start node in debug mode with a break on the first line (node --debug-brk)
- start the node-inspector server
- open the node-inspector url in your default web browser

As soon as you close the node-inspector web application, the node process that is being debugged continues the same as it was before (like it does when there are no attached debuggers).

Node.js Configuration in WebStorm

We saw how to get started with WebStorm for Node.js development in Chapter 1. In particular, we covered how to open and create Node.js projects. Here we will explore its debugging setup a bit more. We've already provided a WebStorm project with the same `server.js` for you as we have been using in this chapter. This project is available under `code/chapter11/webstorm` folder. You might recall from Chapter 1, debugging a file is simply a matter of right clicking inside the file and selecting the debug option, as shown in Figure 11-7.

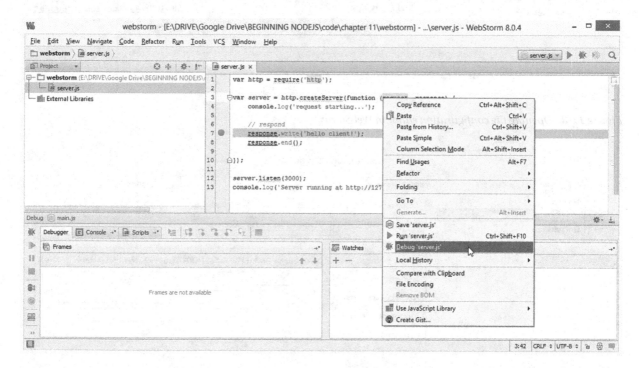

Figure 11-7. *Launching a debug session from WebStorm*

All of the node configuration options are available under the Run menu in the `Edit Configurations` option, as shown in Figure 11-8. Also shown in Figure 11-9 is the edit configurations dialog that opens up.

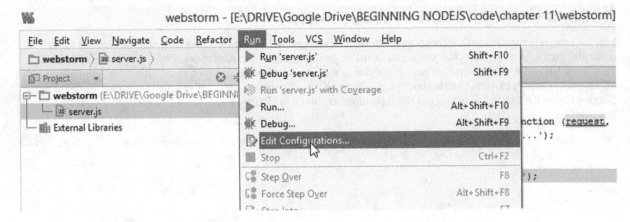

Figure 11-8. Opening the configuration editor in WebStorm

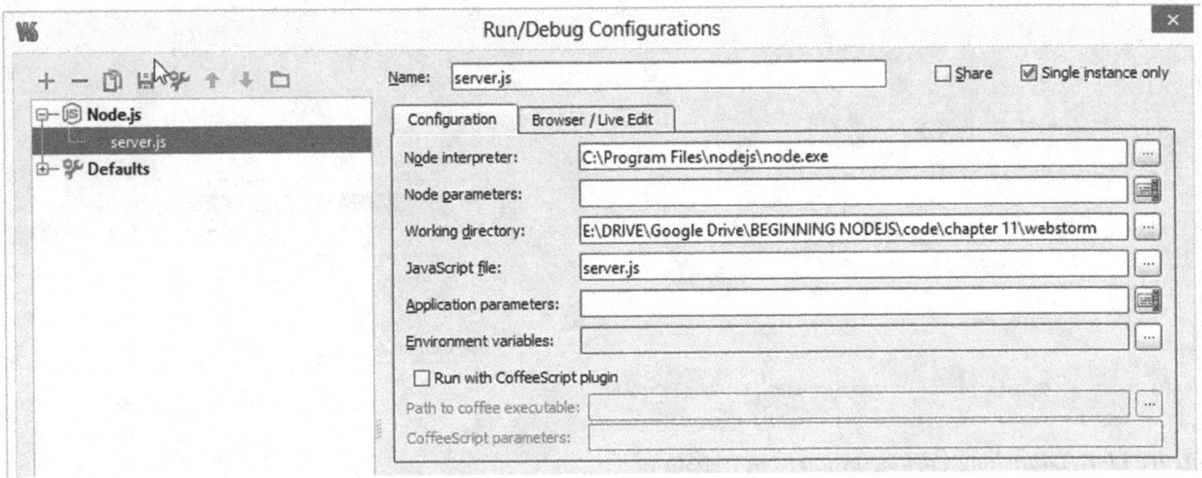

Figure 11-9. Run configuration options in WebStorm

You would provide parameters like `--harmony` using the Node parameters option. Each run configuration has the main JavaScript file that will be passed to node along with any arguments (Application Parameters) that you want passed to the JavaScript file. Based on this configuration, WebStorm *already* knows that to debug this file and you don't need to set anything else explicitly. In fact, if you start the debugging using "Debug server.js" option, as shown earlier, you can see (in Figure 11-10) that it selects a random port to start a debugging session in Node.js.

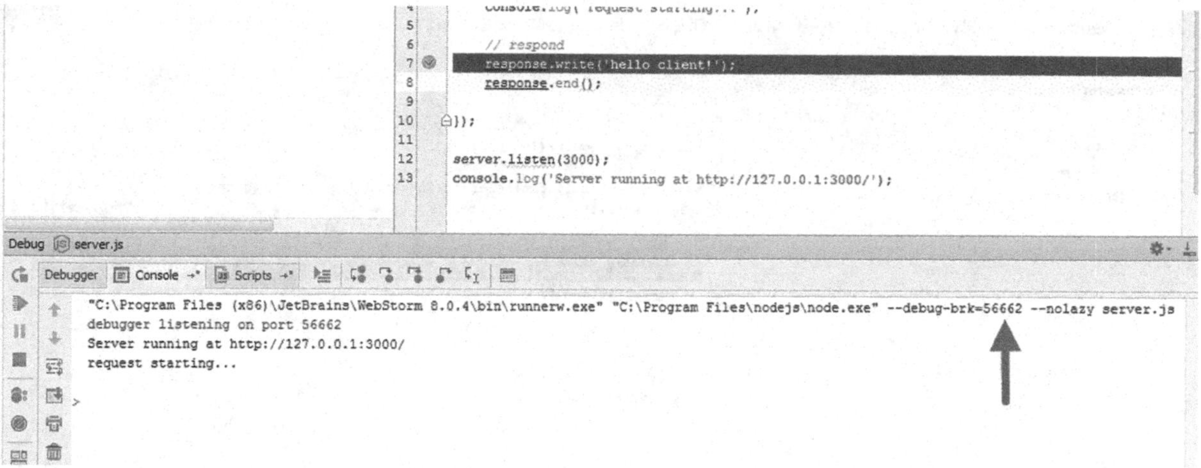

Figure 11-10. The random debug port displayed on the console at the start of a debug session

You can add a breakpoint on any line by clicking the sidebar (shown in Figure 11-11). Also WebStorm will pause if a debugger statement is found.

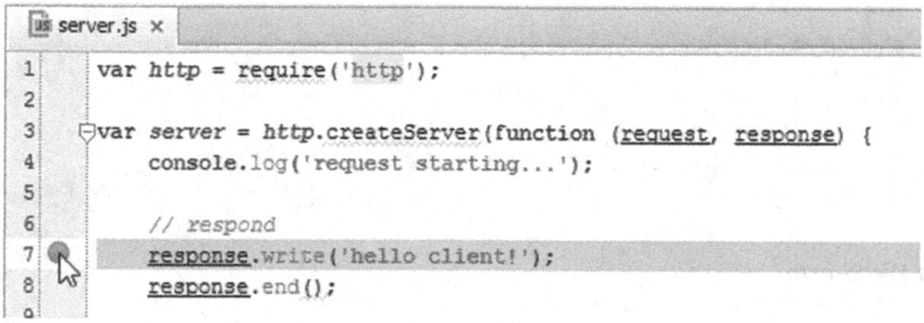

Figure 11-11. Setting a breakpoint in WebStorm

Once a breakpoint is activated (the one in Figure 11-11 can be triggered by a client requesting http://localhost:3000), we have the usual features you would expect from a good debugger (that is, a callstack that you can step through, local variables, watch window, and variable inspection on hover). These are shown in Figure 11-12.

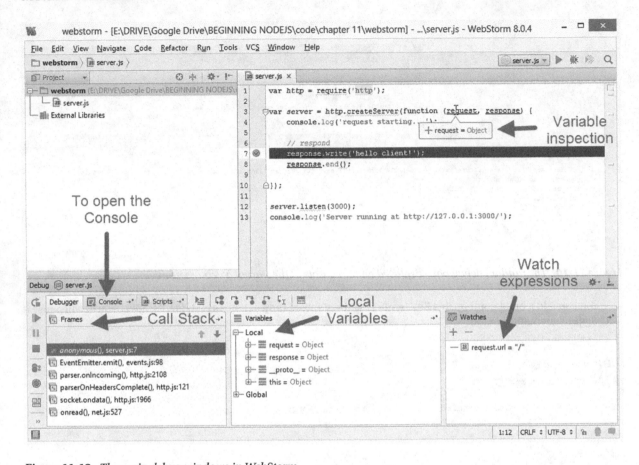

Figure 11-12. *The main debug windows in WebStorm*

You can even execute arbitrary JavaScript in the console. This can greatly improve your software development speed as you can test the code so that you know it gets you the desired outcome before you update the file.

Additional Resources

Information on Node's built-in debugger: `http://nodejs.org/api/debugger.html`
   Source code for Node's built-in debugger: `https://github.com/joyent/node/blob/master/lib/_debugger.js`

Summary

Node.js has excellent support for all the conventional techniques of debugging applications. We started with using the `console` and saw how it can help us make quick observations, do benchmarks, and print stack traces.

   Then we looked at Node.js debuggers, in particular `node-inspector` (free and open source) and WebStorm (a commercial, inexpensive, and very popular cross-platform IDE). In this chapter, we also saw how Node.js provides first-class support for remote debugging out of the box—something that is lacking in many other platforms.

   In the next chapter, we will look at writing tests for our applications so that bugs don't creep into our system.

CHAPTER 12

Testing

I never make stupid mistakes. Only very, very clever ones.

—John Peel

Testing is an integral part of any successful software development life cycle. It ensures that defects are noticed as early as possible. It also prevents feature regressions where things you know to work right now can break because of new code. In this chapter, we will look at various libraries that help test Node.js applications.

Assert

Node.js comes with `assert` as a core module, which you use simply as `require('assert')`. The main objective of `assert` is to provide you with simple logic checks to `throw` errors based on invalid situations. Consider the simple `assert.equal` function tested in a node REPL session in Listing 12-1.

Listing 12-1. Sample Session Demonstrating Assert

```
$ node
> assert.equal(0,0);
undefined
> assert.equal(0,1);
AssertionError: 0 == 1
    at repl:1:8
    at REPLServer.self.eval (repl.js:110:21)
    ... truncated ...
    at ReadStream.onkeypress (readline.js:99:10)
> assert.equal(0,1,"numbers to not match");
AssertionError: numbers to not match
    at repl:1:8
    at REPLServer.self.eval (repl.js:110:21)
    ... truncated ...
    at ReadStream.onkeypress (readline.js:99:10)
```

If the two values passed to `assert.equal` are equal, then the assertion has no effect. However, if they are not equal, an `AssertionError` is thrown. You can optionally also pass in a message to display if the values are not equal. Using custom messages will help you track down the cause of the `AssertionError` faster since you can use a more meaningful message that explains the objective (in other words, the reason for the assertion).

241

■ **Note** Core modules like `assert` and `fs` are available by default in the node REPL. For your code, you will need to use require('assert') as you are already used to doing by now.

Assert is great for simple unit tests. Additionally, it can be used with unit-testing frameworks such as mocha, which we will look at later in this chapter.

As an example of using `assert`, consider a module containing a simple class `List` that manages a list of items. Each item has a unique identifier (stored in member `id`). This class implementation is shown in Listing 12-2.

Listing 12-2. assert/list.js

```javascript
function List() {
    this.items = [];
}
List.prototype.count = function () {
    return this.items.length;
}
List.prototype.add = function (item) {
    if (!item.id) throw new Error('item must have id');
    this.items.push(item);
}
List.prototype.remove = function (id) {
    this.items = this.items.filter(function (item) { item.id !== id });
}
List.prototype.clear = function () {
    this.items = [];
}
List.prototype.getIds = function () {
    return this.items.map(function (item) {
        return item.id;
    });
}
List.prototype.get = function (id) {
    return this.items.filter(function (item) { return item.id == id })[0];
}

module.exports = List;
```

The code is fairly self-explanatory. The `List` class manages a list of arbitrary `items` (as long as each item has an `id`). Let's write a test file (`list.test.js`) to test all of the features of this class using `assert` one by one, starting with count. (See Listing 12-3.)

Listing 12-3. Start from assert/list.test.js

```javascript
var assert = require('assert');

var List = require('./list');
var list = new List();

console.log('testing list.count');
assert.equal(list.count(), 0);
```

If, at the beginning, the count of the items is not zero (because of some bug in our code), then `assert.equal` will throw an error and we will know that the behavior "*it should start with a list of zero items OR count should return the* **actual** *count of items*" is broken. Based on this `AssertionError`, you will be able to track down and investigate broken behavior before it becomes a problem.

Similarly, as an example, we can do some basic testing for all the other members of `List` as well. (See Listing 12-4.)

Listing 12-4. Remaining Code from assert/list.test.js

```
console.log('testing list.add');
list.add({
    id: 'someId',
    value: 'some value'
});
assert.equal(list.count(), 1);

console.log('testing list.clear');
list.clear();
assert.equal(list.count(), 0);

console.log('testing list.getIds');
list.add({
    id: 'someId',
    value: 'some value'
});
assert.equal(list.getIds()[0], 'someId');
list.clear();

console.log('testing list.remove');
list.add({
    id: 'someId',
    value: 'some value'
});
list.remove('someId');
assert.equal(list.count(), 0);

console.log('testing list.get');
list.add({
    id: 'someId',
    value: 'some value'
});
assert.equal(list.get('someId').value, 'some value');
list.clear();

console.log('testing list.add throws an error on invalid value');
assert.throws(function () {
    list.add({
        value: 'some value'
    })
},
function (err) {
    return (err instanceof Error)
    && (err.message == 'item must have id')
});
```

Most of these tests are pretty straightforward. We do an action and assert that it results in the changes that we need. The only tricky one is assert.throws. It takes two functions—one function to carry out an action and a second validation function that is called with the error thrown from the first function. The validation function should return true if the error it received as an argument meets its expectations. Here we try to add an item without an id and expect the error thrown from list.add to be of type Error and have the message 'item must have id'.

Almost all of the member functions in assert take an optional message as a last argument (for example, assert.throws(block, [errorValidator], [message])), which you can use to provide a better development/debugging experience. Assert has a number of other useful functions for doing checks (for example, strictEqual, notEqual, deepEqual) and throwing AssertionError if the check fails.

From a maintainability and usability point of view, there are quite a few issues with these tests. For example, if an AssertionError occurs, we are relying on the console.log preceding the test to tell us which test was running (and hence failed). Also we do a lot of setup (adding an item) and teardown (removing an item) in each of the tests. Another issue is that the test suite exits on the first failing test. It would be nicer if we could be told all the tests that are broken in a single run so have a clearer idea of how much our code has regressed (impact analysis). We could write the logic for all of these things ourselves. However, advanced testing frameworks provide these and other features. We will look at one such framework, mocha, next.

Mocha

From the web site (http://mochajs.org/): "Mocha is a feature-rich JavaScript test framework running on node.js and the browser, making asynchronous testing simple and fun." It is best to think of mocha as a test runner (the mocha executable) as well as test API (for example, describe, it, beforeEach functions). We will look at both of these in this section. Quite a few concepts of mocha (such as the concept of a *suite* and *spec*) are common to other JavaScript frameworks (for example, Jasmine http://jasmine.github.io/). We will discuss these concepts as well.

Installing Mocha

You install the mocha executable from NPM:

```
$ npm install -g mocha
```

Once you do this, the mocha executable becomes available on your system path. Any Node.js file you run using mocha (instead of node) will have access to the mocha API, which we will look at next.

Creating and Running a Basic Test

The two most important functions in the mocha API are describe and it. The describe function is used to encapsulate a *test suite*, which is quite simply a collection of tests. How you decide what goes in a suite is up to you. A common choice on grouping would be based on some functional boundary. For example, tests for a single JavaScript class would normally all go in a single suite.

The it function encapsulates a single test (also called a *spec*). Both the describe and the it functions take a string as a first argument (which is displayed on the console when you run the tests) and a function as a second argument (this is the callback executed when mocha runs the test). Let's look at an example of a simple test suite. Note that it is a normal Node.js file. For example, we can require('assert') like any other file, with just a few global functions (describe and it) added by mocha, as shown in Listing 12-5.

Listing 12-5. mocha/basic.js

```javascript
var assert = require("assert");

describe('our test suite', function () {

    it('should pass this test', function () {
        assert.equal(1, 1, '1 should be equal to 1');
    });

    it('should fail this test', function () {
        assert.equal(1, 0, '1 should be equal to 0');
    });

});
```

Internally, the describe and the it functions basically just register callbacks with mocha that mocha will run in a safe environment. Mocha will execute all the it callbacks, catching all the exceptions (if any) from individual tests (considered a test failure) and logging them for you. In Listing 12-6, we run this test suite by passing it to mocha.

Listing 12-6. Sample Run of mocha/basic.js

```
$ mocha basic.js

  our test suite
    √ should pass this test
    1) should fail this test

  1 passing (7ms)
  1 failing

  1) our test suite should fail this test:
    AssertionError: 1 should be equal to 0
      at Context.<anonymous> (.\mochabasic\basic.js:10:16)
      at callFn (C:\Users\bas\AppData\Roaming\npm\node_modules\mocha\lib\runnable.js:249:21)
      at Test.Runnable.run (.\mocha\lib\runnable.js:242:7)
      at Runner.runTest (.\mocha\lib\runner.js:373:10)
      at .\mocha\lib\runner.js:451:12
      at next (.\mocha\lib\runner.js:298:14)
      at .\mocha\lib\runner.js:308:7
      at next (.\mocha\lib\runner.js:246:23)
      at Object._onImmediate (.\mocha\lib\runner.js:275:5)
      at processImmediate [as _immediateCallback] (timers.js:330:15)
```

We intentionally wrote one test that will always succeed and one test that will always fail. The default reporter used by mocha simply lists each suite description followed by a (√) against every test that succeeded and an incrementing number (only 1 in our case) to indicate the failing tests. At the bottom, it lists the stack trace for every test that failed.

As you can see, getting started with mocha is extremely easy. Just author a new file, put in a few describes and it blocks, and execute this file with mocha.

Mocha API

We've already looked at the describe and it functions. The additional mocha API is quite small (simple but powerful). It can be categorized into hooks and exclusive testing functions.

Hooks

As we mentioned earlier in the chapter, a good test framework should simplify test setup and teardown. For example, when testing our List class, our setup (. adding an item) and teardown (removing an item) was duplicated for each of the tests.

Mocha provides hook functions before(), after(), beforeEach(), and afterEach(), which can be used to simplify our test setup and teardown significantly. All of these functions simply take a callback. This callback is called at the correct instant (hook) when in a test suite (a describe callback). These hook moments are described below with the names pretty much giving away the meaning:

- before: executes the registered callback before it runs the first test (the first it callback)

- after: executes the callback after it runs the last test

- beforeEach: executes the callback before executing *each* test

- afterEach: executes the callback before executing *each* test

As a simple example of using these hooks, consider the following suite where we simply increment a number before we run each test. The test depends upon this number having been incremented to succeed. (See Listings 12-7 and 12-8.)

Listing 12-7. mocha/hooks.js

```
var assert = require("assert");

describe('our test suite', function () {

    var testExecuting = 0;
    beforeEach(function () {
        testExecuting++;
    });

    it('test 1', function () {
        assert.equal(1, 1, 'This should be test 1');
    });

    it('test 2', function () {
        assert.equal(2, 2, 'This should be test 2');
    });
});
```

Listing 12-8. Sample Run of mocha/hooks.js

```
$ mocha hooks.js

  our test suite
    √ test 1
    √ test 2

  2 passing (6ms)
```

This test also demonstrates an important (intentional) feature of mocha. *All tests run in the sequence* that it is called from a describe block. This makes it easy for you argue about the flow of your test suite and makes errors more deterministic.

Also worth mentioning is the fact that mocha will also list out and report any errors (unhandled exceptions) in these hooks separately from the test.

Single Test Runs and Exclusions

The describe and the it functions both have member functions skip and only. If you only want to run one test suite (describe) while you are working on large sets of specs, you can force mocha to only run one suite by simply appending `.only` to the describe (in other words, use describe.only instead of describe). For example, in Listing 12-9, only the first describe will execute.

Listing 12-9. mocha/only.js

```
describe.only('first', function () {
    it('test 1', function () {
    });
});

describe('second', function () {
    it('test 1', function () {
    });
});
```

Similarly, you can use it.only to only run one test. Note that at one time you can only have one usage of 'only' in *all your tests and suites combined*.

If you simply want to exclude a few tests from running (for example, because they are failing and you don't want to investigate why at the moment), use skip, which also exists for describe and it. For example, the second test suite is skipped in the code in Listing 12-10.

Listing 12-10. mocha/skip.js

```
describe('first', function () {
    it('test 1', function () {
    });
});

describe.skip('second', function () {
    it('test 1', function () {
    });
});

describe('third', function () {
    it('test 1', function () {
    });
});
```

You can skip as many describe / it calls as you like. Skip is better than commenting out a test block since you might forget to uncomment the block. But with a skip, mocha will tell you that you have skipped something every time you run it, as shown in Listing 12-11.

Listing 12-11. Sample Run of mocha/skip.js

```
$ mocha skip.js

  first
    √ test 1

  second
    - test 1

  third
    √ test 1

  2 passing (7ms)
  1 pending
```

Async Testing

In its tag line, mocha claims that it "mak[es] asynchronous testing simple and fun." Just because a callback exits doesn't mean that the async work (and therefore the test) is over. For example, consider the test in Listing 12-12 where we test a simulated async operation that returns an error.

Listing 12-12. mocha/asyncbad.js

```
function simulateAsync(cb) {
    setTimeout(function () {
        cb(new Error('This async task will fail'));
    }, 500);
}

describe('our test suite', function () {

    it('test simulateAsync', function () {
        simulateAsync(function (err) {
            if (err) throw err;
        });
    });

});
```

However, since the async operation doesn't take place until after the call to its callback completes, mocha considers the test a success, as shown in Listing 12-13.

Listing 12-13. Sample Run of mocha/asyncbad.js Showing That Tests Pass Incorrectly

```
$ mocha asyncbad.js

  our test suite
    √ test simulateAsync

  1 passing (5ms)
```

To make your test asynchronous, all you need to do is add an argument (conventionally called done) to your it function. Now mocha will wait for the test until done is called. If you call done with an error object, then the test is considered a failure (null is okay). Otherwise, it is considered a success. This is demonstrated in the suite in Listing 12-14 where we have a failing and passing async test. A sample run is demonstrated in Listing 12-15.

Listing 12-14. mocha/asyncgood.js

```
describe('our test suite', function () {

    it('this should pass', function (done) {
        setTimeout(function () {
            done(); // same as done(null);
        }, 500);
    });

    it('this should fail', function (done) {
        setTimeout(function () {
            done(new Error('fail'));
        }, 500);
    });

});
```

Listing 12-15. Sample Run of mocha/syncgood.js

```
$ mocha asyncgood.js

  our test suite
    √ this should pass (501ms)
    1) this should fail

  1 passing (1s)
  1 failing

  1) our test suite this should fail:
     Error: fail
       at null._onTimeout (.\mochabasic\asyncgood.js:11:18)
       at Timer.listOnTimeout [as ontimeout] (timers.js:110:15)
```

The same optional done argument exists for all of the hooks (before, after, beforeEach, afterEach functions) so they can be asynchronous as well.

As we said before, executing tests in order makes them easier to reason about. This rule is followed for async tests as well. Mocha will not execute the next test unless the previous one completes. Because async operations might hang, mocha takes a command line flag (--timeout or -t for short) to set a global timeout for all the tests. For example, --timeout 1000 will set a one-second timeout for each test. If a test does not complete in the specified time, it is considered to fail and mocha will move on the next test (if any). You can optionally change a timeout for an individual test by calling `this.timeout(msValue)` within the it callback.

249

Testing Promises

Mocha has excellent support for promises. Instead of using a `done` argument, you can simply return a promise from your test or any of the hooks. Mocha will wait until the promise settles. If it gets fulfilled, the test/hook succeeds. Similarly, if it is rejected, the corresponding test/hook will fail. This is shown in Listing 12-16.

Listing 12-16. mocha/asyncpromise.js

```javascript
var Q = require('q');

describe('our test suite', function () {

    it('this should pass', function () {
        return Q.when('pass');
    });

    it('this should fail', function () {
        return Q.reject(new Error('fail'));
    });

});
```

Just one more reason to use promises in your codebase.

Mocha Command Line Options

As we said earlier, mocha is split between an API and an executable. We've seen the API and we've seen simple usage of the mocha executable (which simply executes a Node.js file). Among the command line options for mocha, we have already mentioned the `--timeout` flag used to increase the duration for which mocha will wait on an asynchronous test to settle. Now let's look at other options we feel will be the most helpful to you.

Specify Files to Test

Mocha can take not only individual files (like we have been giving it on the command line), but it can also take file globs (pattern matching arguments). If you don't provide a file argument, by default, the mocha executable will run all the JavaScript files in the `'./test'` folder (that is, the test folder in the current working directory). You can optionally specify the file pattern on the command line. In this code snippet, we ask it to run all the JavaScript files in mytestdir:

```
mocha "./mytestdir/*.js"
```

Earlier we showed the `'only'` member function of describe and it. We recommend avoid doing this as you need to be careful to revert this before you commit your code. Otherwise, automated deployment systems could potentially run only one suite (or test) and think that all tests are green. Instead, use the `'-g'` (short for `--grep`) command line flag to specify a regular expression match for the tests you want to run. For example, the following will only run tests that contain the phrase my awesome test:

```
mocha -g "my awesome test"
```

Debugging Mocha Tests

The mocha executable provides the command line flags --debug and --debug-brk that behave similarly to the node --debug and --debug-brk flags we saw in Chapter 11. The flags are actually just passed to the underlying node process that mocha starts so you can attach a debugger to localhost (port 5858 by default, if you recall). This means there is nothing special to debugging tests started with mocha and it is pretty much same as what you learned in the previous chapter.

The simplest workflow is to start your tests with mocha --debug-brk to begin a paused node process. Then launch node-inspector (by simply running it on the command line like we did in Chapter 11) to start the web server and visit http://localhost:8080/debug?port=5858 to debug the paused node process that mocha starts.

One thing to be aware of is that if you put a breakpoint in an async test, it will probably cause it to time out. So, actually, you will most commonly run mocha --debug-brk -t=100000 -g "my awesome test". Also, recall the debugger keyword, which will still work (for obvious reasons).

Chai

Good tests follow the **AAA** pattern:

- **Arrange** all the necessary preconditions and inputs.
- **Act** using the object / method under test.
- **Assert** that the expected results have occurred.

We've already seen the core Node.js assert module, which provides a basic set of functions for simple assertions. Chai is a library (npm install chai) that provides you with additional assertion functions.

Additional Assertions in Chai

The member function list in require('chai').assert is quite large. The additional functions provided by chai mostly focus on stronger type checks (for example, isNull/isNotNull, isDefined/isUndefined, and isFunction/isNotFunction). Usage of one of these is demonstrated in Listing 12-17.

Listing 12-17. Sample Session Demonstrating chai.assert

```
$ node
> var assert = require('chai').assert;
undefined
> assert.isNull(null,'Null should be null');
undefined
> assert.isNull(undefined,'undefined should be null');
AssertionError: undefined should be null: expected undefined to equal null
```

In addition to these functions, the node's core assert functions are duplicated in require('chai').assert so you only have one assert module loaded.

Chai Plug-ins

Another advantage of chai is that it provides a plug-in framework for others to easily add additional assertions to. For example, chai-datetime plug-in (npm install chai-datetime) provides several assertions that make comparing dates easy. Example functions are equalTime, beforeTime, afterTime, equalDate, beforeDate, and afterDate.

To use a chai plug-in, you call the chai.use function to register it with chai. An example with chai-datetime is demonstrated in Listing 12-18.

Listing 12-18. Sample Session Demonstrating Using a Chai Plug-in

```
$ node
> var chai = require('chai');
> chai.use(require('chai-datetime'));
> var t1 = new Date();
> chai.assert.equalTime(t1,t1);
> chai.assert.equalTime(t1,new Date());
AssertionError: expected Thu Aug 14 2014 19:30:40 GMT+1000 (AUS Eastern Standard Time) to equal Thu
Aug 14 2014 19:31:22 GMT+1000 (AUS Eastern Standard Time)
    at Function.assert.equalTime (.\node_modules\chai-datetime\chai-datetime.js:147:40)
    at repl:1:13
    at REPLServer.self.eval (repl.js:110:21)
    at repl.js:249:20
```

BDD Style Assertions

Chai also provides BDD (behavior-driven development) style assertions. Here are a few reasons why this is worth your consideration (examples to follow):

- These are easily chainable.

- These read in better *English*, so the test code is closer to the **behavior** that you are trying to test.

These are demonstrated in the code sample in Listing 12-19.

Listing 12-19. chai/chain.js

```
var expect = require('chai').expect;
var assert = require('chai').assert;

// Some variable to assert on
var beverages = { tea: ['chai', 'matcha', 'oolong'] };

// assert
assert.lengthOf(beverages.tea, 3);
// BDD
expect(beverages).to.have.property('tea').with.length(3);
// same as
expect(beverages).property('tea').length(3);
```

Note that chai provides a number of useful properties that, by default, have no effect (`to, have, with` in our example). These exist to make it easier to read the specification.

We recommend that you use whatever style feels more natural to you and *your team*. With chai *you* have the option. Also, you might be more familiar with this format if you are coming from other languages where such format is common such as Ruby (`RSpec`).

Additional Resources

Assert API documentation: `http://nodejs.org/api/assert.html`

Mocha documentation: `http://visionmedia.github.io/mocha/`

Chai plug-ins: `http://chaijs.com/plugins`

At the start of this chapter, we saw how easy it is to write quick and simple unit tests using the core `assert` module. We followed this by a discussion of `mocha` (a testing framework) and `chai` (an assertion framework). As usual, instead of listing all the API details for all the libraries, we have focused on the why and the general how, providing you with a deeper understanding of the concepts so that you can jump right in and explore the APIs as you use them.

The next chapter is the last in the book. We will look at deploying and sharing our web applications with the world.

CHAPTER 13

■ ■ ■

Deployment and Scalability

It's better to have infinite scalability and not need it than to need infinite scalability and not have it.

—Andrew Clay Shafer

We will start this chapter by looking at ways to ensure the stability of our web server. The objective here is to automatically re-spawn our server so that we continue responding to web requests even if there were some unhandled errors that caused our Node.js server to crash.

Next, we will discuss how we can easily scale our application to utilize all the CPU cores of a multi-core single machine. We will follow this with a guide to deploying our application on Amazon Web Services (AWS). To make sure that changing AWS screens does not decrease the usefulness of this guide, we will present the concepts in isolation before doing a step-by-step guide.

Ensuring Uptime

Like all application platforms, it is not difficult to imagine our server raising an unhandled error and crashing. For example, in Listing 13-1, the Node.js server will only serve the first request and crash due to a programming mistake.

Listing 13-1. uptime/crash.js

```
var http = require('http');
http.createServer(function (req, res) {
    res.write('Hello\n');
    res.foo.bar; // Programming error. Tried to read property 'bar' on an undefined member 'foo'
    res.end('World!');
}).listen(3000);
console.log("Server running on http://localhost:3000");
```

If you run this server, the first client request will result in an error and the client connection will be dropped. After that, no more client requests will be processed, as shown in Listing 13-2.

Listing 13-2. Sample Client Requests with uptime/crash.js

```
$ curl localhost:3000
Hello
curl: (56) Recv failure: Connection was reset

$ curl localhost:3000
curl: (7) Failed connect to localhost:3000; No error
```

Such programming errors can be handled quite gracefully with something like Connect and ExpressJS, which we have already looked at (Chapters 6 and 7). This is because they offer a simple way to add an error handler middleware. This error handler middleware limits the scope of the error to a single client request. For example, the following server, despite giving an error on *each* request (same error as previous example), will gracefully respond to the request and additionally continue to service future client requests. (See Listings 13-3 and 13-4.)

Listing 13-3. uptime/graceful.js

```
var express = require('express');
express()
    .use(function (req, res, next) {
        res.write('Hello\n');
        // Programming error. Tried to read property 'bar' on an undefined member 'foo'
        res.foo.bar;
        res.end('World!');
    })
    .use(function (err, req, res, next) {
        console.log('Error in server', err);
        res.end('Error!');
    })
    .listen(3000);
console.log("Server running on http://localhost:3000");
```

Listing 13-4. Sample Client Requests with uptime/graceful.js

```
$ curl localhost:3000
Hello
Error!
$ curl localhost:3000
Hello
Error!
```

This is useful for cases where the error is only a rare occurrence. Using an error middleware, it can be logged and the server can continue to service cases where the error path isn't triggered.

Nonetheless, there might be other errors that can take the server down, such as errors within ExpressJS itself. The situation is slightly dire in Node.js (compared to traditional servers) because everything is handled on a single JavaScript thread. The reason behind this single-threaded nature, of course, is performance. In traditional systems, requests are handled on a thread-pool thread. That means that if something bad happens in a thread, the thread can be discarded and a new thread allocated without taking the whole server down. In Node.js, however, since it's single-threaded, we need to take the Node.js process down and restart it. This is exactly what applications like forever do.

Using Forever

Forever is available as an NPM package (npm install -g forever). It is a simple command line tool for ensuring that a given script runs continuously (that is, forever). After you install forever, you get access to the forever executable. You can ask it to start any command (not just Node.js scripts) using the -c command line flag. Let's run the crashing server script (from Listing 13-1) using forever (shown in Listing 13-5).

Listing 13-5. Starting uptime/crash.js with Forever as a Custom Command

```
$ forever -c node crash.js
warn:    --minUptime not set. Defaulting to: 1000ms
warn:    --spinSleepTime not set. Your script will exit if it does not stay up for at least 1000ms
Server running on http://localhost:3000
```

Now if a client makes an HTTP request, even though the server will crash, it will be restarted so that future requests can (potentially) succeed, as shown in Listing 13-6.

Listing 13-6. Sample Client Requests When Running uptime/crash.js with Forever

```
$ curl localhost:3000
Hello
curl: (56) Recv failure: Connection was reset

$ curl localhost:3000
Hello
curl: (56) Recv failure: Connection was reset
```

For most purposes, using forever really is that simple. Note that it is always better to try and handle as many errors as possible and only use forever in the background as a backup for the unexpected. If you use forever as your main error-handling strategy, the server performance will be horrible.

Node.js Clustering

As you know, Node.js is single-threaded, which means it is optimized for a single processor. However, it is not difficult to make our application utilize all the CPU cores available to us on a multi-core system. This is made simple for an HTTP server thanks to the clustering API, which is a part of core Node.js. We simply use it via require('cluster').

Other platforms have multi-threaded servers. Since a single Node.js process only has a single thread, we effectively need to look at multi-process servers. The main issue is that only a single process is allowed to listen on a particular port by the operating system. Otherwise, the OS would not know which process should get the packet received on a particular port. Therefore, we need a design where one process is the master (and actually listens on the TCP/IP port), and it spawns child processes and distributes the received HTTP traffic between them. This is exactly what the cluster module does.

Spawning Workers

When you run a script that uses the cluster module, it will, by default, start in master mode:

```
var cluster = require('cluster');
console.log(cluster.isMaster); // true
```

To start a new worker process (a child process) with the *same* script as the one that is currently executing, you simply call cluster.fork, demonstrated in the previous code snippet. If the script is running in master mode, we get a Node.js process running the same script in worker mode. This is shown in Listings 13-7 and 13-8.

Listing 13-7. cluster/fork.js

```
var cluster = require('cluster');
if (cluster.isMaster) {
    console.log("Starting a worker");
    cluster.fork();
} else {
    console.log("Worker started");
    process.exit();
}
```

Listing 13-8. Sample Session Running cluster/fork.js

```
$ node fork.js
Starting a worker
Worker started
```

In Listing 13-7, once we are running as a worker, we log to the console and just exit. The output from this sample is demonstrated in Listing 13-8.

The objective of spawning workers is that each worker does the heavy lifting of responding to HTTP requests, while the master simply orchestrates this workflow.

Note that since the script is re-executed for each new worker, you have no shared memory and data structures. Therefore, you don't need to handle the complexity of locking shared memory to prevent un-deterministic mutation by different worker processes. All communication must take place via events that we will see later in this section.

The Ideal Worker Count

Since workers do the heavy lifting, ideally you want workers equal to the number of CPUs you have on your system. Assuming that each worker process, with its single JavaScript thread, is able to fully utilize a CPU, this is the maximum performance you can drive from a system using Node.js.

Determining the number for CPUs is trivial, thanks to the core os module's cpus function. This is demonstrated in Listing 13-9, where we fork the ideal number of worker processes.

Listing 13-9. cluster/cpus.js

```
var cluster = require('cluster');
var numCPUs = require('os').cpus().length;

if (cluster.isMaster) {
    // Fork workers
    for (var i = 0; i < numCPUs; i++) {
        console.log("Starting a worker");
        cluster.fork();
    }

    // Listen to any worker exiting
    cluster.on('exit', function (worker, code, signal) {
        console.log('worker ' + worker.process.pid + ' exited');
    });
} else {
    console.log("Worker started");
    process.exit();
}
```

Also demonstrated in this example, the cluster.on event subscription mechanism allows us to manage started workers in the master using events.

Handling HTTP Requests in Workers

If any worker calls the server.listen function, cluster serializes the arguments and passes the request to the master process. If the master process already has a listening server matching the worker's requirement (port), then it passes the handle to the worker. Otherwise, the master creates a listening server with those requirements and then passes the handle to the worker.

From the code perspective, the worker code remains unchanged from what you already know, that is, something as simple as http.createServer().listen. All of this complexity of the master actually doing the listening and distributing the request load to the workers is handled for you by the cluster module. Sharing the HTTP load between workers is demonstrated in Listing 13-10.

Listing 13-10. cluster/http.js

```
var cluster = require('cluster');
var http = require('http');
var numCPUs = require('os').cpus().length;

if (cluster.isMaster) {
    // Fork workers
    for (var i = 0; i < numCPUs; i++) {
        var worker = cluster.fork();
        console.log("Started a worker with pid: " + worker.process.pid);
    }

    // Listen to worker exiting
    cluster.on('exit', function (worker, code, signal) {
        console.log('worker ' + worker.process.pid + ' exited');
    });
} else {
    // Workers can share any TCP connection
    http.createServer(function (req, res) {
        res.writeHead(200);
        res.end("Hello world from worker: " + cluster.worker.process.pid);
    }).listen(3000);
}
```

Communicating with the Master

As we stated earlier, there is no shared JavaScript state between workers. All information sharing must take place with events. You can send a data structure to the master using process.send from the worker. You can receive such a data structure in the master simply by subscribing to the worker's 'message' event. In the sample in Listing 13-11, we send a simple string to the master. A sample run is presented in Listing 13-12.

Listing 13-11. cluster/message.js

```
var cluster = require('cluster');
if (cluster.isMaster) {
    var worker = cluster.fork();
    worker.on('message', function(msg) {
        console.log('Message received from worker:', msg);
    })
} else {
    console.log('Worker started');
    process.send('Hello world!');
    process.exit();
}
```

Listing 13-12. Sample Output from message.js

```
$ node message.js
Worker started
Message received from worker: Hello world!
```

As we have demonstrated, starting multiple Node.js HTTP processes to fully utilize the system resources is trivial. However, you are generally better off deploying multiple servers, each with a single CPU instead of a single server with multiple CPUs. Then you would distribute the load via a traditional load balancer, such as a reverse proxy like nginx (http://nginx.org/en/docs/http/load_balancing.html). It is still comforting to know that single server clustering is supported by Node.js.

Core AWS Concepts
Why Amazon Web Services

There are a lot of cloud providers out there, but we choose AWS for good reason. It is by far the most popular, and it has the greatest number of resources available at its disposal. Also, you will find plenty of help online for any issues that you might run into, and the concepts you learn from AWS are easily transferrable to other cloud providers.

AWS is free for one year when you start. Most AWS features at a reasonable scale are free for one year after you sign up. This means that you can test your application without paying any fee. After you sign up, the first thing you should do is log on the AWS console (https://console.aws.amazon.com/).

AWS Console

The AWS console is the single launching point for provisioning and managing your usage of various AWS products. At any point in the console, you have the choice of picking an availability zone, as shown in Figure 13-1. Here you would choose the region of the world you are developing your software for (we selected "Sydney" for this). Also highlighted in the figure is the EC2 service. EC2 is arguably the most fundamental AWS service you need to use for a Node.js deployment and will be discussed shortly.

Figure 13-1. AWS console

Clicking any of these services will take you to that service's dashboard. For now, jump into the EC2 dashboard, which is shown in Figure 13-2.

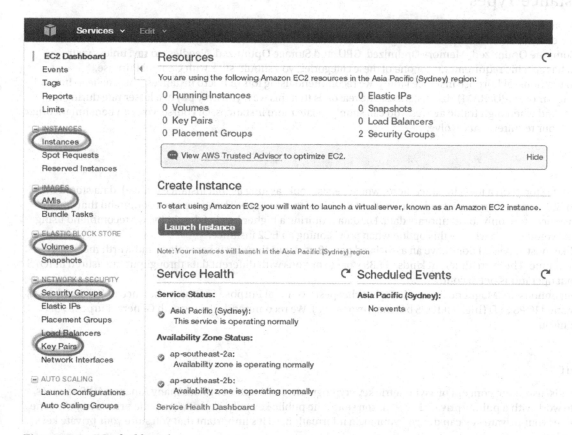

Figure 13-2. EC2 dashboard

The important sections of the EC2 dashboard are highlighted and the related concepts are presented next.

EC2

Elastic Compute Cloud (EC2) is a service to launch virtual machines hosted by Amazon. A virtual machine in this context is a single, isolated computer running on Amazon infrastructure. The initial contents of the virtual machine are driven by an Amazon Machine Image (AMI). We will be using the Amazon Linux AMI with EBS-backed storage. Concepts regarding these are explained next.

Which EC2 AMI?

Amazon Web Services provides ongoing security and maintenance updates to all instances running the Amazon Linux AMI, so this is the one we recommend. Anything else and you will need to be more hands-on with ensuring the integrity and security of your system. We would rather let Amazon deal with it for us. Another advantage of using some form of a Linux distribution is that it allows you to easily migrate to other cloud providers since more providers offer Linux compared to Windows.

One thing worth mentioning is that the default user for Amazon Linux is `ec2-user`. We will need this username to connect to our instance.

EC2 Instance Types

The EC2 instance type determines the quantity of CPU, RAM, and type of disk storage available to the VM (virtual machine) when it starts. These types are categorized into instance families. Currently, these families are General Purpose, Compute Optimized, Memory Optimized, GPU, and Storage Optimized. Needless to say, unless your application has specific requirements for one of these categories, you should stick with General Purpose.

Within the General Purpose instance family, we recommend using lots of micro instances (the smallest) instead of one heavier (more CPU, RAM) size instances. The reason is that this way, you only pay at a lesser rate during low traffic times. And when high traffic arrives, you can simply create more instances. Of course, you can benchmark other instances as your requirements evolve.

EBS

Unlike the data stored on a local instance store (which persists only as long as that instance is alive), data stored on an Amazon EBS volume can persist independently of the life of the instance. Therefore, we recommend that you use the local instance store only for temporary data. For data requiring a higher level of durability, we recommend using Amazon EBS volumes. We will see this option when provisioning an EC2 instance.

EBS (like most services) does have an associated per GB cost, but this cost is very minor and worth the quick instance boot time. There are different kinds of EBS storage options with different data throughput (measured in IOPS, input/output operations per second).

Current options are Magnetic (lowest IOPS but cheapest), General Purpose SSD (good balance of IOPS and cost), and Provisioned IOPS SSD (highest IOPS but most expensive). We recommend sticking with General Purpose SSD when starting out.

Key Pair

We already discussed the concept of asymmetric key cryptography in Chapter 6. To use many Amazon AWS services, you need to work with a public/private key. Amazon stores the public key only, and you store the private key. Anyone who possesses your private key can decrypt your login information, so it's important that you store your private keys in a secure place.

VPC

Amazon Virtual Private Cloud (VPC) enables you to launch AWS resources into a virtual network. The VPC determines the interconnection IP networking between various AWS resources (such as different EC2 instances) and external interaction. The external interaction and the TCP/IP ports are significant because they allow you to have a database server that is only accessible within the VPC from other EC2 instances, but not accessible from the outside world. A new AWS account comes with a default VPC for each AWS region. By default, this VPC allows internal traffic only. We will alter this VPC security to allow web traffic.

And that's it. You now have a basic understanding of the fundamental concepts you need when working with AWS.

Creating Your First EC2 Instance

Now we present a step-by-step guide.

Create a Key Pair

The first step is to create a key pair (your login for the EC2 instance you will create later). This is done from the EC2 dashboard, as shown in Figure 13-3.

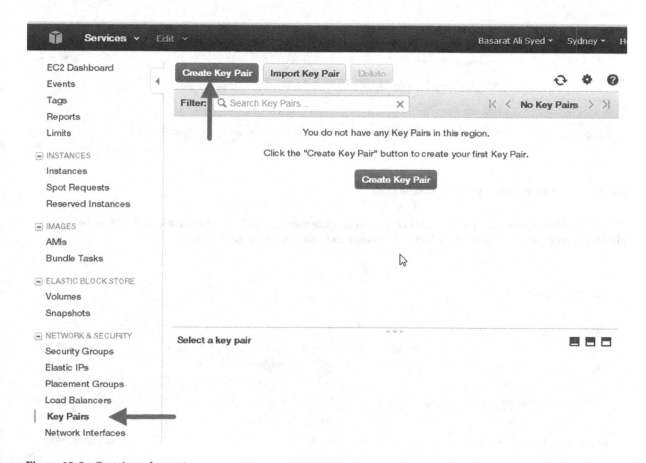

Figure 13-3. Creating a key pair

You will be asked to name the key pair and, as soon as you do, the dashboard will create a <name>.pem file you can download. Keep this pem file in a safe place. You will need this to SSH to the EC2 instance that you will create.

Configuring the Security Group

As we stated earlier, the default VPC/Security Group only allows internal traffic within the AWS resources. We will open it up to allow external web traffic. Click the Security Groups section in the EC2 Dashboard, select the default VPC security group, and click to edit the inbound traffic rules, as shown in Figure 13-4.

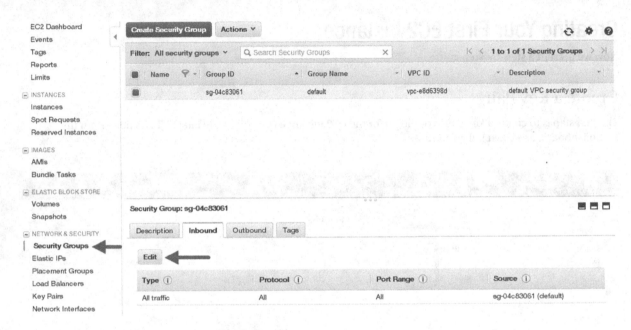

Figure 13-4. *Edit the security group inbound ports*

In the inbound rules, add SSH and HTTP to be accessible from any address. Also enable all ICMP so that you can ping the server. Finally, click the Save button to commit the changes. (See Figure 13-5.)

Edit inbound rules

Type	Protocol	Port Range	Source	
All traffic	All	0 - 65535	Custom IP / sg-04c83061	⊗
SSH	TCP	22	Anywhere / 0.0.0.0/0	⊗
HTTP	TCP	80	Anywhere / 0.0.0.0/0	⊗
All ICMP	ICMP	0 - 65535	Anywhere / 0.0.0.0/0	⊗

Add Rule   Cancel **Save**

Figure 13-5. *Values for the security group inbound ports*

Provisioning an Instance

Select the instances section on the dashboard and click Launch Instance, as shown in Figure 13-6.

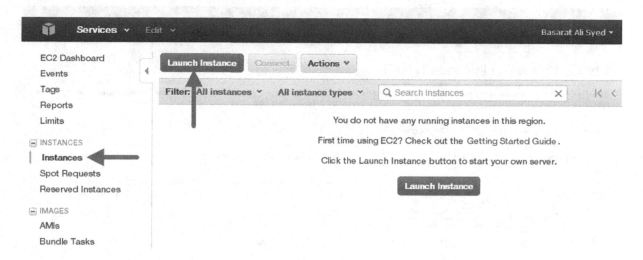

Figure 13-6. *Creating an new EC2 instance*

This will take you into the AMI selection screen. As we already mentioned, we recommend the Amazon Linux AMI. (See Figure 13-7.)

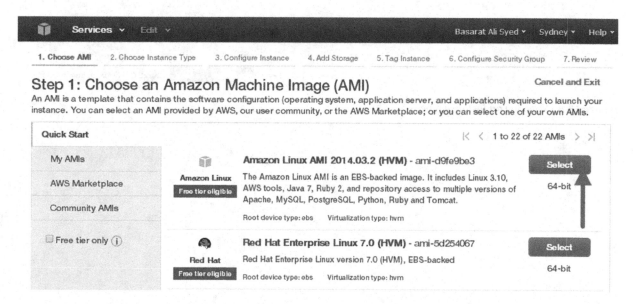

Figure 13-7. *Select the Amazon Linux AMI*

Now you will be prompted to select an instance type. We will go with a general purpose `t2.micro` instance, which is a single processor server, as shown in Figure 13-8.

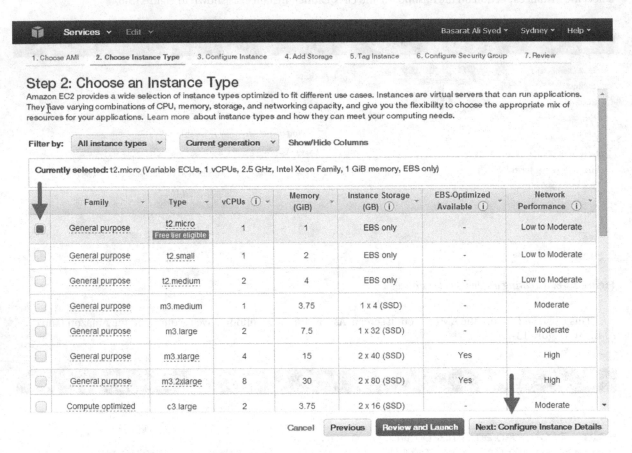

Figure 13-8. *Selecting an instance type*

Next, in the instance details, you will be able to configure networking (such as the VPC, for which we recommend default as that is the one we modified) and shutdown behavior. The defaults options are perfectly fine. The *Stop* shutdown behavior (instead of *Terminate*) ensures that your data is not cleared on machine shutdown. (See Figure 13-9.)

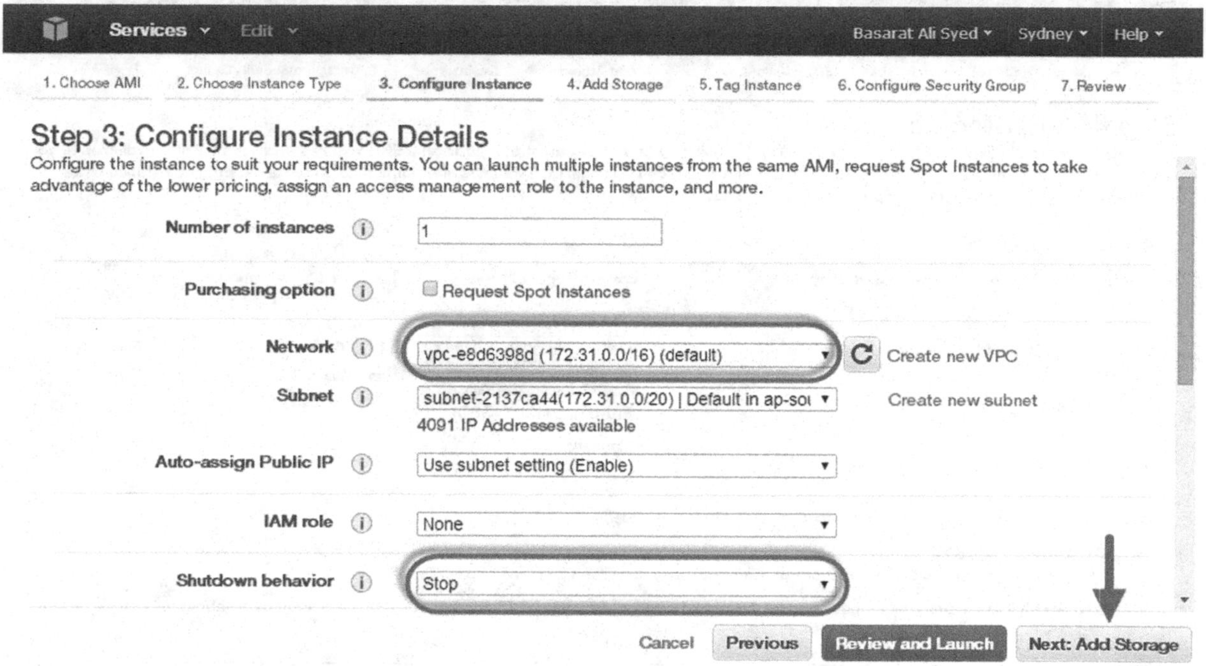

Figure 13-9. *Configuring instance details*

The next screen allows you to configure the storage. The default space of 8GB space is more than enough. As we discussed previously in EBS concepts, we recommend you use the general purpose SSD storage (the default at this time was magnetic). You can later modify the configuration for EBS volumes from the EBS section of the EC2 management dashboard. (See Figure 13-10.)

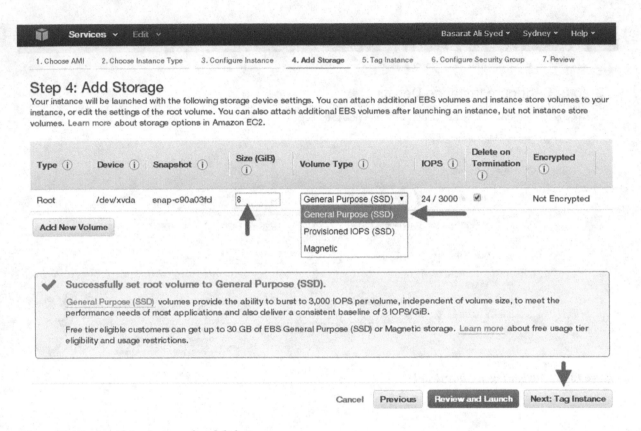

Figure 13-10. Specifying instance hard disk storage

The next screen allows you to tag the instance. Tags help you manage a collection of instances, but you can ignore that for now. The final configuration screen allows you to configure a security group. In Figure 13-11, we will utilize the Security Group inside the default VPC (which we already modified to allow HTTP traffic).

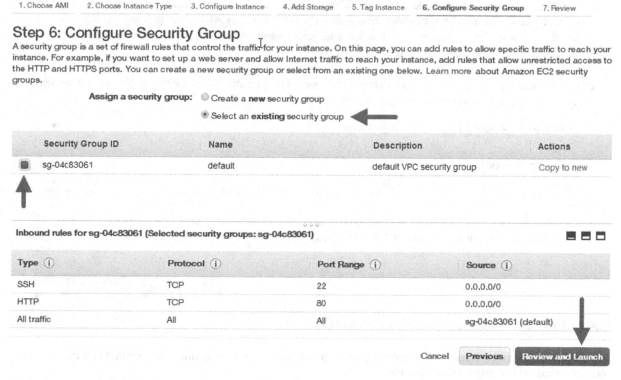

Figure 13-11. Selecting the security group

In the review screen, you will click the Launch button, at which point you will be asked to select a key pair. In Figure 13-12, we will utilize the key pair we already created from the dashboard.

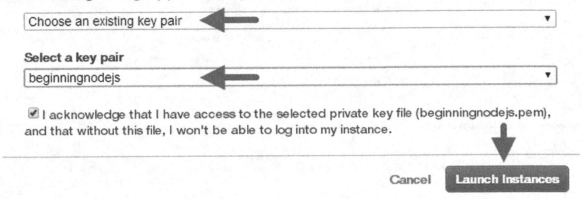

Figure 13-12. Selecting a key pair for instance credentials

Click Launch Instance and you are good to go. Congratulations—you have configured your first EC2 instance and you understand every option of significance!

Connecting to the EC2 Instance for the First Time

We will use the PEM file (key value pair) that we downloaded, along with SSH.

■ **Note**   On Windows, ssh is a part of Cygwin, www.cygwin.com/, which we have been using for bash as well. Many Windows users prefer using PuTTY though (www.chiark.greenend.org.uk/~sgtatham/putty/). However, we will stick with ssh for consistency.

Setting Up a SSH Connect Script

From the dashboard, select your running instance and note down its public IP address, as shown in Figure 13-13. Note that this IP address and public DNS are only valid for the duration that this instance is running. Restarting the instance results in a new IP and DNS allocation. (See Figure 13-13.)

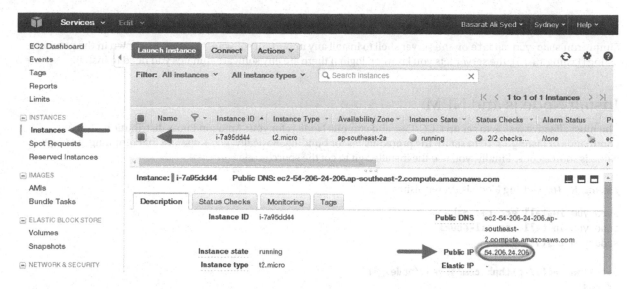

Figure 13-13. *Getting the instance's public IP address*

Now create a simple `connect` script (shown in Listing 13-14) in the same directory as the `.pem` file to easily `ssh` to your server using its public IP address.

Listing 13-14. Connect Script

```
#!/bin/bash

## Connect to our EC2 instance using SSH. To do this, we have to
## supply the PEM file using -i (Identity File) during connection.
## For the user, we can use "ec2-user" and the public IP Address.
ssh -i ./beginningnodejs.pem ec2-user@54.206.24.206
```

Make this `connect` script executable and run it, as shown in Listing 13-15.

Listing 13-15. Initial Configuration for Connect Script and Sample Usage

```
$ chmod +x ./connect
$ ./connect
Last login: Sun Aug 17 11:17:12 2014 from cpe-121-213-245-111.static.vic.bigpond.net.au

       __|  __|_  )
       _|  (     /    Amazon Linux AMI
      ___|\___|___|

https://aws.amazon.com/amazon-linux-ami/2014.03-release-notes/
9 package(s) needed for security, out of 19 available
Run "sudo yum update" to apply all updates.
[ec2-user@ip-172-31-2-33 ~]$
```

Now you have access to the server terminal (server shell). To reiterate, from now on, you simply run `./connect` whenever you want to connect to the server.

Keeping Your Server Safe

Simply run `sudo yum update` on the server shell to install any important software updates. As shown in the previous listing (Listing 13-15), the server lets you know on login if there are any software updates you need to install.

Install Node.js and NPM

The most effective way is to set up GCC/C++ and compile Node.js for your Amazon Linux distribution. Run the commands in Listing 13-16 to set up the prerequisites for building. Basically, gcc + openssl for compiling, git to get Node.js source code. Finally, you use the installed git to get the source code.

Listing 13-16. Getting Node.js Prerequisites

```
sudo yum install gcc-c++ make
sudo yum install openssl-devel
sudo yum install git

git clone git://github.com/joyent/node.git
cd node
```

Now the next decision is which version of Node.js do you want to run. To see which versions are tagged inside the Node.js source code, you can use `git tag -l` to list them. We recommend the latest stable version (listed on nodejs.org), as shown in Listing 13-17.

Listing 13-17. Building/Installing a Particular Version of Node.js

```
git checkout v0.10.30
./configure make
sudo make install
```

It might be a while until it's all done so you might want to grab a coffee. The output will show quite a few warnings, but it is normal as a part of compilation. To verify that it all went smoothly, check that the following (Listing 13-18) code works.

Listing 13-18. Checking a Successful Installation

```
$ node -v
v0.10.30
$ npm -v
1.4.21
$ which node
/usr/local/bin/node
$ which npm
/usr/local/bin/npm
```

Allowing Global Package Installation

As shown in the output in Listing 13-18(from the `which node` command), node and npm will be installed in `/usr/local/bin` directory. To be able to install global NPM packages, you will need to run npm using sudo (**super user do**). This means you need to add this path to the secure bin paths for sudo. You can do that by editing the `/etc/sudoers` file and adding to the secure_pathfile. We will be using vi for this. Just in case you are not familiar with vim, we show the keyboard shortcuts below. At any time to exit vim, type in :q and press enter to quit. Now open the file in vim as super user:

```
sudo vi /etc/sudoers
```

Find the following within this file (vim tip, type in /secure and press enter):

```
Defaults secure_path = /sbin:/bin:/usr/sbin:/usr/bin
```

Go to the end of the line (vim tip, it's okay to use arrow keys), go into append mode (vim shortcut a), and append what we show in bold:

```
Defaults secure_path = /sbin:/bin:/usr/sbin:/usr/bin:/usr/local/bin
```

Now exit insert mode (vim shortcut: ESC key) and save the file overwriting original (vim shortcut `:w!`). Finally, quit vim `:q`. Now to test that it went as planned, install forever globally:

```
$ sudo npm install -g forever
```

Congratulations—you are now a Linux node setup guru.

Running Your Node.js Application in AWS

This part should be fairly trivial. You simply execute your script on the server the same way you have been executing on your machine. The best way to get the code on the server is simply to use a source control repository (such as github) and clone the code on the server. For example:

```
git clone git://github.com/youcompacy/yourproject.git
git checkout master
npm install
node app.js
```

And that's pretty much it. Your application is now ready for public consumption.

Additional Resources

AWS EC2 Instance Types: http://aws.amazon.com/ec2/instance-types/
    EBS Types: http://aws.amazon.com/ebs/details/
    Amazon EBS FAQ: http://aws.amazon.com/ebs/faqs/
    Amazon Linux AMI: http://aws.amazon.com/amazon-linux-ami/
    Amazon AWS getting started video series: https://aws.amazon.com/getting-started/
    The default VPC: http://docs.aws.amazon.com/AmazonVPC/latest/UserGuide/default-vpc.html

Summary

We started the chapter by discussing how you can ensure better uptime in your web servers. One hundred percent uptime is something that is highly desirable. Libraries like ExpressJS and Connect help making error handling highly localized to a single HTTP request. Additionally, applications like forever can help keep your server running even in the case of drastic errors.

Next, we demonstrated that starting multiple Node.js processes to fully utilize the system resources for an HTTP server is trivial. However, it is worth mentioning that the API is still experimental. Additionally, you are generally better off deploying multiple servers, each with a single CPU (like the AWS micro EC2 instance) instead of a single server with multiple CPUs since you only pay for what you use. It is still comforting to know that single multi-core server clustering is supported by Node.js.

Finally, we covered deployment. Before presenting a step-by-step AWS setup guide, we tried to present the important concepts. This ensures that you will be able to navigate your way around the dashboard if Amazon chooses to update the administration interface design. We also made clear the factors that swayed us in giving you a recommended hardware selection so if those change, you can make similar rational choices.

Index

Get the eBook for only $10!

> Now you can take the weightless companion with you anywhere, anytime. Your purchase of this book entitles you to 3 electronic versions for only $10.

This Apress title will prove so indispensible that you'll want to carry it with you everywhere, which is why we are offering the eBook in 3 formats for only $10 if you have already purchased the print book.

Convenient and fully searchable, the PDF version enables you to easily find and copy code—or perform examples by quickly toggling between instructions and applications. The MOBI format is ideal for your Kindle, while the ePUB can be utilized on a variety of mobile devices.

Go to www.apress.com/promo/tendollars to purchase your companion eBook.